收获

Harvest

Intermediate Chinese
Textbook

许嘉璐 主编
XU Jialu

陈绂   王若江   朱瑞平
CHEN Fu   WANG Ruojiang   ZHU Ruiping

娄毅   杨丽姣   李凌艳   Pedro ACOSTA
LOU Yi   YANG Lijiao   LI Lingyan

CENGAGE
Learning™

北京师范大学出版集团
BEIJING NORMAL UNIVERSITY PUBLISHING GROUP
北京师范大学出版社

收获

Harvest

Intermediate Chinese
TEXTBOOK

CENGAGE
Learning™

北京师范大学出版集团
BEIJING NORMAL UNIVERSITY PUBLISHING GROUP
北京师范大学出版社

Publishing Director: Paul Tan
Language Product Director: Joh Liang Hee
Product Manager (U.S.): Mei Yun Loh
Development Editor: Lan Zhao
Associate Development Editor: Coco Koh
Product Manager (Asia): Joyce Tan
Senior Account Manager (China): Caroline Ma
Account Manager (China): Arthur Sun
CLT Coordinator (China): Mana Wu
Publishing Executive: Gemaine Goh
Graphic Designer: Debbie Ng

Executive Editors: Fan Yang, Lili Yin
Graphic Designer: Baofen Li
Illustrator: Hai Bo
Proofreader: Han Li
Sound Engineers: Guangying Feng, Wei Wang, Shuai Wang
Sound Editor: Zhangji Wei

Cover and Layout Design: Redbean De Pte Ltd
Photos: Getty Images, unless otherwise stated

CENGAGE LEARNING

Asia Head Office (Singapore)
Cengage Learning Asia Pte Ltd
5 Shenton Way #01-01
UIC Building
Singapore 068808
Tel: (65) 6410 1200
Fax: (65) 6410 1208
Email: asia.info@cengage.com

United States
Heinle - Cengage Learning
25 Thomson Place
Boston, MA 02210
Tel: (1) 800 354 9706
     (1) 617 757 7900
Fax: (1) 800 487 8488

China
Cengage Learning Asia Pte Ltd
(Beijing Rep Office)
Room 1201, South Tower, Building C
Raycom Info Tech Park
No. 2, Kexueyuan South Road
Haidian District, Beijing, China 100080
Tel: (86) 10 8286 2096
Fax: (86) 10 8286 2089
Email: asia.infochina@cengage.com

Beijing Normal University Press

China
No. 19 Xinjiekouwai Street
Beijing, China 100875
Tel: (86) 10 5880 2833
Fax: (86) 10 5880 6196
Email: yll@bnup.com.cn
      fan@bnup.com.cn

Author's Message

Harvest: Intermediate Chinese is specially written for anyone who seeks to learn about the Chinese culture and people, and to use this knowledge in the context of the global community.

The most important aim of learning another language is to be able to exchange ideas with people of another culture. In order to achieve this, you need to learn about the culture of the people you wish to communicate with. From this perspective, a good textbook should contain rich cultural content. It should also provide the learner with a variety of exercises and reference materials so that they can get more practice in using the language.

It was in accordance with the above principles that we wrote this textbook series. It was created by a team of distinguished Chinese and American scholars who are experts in both Chinese language teaching, and subjects such as educational psychology, Chinese history, and culture.

If you already have some knowledge of Chinese and would like to go on learning, then this textbook series is definitely suitable for you. We hope it will inspire you to lifelong learning about the Chinese language and people.

We are keen to hear feedback from students and teachers who use this textbook series. This will be of great help to us, and will also help in strengthening friendship between the Chinese and American people.

Xu Jialu

PRINCIPAL
College of Chinese Language and Culture
Beijing Normal University, China

Acknowledgments

We would like to express our most sincere gratitude to Cengage Learning and Beijing Normal University Press Publishers, for their vision and leadership in the development of quality Chinese language materials. Our thanks to all the editorial and production staff for their hard and meticulous work, enthusiasm, and commitment to the success of this project.

Our deepest appreciation to our colleagues, whose ideas and suggestions at the initial stages helped shaped the development of this program.

Richard Chi, *Utah State University, Utah*
Tao-chung Yao, *University of Hawaii*
Yu-Lan Lin, *Boston Public Schools, Massachusetts*
Lucy Lee, *Livingston High School, New Jersey*
Feng Ye, *Punahou High School, Hawaii*
Qinru Zhou, *Harvard Westlake High School, California*

Jianhua Bai, *Kenyon College, Ohio*
Zhaoming Pan, *South Seas Arts Center, USA; Peking University*
Xiaolin Chang, *Lowell High School, California*
Carol Chen-Lin, *Choate Rosemary Hall, Connecticut*
Shuqiang Zhang, *University of Hawaii*

Special thanks to Mr. Gaston Caperton (President), Mr. Thomas Matts and Ms. Selena Cantor from the College Board for their help and hospitality during our study tour in the United States. Our thanks also go to Ms. Xu Lin (Director, Office of Chinese Language Council International) and her colleagues for their support of this project.

We are deeply grateful to all reviewers for their constructive comments and suggestions. Your contribution enriched the *Jia You!* program with your wealth of expertise and experience.

Miao-fen Tseng, *University of Virginia*
Xiaolin Chang, *Lowell High School, California*
Xiaohong Wen, *University of Houston, Texas*
Jinghui Liu, *California State University, Fullerton*
Pifeng Esther Hsiao, *The Bishop's School, California*
Xiaohua Yu, *Piedmont High School, California*

Baocai Paul Jia, *Cupertino High School, California*
Bih-Yuan Yang, *Mira Loma High School, California*
Chao-mei Shen, *Rice University, Texas*
Xing King, *The Bishop's School, California*
Yangyang Qin Daniell, *Lawrenceville School, New Jersey*
Yumei Chu, *Saratoga Community Chinese School, California*

Our gratitude also goes to Prof. Guohua Chen, Beijing Foreign Studies University, who helped us a great deal with the English translation.

We are indebted to PhD candidates Xiangping Jiang, Yun Lu, Xiang Chen, Xin Tian, Yanxin Bu, Yan Liu and MA students Lina Tang, Manrong Wu, Xiaoye Dai, Ying Zhao at the School of Chinese Language and Culture, Beijing Normal University, MA students Lihua Li and Qing Li at the Foreign Language Department of Beijing Normal University, and MA student Yan Zhang at Beijing University for their assistance and support during the compilation of this book.

Finally, we are grateful to everyone who chooses to use our textbooks. We look forward to your comments and feedback.

Preface

Harvest is a one-year intermediate-level Chinese program ideally suited for high school students who have studied Chinese for at least 3 years and those who are preparing for the AP Chinese language and culture exam. It includes a student text, a workbook and accompanying audio program for all listening activities.

Developed in accordance to the ACTFL's "Five Cs" - Communication, Culture, Connections, Comparisons, and Communities, the program aims to equip students both linguistically and culturally, and prepare them to speak, read and converse in Chinese successfully within and beyond the school setting.

Harvest incorporates both well-established traditions and new developments in foreign language pedagogy. Below are some of the features of *Harvest* that distinguish it from other Chinese language textbooks.

It Interweaves Chinese Language and Culture

Harvest places a premium on communication through cultural understanding and strives for real-world use of the Chinese language. Culture is integrated into every facet of the textbook and is featured in carefully crafted speaking, listening, reading and exercises.

The program is structured into six units or themes: School & Family, Festival & Customs, Travel & Transportation, People & Society, Famous People & History, and Literature & Arts. Each unit contains two lessons designed around the theme.

Students are regularly placed in a real-life context to discuss the similarities and differences between cultural practices and perspectives. They are encouraged to express their views and opinions while considering the views and opinions of others, and to think critically about issues. Through these classroom discussions and debates, *Harvest* hones students' four language skills of speaking, listening, reading, and writing; fosters their reflective and critical thinking skills; and broadens their world view.

It Integrates Materials of Different Varieties and Discourse Styles

A mix of authentic and carefully crafted Chinese texts of different forms (dialogs and narratives) and discourse styles (formal and spoken) are incorporated into *Harvest* to expose students to a broad range of written texts.

Students develop their reading proficiency through exposure to contextualized written materials ranging from notices, messages, and signs, to more dense texts taken or adapted from newspapers, magazine articles, interview transcripts, letters, and essays. The reading texts in *Harvest* are current, engaging, informative, and thought-provoking; they promote classroom discussion and individual reflection. Each lesson has a supplementary text that is carefully chosen to complement the theme of the lesson. This allows students to practice immediately what they have learned from their study of the main text, as well as to develop reading skills in predicting and guessing the meanings of new words and phrases from context.

It Integrates Content-based Vocabulary, Grammar, Exercises, and Activities

In keeping with *Harvest*'s content-driven, functional pedagogical focus, the vocabulary, grammar, and common expressions are presented based on their relevance to the theme of each unit, and then practiced in contextualized, meaningful, and relevant exercises and classroom activities.

Besides traditional exercises such as fill-in-the-blanks, sentence completion, and paraphrasing, the program also offers a broad range of communicative exercises, such as instructor-directed discussions, pair or group discussions, role plays, games, interviews, and debates. Through these activities, students learn to initiate and sustain conversations, and communicate appropriately in a variety of social and cultural contexts.

Collaborative group projects and research projects that involve direct contact with the community and the use of the Internet are also incorporated into *Harvest*. This encourages students to become independent, lifelong language learners.

It Integrates Process Pedagogy into Speaking and Writing Tasks

To make writing and speaking tasks less daunting and much more manageable for students, the *Harvest* program breaks each communicative task into parts. It provides prompts or questions at every step of the process to initiate ideas and guide students through the process of organizing their thoughts. Students are also encouraged to make use of the grammar patterns and new vocabulary they have learned from the study of the main text.

The Workbook is Designed to Resemble the AP Chinese Language & Culture Exam Format

Exercises in the Workbook are designed around the lesson topics and are modeled after the question types in the AP Chinese Language and Culture exam. The exercises test students on cultural knowledge and all four language skills of listening, reading, speaking, and writing.

Students who are sitting for the AP Chinese Language and Culture exam can get extensive practice on the exam format. Those who are not will find the Workbook a useful tool for assessing their grasp of the materials learned and for furthering their communication and language skills.

Scope and Sequence

UNIT 1:
SCHOOL AND FAMILY 学校与家庭

<table>
<tr>
<td>COMMUNICATIVE GOALS</td>
<td colspan="2">
<ul>
<li>Talk about what you like and give reasons why you like it</li>
<li>Ask follow-up questions to obtain detailed answers</li>
</ul>
</td>
</tr>
<tr>
<td rowspan="1">CHINESE TEXTS</td>
<td>
Lesson 1:

Chinese is Fun!
我爱学中文
Anecdotes of Learning Chinese
学汉语的趣事
</td>
<td>
Lesson 2:

My Father, Laoshe
儿子眼中的父亲
Raising Children in a
Cross-Cultural Marriage
跨国婚姻家庭中的孩子
</td>
</tr>
<tr>
<td>LANGUAGE CONNECTION</td>
<td>
<ul>
<li>别看……可是…… (even though…, but…)</li>
<li>并+ Neg. (not really)</li>
<li>"被"字句 (a passive sentence construction)</li>
<li>"把"字句 (to express how a matter is handled)</li>
</ul>
</td>
<td>
<ul>
<li>从……说起 (to begin a narration)</li>
<li>……极了 (extremely)</li>
<li>正好相反 (on the contrary)</li>
<li>净 (always)</li>
<li>或者说 (in other words)</li>
<li>何况 (even less; more so)</li>
<li>当…… (when…)</li>
<li>万一 (in case)</li>
</ul>
</td>
</tr>
<tr>
<td>COMMON EXPRESSIONS</td>
<td>
<ul>
<li>首先, 其次, 最后 (firstly, secondly, in addition…)</li>
<li>我爱……是因为…… (I like…, because…)</li>
<li>非常欣赏它 (他) 的…… (…really like…)</li>
<li>在我看来, ………… (in my opinion…)</li>
</ul>
</td>
<td>
<ul>
<li>为什么 (why…)</li>
<li>有什么…… (to ask about the details of something)</li>
<li>怎么了 (What's wrong/up?)</li>
<li>怎么+V (how…)</li>
<li>有没有…… (a selective question)</li>
</ul>
</td>
</tr>
<tr>
<td>CULTURAL INFORMATION</td>
<td colspan="2">
<ul>
<li>Traditional Chinese family values</li>
<li>Changes in Chinese culture as reflected in modern Chinese family life</li>
<li>Famous Chinese novelist and dramatist, Laoshe</li>
</ul>
</td>
</tr>
</table>

UNIT 2:
FESTIVALS AND CUSTOMS 节日与风俗

COMMUNICATIVE GOALS

- Talk about the similarities and differences in the way two festivals are celebrated
- Express agreement, excitement, or approval
- Explain the source or origin of something

CHINESE TEXTS

Lesson 3:	Lesson 4:
Celebrating Chinese New Year 过年 The Origin of Chinese Valentine's Day 七夕节的传说	**Moon Festival** 中秋节 Making *Zongzi* during the Dragon Boat Festival 端午节包粽子

LANGUAGE CONNECTION

• 学会 + V (learned to do something) • 少于…… (less than…) • 就 (then) • 不管怎样, ……还是…… (no matter…, still…)	• 把A看作B (to regard A as B) • 一边……一边…… (while…) • 什么……啦……啦……啦…… (*to list different things*) • 每到…… (every time that…)

COMMON EXPRESSIONS

• 肯定 (definitely) • 那当然了 (of course) • 特别……/……极了/……得 + 不得了/太……了 (very; extremely)	• ……所以称作…… (therefore known as…) • ……因此……又叫…… (therefore it's also known as…) • 据说…… (it is said that…) • 相传…… (legend has it that…)

CULTURAL INFORMATION

- The Chinese lunar calendar and the animal zodiac
- Major Chinese festivals and celebrations
- Festive foods and their symbolic meanings
- Origins and legends of Chinese festivals

UNIT 3:
TRAVEL AND TRANSPORTATION 旅游与交通

COMMUNICATIVE GOALS	• Describe travel plans and itineraries • Offer suggestions and reminders • Consult with and persuade someone to accept your recommendations • Describe complex topics and situations • Express and describe a complex series of actions	
CHINESE TEXTS	**Lesson 5:** **Planning a Trip to China** 我要去中国旅游 Old China, Modern China 中国不是博物馆	**Lesson 6:** **I Climbed the Great Wall** 我登上了长城 100,000 Miles Long and 3,000 Years Old 三千年，十万里
LANGUAGE CONNECTION	• 疑问句及疑问语气词 (interrogatives) • ……怎么办 (what if…) • 先……再……然后…… (first…, next…, then…) • 经过…… (to pass by…) • ……才能…… (only if…)	• 缩略语 (Abbreviations) • V₁着V₁着+V₂ (to show a second action has started as the first one is taking place) • 连动句 (a sentence with two or more verbs referring to the same subject) • 到底 (after all; exactly) • 显然…… (obviously…) • 居然…… (unexpectedly…)
COMMON EXPRESSIONS	• 怎么能…… (how could you possibly…) • 要不……，……也行 (alternatively…) • 最好+V (you'd better…) • ……怎么样 (what do you think of…) • ……好不好 (a "yes/no" question to ask for someone's opinion)	
CULTURAL INFORMATION	• Major tourist attractions in China and their historical significance • Geography and environment of different parts of China • Major cities in China – their cultural and historical significance, local delicacies, and means of transportation • History and features of the Great Wall of China	

UNIT 4:
PEOPLE AND SOCIETY 民族与社会

COMMUNICATIVE GOALS	• Express disbelief and surprise • Relate a different cultural practice or a social phenomenon • Express regret for things that happened (or didn't happen) in the past

	Lesson 7:	**Lesson 8:**
CHINESE TEXTS	**The Hospitable Southwest** 远方的客人请你留下来 The Kazak Girl's Chase "姑娘追"	**Moving into a Modern Apartment** 搬家手记 "Pushing Hands" 老年人的烦恼
LANGUAGE CONNECTION	• Split Verb (*e.g.* 跳个舞, 担着心) • V + 在 + noun of place (*e.g.* 放在门外) • Writing Conventions on an Envelope • V + 得 + another element (*e.g.* 举得高高的)	• Prepositions "从" and "离" • A比不上B (A is not as good as B) • "Object + Complement" Construction (*e.g.* 请老邻居来家里吃饭) • V₁的V₁, V₂的V₂ (*e.g.* 跳舞的跳舞, 唱歌的唱歌) • Demonstrative Pronoun (*e.g.* 这, 那, 这儿, 那儿) • Prefix and Suffix (*e.g.* 老, 小, 子, 儿, 头, 者)

CULTURAL INFORMATION	• Chinese ethnic minorities (e.g. Bai, Dai, Tibetan, Kazak) and their cultural practices • Types of residences in China: courtyard house, shared dormitory housing and apartment • "Pushing Hands", a film directed by Ang Lee that explores the clash of eastern and western family values

UNIT 5:
FAMOUS PEOPLE AND HISTORY 名人与历史

<table>
<tr>
<td rowspan="2">COMMUNICATIVE GOALS</td>
<td colspan="2">
<ul>
<li>Explain an idea by including examples and relevant details</li>
<li>Describe admirable characteristics of a person</li>
<li>Summarize key points</li>
</ul>
</td>
</tr>
<tr>
</tr>
<tr>
<td>CHINESE TEXTS</td>
<td>

Lesson 9:

Who Was Confucius?

孔子是谁?

Father of Modern China

参观中山陵

</td>
<td>

Lesson 10:

China Highlights

我知道的中国历史和文化

The Silk Road

丝绸之路

</td>
</tr>
<tr>
<td>LANGUAGE CONNECTION</td>
<td>
<ul>
<li>Rhetorical Question</li>
<li>难怪 (no wonder)</li>
<li>Quasi-Prefix (e.g. 可, 不)</li>
<li>The Conjuction "而"</li>
</ul>
</td>
<td>
<ul>
<li>既然……就…… (since/as…)</li>
<li>大都 (almost all)</li>
<li>所谓 (so-called)</li>
<li>从……起 (since)</li>
<li>由/通过…… + V (by which something is done)</li>
</ul>
</td>
</tr>
<tr>
<td>CULTURAL INFORMATION</td>
<td colspan="2">
<ul>
<li>Confucius, the famous Chinese thinker and social philosopher</li>
<li>Dr Sun Yat-Sen, the founder of modern China</li>
<li>China's two major rivers and five sacred mountains</li>
<li>China's seven ancient capitals</li>
<li>The Silk Road and trade in Chinese history during the Han and Tang dynasties</li>
<li>Fuwa, the official mascots of the Beijing 2008 Olympic Games</li>
</ul>
</td>
</tr>
</table>

UNIT 6:
LITERATURE AND ARTS 文学与艺术

COMMUNICATIVE GOALS	• Discuss problems and seek others' advice or opinions amicably and cooperatively • Describe the process of making something (physical object)

	CHINESE TEXTS	
	Lesson 11: **"To Borrow Arrows with Thatched Boats"** 草船借箭 The "Peach-Blossom" Face 人面桃花	**Lesson 12:** **Chinese Papercutting** 中国剪纸 The Butterfly Lovers 小提琴协奏曲梁祝

LANGUAGE CONNECTION

• 未必 (not necessarily; maybe not) • Existential Sentence (*e.g.* 江面上起了大雾) • Directional Adjunct (*e.g.* 借回来十万支箭) • Extended Usage of Directional Adjuncts • The Adverb "一向" (always, usually) • Compare "沿着" and "顺着"	• The Deductive Method of Narration • 为……所…… *(a passive construction)* • V₁ + 什么 + 就 + V₂ + 什么 *(e.g.* 唱什么就剪什么) • Quasi-Suffix *(e.g.* 力, 感, 化, 吧) • Parallelism

CULTURAL INFORMATION

- *Romance of the Three Kingdoms*, one of the Four Great Classical Novels of Chinese literature
- *Book of Songs*, the earliest existing collection of Chinese poems
- Chinese Papercutting
- Butterfly Lovers' Violin Concerto, one of the most famous works of Chinese music outside of China

Contents

UNIT **1**
SCHOOL AND FAMILY

学校与家庭

Communicative Goals
- Talk about what you like and give reasons why you like it
- Ask follow-up questions to obtain detailed answers

Cultural Information
- Traditional Chinese family values
- Changes in Chinese culture as reflected in modern Chinese family life
- Famous Chinese novelist and dramatist, Laoshe

Warm up

　　学校和家庭是我们生活的主要环境，它们就像一个广阔的舞台，每天都上演着丰富多彩的节目。你、你的同学和你的家庭在这个舞台上扮演着怎样的角色呢？

1.　你的学校生活是怎样的？你认为在学校生活中最有意思的是什么？请仿照下列表格，记录你一天的学习和活动安排，你也可以使用你熟悉和喜欢的各种图表。

	时间段	课程／活动	喜爱程度
课堂学习	8:00–9:00	中文课	比较喜欢
课余生活	3:00–4:00	打篮球	喜欢
	晚上		

2. 根据下面这个家庭关系图，说一说这些家庭成员之间的关系和称呼。

Photo: Getty Images

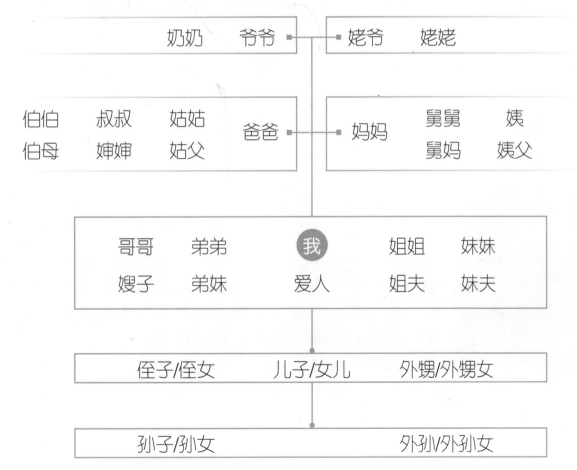

奶奶 爷爷	姥爷 姥姥

伯伯 叔叔 姑姑 伯母 婶婶 姑父	爸爸	妈妈	舅舅 姨 舅妈 姨父

哥哥   弟弟   **我**   姐姐   妹妹 嫂子   弟妹   爱人   姐夫   妹夫

侄子/侄女   儿子/女儿   外甥/外甥女

孙子/孙女   外孙/外孙女

Chinese is Fun!

第一课
我爱
学中文

Pre-reading

■ 你喜欢学中文吗？为什么？
■ 你觉得应该怎样学习中文？

外语不能只在教室里学，我在学中文的时候深深地体会到了这一点，因此越来越爱学中文。

　　首先，我爱学中文的原因是非常欣赏它的实用性。在我看来，在学校里跟老师学习语法、词汇固然重要，但更重要的是把这些知识用在实际的生活中，而且我觉得在街道、超市、篮球场学来的话更实用。当我说这些话时觉得很自然，中国人都能听得懂。

　　其次，我爱学中文，是因为汉语能帮助我了解中国文化。我在中国留学的经验证明，真正的中文学校是没有围墙的。我曾在北京留学五个星期，住在中国人家里，每天和家里的姥姥、姥爷聊天。在看电视时、在火锅店点菜时、在上街购物时，我慢慢学会了在各种情况下应该说什么，什么时候可以开玩笑，什么时候应该认认真真地谈话。

　　另外，没有人可以<u>否认</u>跟小贩聊天也是很好的学习方法。别看他们说的普通话不太标准，可是跟他们交谈对提高听力是非常有用的。我还从朋友、服务员、队友那里学会了很多常用的词语和一些成语、方言俚语。<u>好像</u>会说中文的十几亿人<u>不知不觉</u>都成了我的老师。在学习中，我也慢慢了解了中国。

　　最后，我爱学中文是因为学习有挑战性。很多人说中文难学，但我并没有被吓倒。我知道如果只学习课本知识，进步一定很慢。这就意味着要想让你的中文进步快，就需要有勇气利用各种听、说、读、写的机会。在我看来，学习中文真的是"师傅领进门，修行在个人"，只要对中文感兴趣，学得努力，中文水平很快就可以提高。

　　比如说我喜欢看足球，可是在学校没有学过怎么说球队、球星的名字，后来问别人，知道曼彻斯特联队也叫"曼联"，皇家马德里也称"皇马"。这件事更坚定了我学习中文的态度，那就是：想知道什么，就马上问别人，千万别不好意思。爱学中文的话，害羞是有害无益的。

(作者：麦特，美国东部地区某中学学生，学过三年中文，曾获全美中文论文比赛中级组第一名。本文在选入时有所删改。)

VOCABULARY
生词表

1	体会	tǐhuì	to understand, experience

【动】你自己*体会*一下这个动作。 | 我们总能*体会*到父母的爱。

2	首先	shǒuxiān	first of all

【连】我们重视的，*首先*是一个人的能力，其次是他的人品。 | 等到了北京，大家*首先*去长城，然后去天坛等景点。📖首：第一，最初。📖*首次* | *首位* | *首日* | *首班车*。

3	欣赏	xīnshǎng	to appreciate

【动】大家都很*欣赏*他的做法。 | 我不太*欣赏*这种风格的建筑。

4	实用性	shíyòngxìng	practicality

【名】没有什么*实用性* | *实用性*是首先要考虑的。 | 这种技术*实用性*很强。📖性：性质；性能。📖*专业性* | *知识性* | *统一性*。

5	词汇	cíhuì	vocabulary

【名】*词汇*手册 | 汉语常用*词汇*。

6	固然	gùrán	certainly, of course

【连】这里风景*固然*不错，但是交通太不方便了。 | 学汉语背生词*固然*重要，在生活中多练习听和说更重要。

7	街道	jiēdào	street

【名】一条*街道* | 打扫*街道* | *街道*委员会 | *街道*上冷冷清清。

8	超市	chāoshì	supermarket

【名】一家*超市* | 我家旁边有个小*超市*。 | *超市*里的东西比较便宜。📖市：市场。📖*股市* | *集市* | *菜市* | *早市*。

9	篮球场	lánqiúchǎng	basketball court

【名】学校有五个*篮球场*。 | 足球场大概有十七个*篮球场*那么大。📖场：某些比较大的地方。📖*足球场* | *排球场* | *运动场* | *停车场*。

10	自然	zìrán	natural

【形】表情*自然* | 今天大家的表演都很*自然*。

11	其次	qícì	secondly

【连】学汉语首先要学拼音，*其次*要学写汉字。 | 今天我来这里，首先是要看一看大家，*其次*也想和大家讨论几个问题。

12	经验	jīngyàn	experience

【名】*经验*丰富 | 先进*经验* | 大家都没有什么*经验*。

13	证明	zhèngmíng	to prove

【动】事实*证明*你说得对。 | 时间可以*证明*一切。 | 如果你有能力，你就*证明*给大家看。

14	围墙	wéiqiáng	surrounding wall

【名】一道*围墙* | 学校的*围墙*外有一家商店。📖*城墙* | *院墙* | *砖墙* | *土墙*。

15	<u>曾</u>	céng	ever

【副】有谁曾到过中国？ | 这家餐厅我们曾来过。

16	留学	liúxué	to study abroad

【动】到国外留学 | 在欧洲留过三年学 | 谁留过学？ | 小王到日本留学去了。

17	姥姥	lǎolao	maternal grandmother

【名】我姥姥家住天津。

18	姥爷	lǎoye	maternal grandfather

【名】姥爷今年七十八岁了。 | 姥姥和姥爷只有一个女儿。

19	聊天（儿）	liáotiān(r)	to chat

【动】上网聊天 | 和奶奶聊一会儿天 | 我们只聊过两次天。 | 咱们聊聊天儿吧。

20	火锅店	huǒguōdiàn	hot-pot restaurant

【名】一家火锅店 | 马路对面的火锅店生意很好。

21	点菜	diǎncài	to order dishes in a restaurant

我们现在可以点菜了。 | 每个人点一道自己最喜欢的菜。

22	上街	shàngjiē	to go shopping

今天上街吗？ | 昨天上了一回街，什么都没买到。

23	购物	gòuwù	to shop, to buy things

【动】上街购物 | 一周外出购一回物。 ⑤ 购：买。物：东西。

24	开玩笑	kāiwánxiào	to joke

他不喜欢开玩笑。 | 大家经常开他的玩笑。 | 我只是和你开一个小玩笑。

25	<u>否认</u>	fǒurèn	to deny

【动】他否认自己曾来过这里。 | 事实是无法否认的。

26	小贩	xiǎofàn	street vendor, hawker

【名】几个小贩 | 小贩们叫卖着自己的商品。

27	服务员	fúwùyuán	salesperson, waiter

【名】招三名服务员 | 请服务员把盘子拿走。

28	队友	duìyǒu	teammate

【名】她是我的队友。 | 队友们都走了。

29	成语	chéngyǔ	idiom, set expression

【名】一条成语 | 成语词典 | 用成语造句。

30	方言	fāngyán	dialect

【名】一种方言 | 上海方言 | 中国各地方言差别很大。

31	俚语	lǐyǔ	slang

【名】有些俚语很粗俗。 | 使用俚语能使你的话听起来更有意思。

32	好像	hǎoxiàng	to seem like

【副】天好像要下雨。 | 他好像忘记了自己曾经说过的话。

33	<u>不知不觉</u>	bùzhī-bùjué	without realizing

不知不觉就到了冬天。 | 我们在不知不觉中就做完了所有工作。

34	挑战性	tiǎozhànxìng	challenge (n.)
	【名】具有*挑战性*	这样的工作对我没什么*挑战性*。		
35	课本	kèběn	textbook
	【名】一套*课本*	几本*课本*	我们用的*课本*都是新的。		
36	进步	jìnbù	to progress, improve
	【动】没有*进步*	只有努力才能*进步*。	一年的学习使我的汉语水平向前*进*了一大步。		
37	意味着	yìwèizhe	to mean
	【动】你没有不舒服的感觉并不*意味着*你没有病。	这种现象*意味着*大家都不喜欢他。		
38	勇气	yǒngqì	courage
	【名】有*勇气*	一股*勇气*	鼓起*勇气*。◨ 土气	洋气	锐气	志气。		
39	师傅领进门，修行在个人	shīfu lǐng jìn mén, xiūxíng zài gèrén	"The master teaches the trade, but an apprentice is self made."
	我只是教大家一些最基本的东西，以后全靠大家自己学了。"*师傅领进门，修行在个人*"嘛! ◨ 师傅: 老师。领: 带, 引。修行: 实践; 做。在: 取决于, 由……决定。个人: 自己。		
40	球队	qiúduì	team (in a ball game)
	【名】组建一支新*球队*	我们的*球队*取得了胜利。		
41	球星	qiúxīng	star athlete (in a ball game)
	【名】一名*球星*	一位*球星*	所有的*球星*都登场亮相了。		
42	坚定	jiāndìng	to strengthen, solidify
	【动】*坚定*立场	*坚定*信心	这更*坚定*了我的看法。		
43	害羞	hàixiū	shy, timid
	【形】这个小孩有点*害羞*。	别*害羞*, 胆子大一点!		
44	有害无益	yǒu hài wú yì	harmful, not beneficial
	你这么想, 对你自己*有害无益*。	这样的做法*有害无益*。◨ 害: 坏处。益: 好处。		

PROPER NOUNS			
45	曼彻斯特联队	Mànchèsītè Liánduì	Manchester United
46	皇家马德里	Huángjiā Mǎdélǐ	Real Madrid

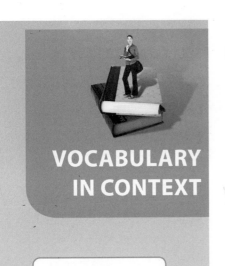

VOCABULARY IN CONTEXT

体会

首先

其次

最后

固然

曾

否认

好像

不知不觉

✓ 意味

后来

A Read the passage below.

　　一说到中文，你马上会联想到哪些词呢？汉字，对你又意味着什么？

　　谈起自己学中文的经历，你又有哪些有趣或者难忘的故事呢？

　　你曾很害怕学中文吗？对学习写汉字又有哪些体会？

　　你也许会说："中国文化固然对我有吸引力，但是不能否认，中文确实不太好学，尤其是汉字不好写。"

　　其实，我也经历了和你非常相似的过程。别看我现在的普通话好像很流利，可三年前我连一个中文词都不会说，后来经过努力，才达到今天的水平。

　　我的经验告诉我：要学好中文，首先，一定要有兴趣，要真正愿意学习中文；其次，要努力寻找一个学习中文的好环境，这样才能多练习；最后，一定要有信心！

　　只要你肯坚持，在不知不觉中你会发现，学中文可以带给你一个完全不同的、神奇的世界。

B Find the words in the boxes in the passage above.

C Talk with your partner about your experiences in learning Chinese. Use the words from the boxes in your conversation.

LANGUAGE CONNECTION

别看……可是……

is used to express that even though something is true, the resulting situation is not necessarily affected by it. "别看" may be followed by a short phrase or a short sentence.

For example

- 别看他小小的年龄，可是知道的事情却不少。
- 别看他得了冠军，可是一点儿也没有高兴的样子。

并+Neg.

is used before the negative expressions "没(有)" "不" to emphasize the negative tone. "并" may be used after words such as "但是" "可是", which indicate a shift in tone.

For example

- 他说他已经给我发了邮件，可是我并没有收到。
- 现在已经是冬天了，但天气并不太冷。

A　别看……可是…… (even though..., but...)

"别看他们说的普通话不太标准，可是跟他们交谈对提高听力是非常有用的。"

Complete the sentences using "别看……可是……"

1.　别看这件衣服价格不高，_____

　　_____。

2.　_____，可是他心里

　　却没有这么想。

3.　别看这个老师平时笑眯眯的，_____
　　_____。

B　并+Neg. (not really)

"我并没有被吓倒。"

Complete the dialogs using "并."

1.　甲：你怎么能随便说朋友的坏话？

　　乙：_____。

2.　甲：看你，一点小小的麻烦用不着这么着急嘛。

　　乙：_____。

3.　甲：我上周寄给你的礼物收到了吗？

　　乙：_____。

"被"字句

is a passive sentence construction. "被" is used before a noun, a pronoun, or a noun phrase. The verb used generally takes an object. In circumstances when the context is clear, the part after "被" may be omitted.

For example
- 我们被这里的景色迷住了。
- 那个箱子已经被拿走了。

"把"字句

is used to express how a matter is handled, and the results produced by the behavior. The common pattern is "把+N+V+其他".

For example
- 我把作业做完了。
- 请把你的地址告诉我。

C "被"字句

"我并没有被吓倒。"

Complete the sentences using "'被'字句."

1. 这里的情况太可怕了, _____

_____ 。

2. 今天我真是太倒霉了, _____

_____ 。

3. _____ ,

瓶子里一点牛奶都没剩下。

D "把"字句

"更重要的是把这些知识用在实际的生活中。"

Complete the dialogs using "'把'字句."

1. 甲：外面好冷哦!

乙：我建议你 _____ 。

2. 甲：_____ !

乙：我从来没有碰过你的电脑。

3. 甲：我觉得这件事情一定没有这么简单。

乙：这件事情就是这么简单, _____

_____ 。

COMMUNICATION CORNER

Intructions:

- In groups, prepare a list of interview questions on the topic "Your favorite school activity."

- Individually, interview other classmates on this subject. Take notes during the interviews. Collate the interview results.

- Appoint a representative to give a presentation of your group's findings. Summarize clearly what you discovered about your classmates' favorite activities and why they like them.

- Keep your presentation to about 300 words.

你喜欢学校里的哪些活动？

Guidelines:

🗣 You can use the common expressions you have learnt in this lesson to answer interview questions about what you like and why. These expressions are also useful when you are recording your interview findings.

首先，其次，最后

A：你为什么喜欢旅游？

B：首先，旅游可以增长我的见识。其次，我可以欣赏各地的风光。最后，我还可以品尝不同地区以及不同国家的美食。

我非常欣赏它（他）的……

A：你为什么喜欢那个小伙子？

B：我非常欣赏他的才能。

我爱(喜欢)……是因为……

🔊 我喜欢去云南旅游，是因为我希望更多地了解当地少数民族的风俗习惯。

🔊 我爱参加学校音乐社团活动的原因是非常欣赏乐团的指挥。

🔊 我喜欢这个活动，是因为在学校的万圣节舞会上，我可以邀请任何一位姑娘做我的舞伴。

在我看来，……

A：你为什么想去上海学习汉语？

B：在我看来，上海是个非常现代化的城市，所以我愿意去那里学习汉语。

🗣 Here are some other useful expressions to list reasons why a particular activity is well-liked.

🔊 他喜欢参加学校的中文演讲比赛，一是因为通过这项活动可以提高他自己的中文水平，二是由于在活动的过程中可以结交新的朋友。

🔊 学校每年一次的话剧节规模大、参与人员多、活动气氛热烈、持续时间长达一个月，很多人非常喜欢。

🔊 我调查的五个人都对学校篮球协会的比赛非常感兴趣，因为比赛激烈、刺激、紧张。

WRITING TASK

夏令营活动申请表

Instruction:

Fill out the form below.
Provide as much detail as possible.

"快乐中国行" 暑假夏令营活动申请表

姓名： 梁果	性别： 男	照片或自画像

国籍： 美国	所在城市： 城ville	出生年月： 胡 2014年

所在学校： MBA

详细通讯地址： 90 Ave ICT
Nashville TN ~ 185

电子邮件信箱： hoage@naeby-morytell.edu

电话： (615)444-6644

是否参加过同类夏令营活动： 没有 如"是"，最近一次活动时间：	你从哪里得知本次夏令营的信息？ 请在符合你情况的选项后划"√"。
	同学或朋友　　　　（　　）
	老师　　　　　　　（ √ ）
	海报或其他广告　　（　　）
	网络　　　　　　　（　　）
	其他　　　　　　　（　　）

申请参加本次夏令营的原因： 我想找到好的职业。

本次夏令营中你最大的愿望是什么？为什么？
我想吃许多的中国菜因为我喜欢中国饭。

你对本次夏令营活动安排有什么具体建议，并请简要说明建议理由：
我希望可以去卡威州看望中国的成熟之一。

在你所参加过的其他夏令营或其他校外活动中，你最喜欢哪一次活动？为什么？
并请简要描述那次活动的主要过程。

Anecdotes of Learning Chinese

副课文

学汉语的趣事

Pre-reading

■ 你学习汉语多长时间了?

■ 你在学习汉语过程中有哪些有趣的事情?

有几位来自世界各国,并且都在北京学习汉语的留学生,在一次周末聚会时,聊起他们汉语学习的经历以及一些有趣的故事。

🇰🇷 金俊雄(韩国人)	🇬🇧 安娜(英国人)
🇺🇸 赵刚(美国人)	🇺🇸 大卫(美国人)
🇹🇭 文丽(泰国人)	

1.服务员为什么会把"盐"听成了"烟"?二者的区别在哪里?

2.什么是"儿化音"?

3.北京人说话的重要特点是什么?能举几个例子吗?

4.安娜为什么会把"银行"看成了"很行"?它们在形、音、义方面有什么区别?

金俊雄: 上个星期,我和几个朋友一起去附近的饭馆吃饭,我们点了几个菜,其中一个菜的味道特别淡,我把服务员叫过来,跟他说:"请给我拿点儿盐!"没想到过了一会儿,服务员拿了一包烟放在我的桌子上!

赵　刚: 你的声调有问题吧?盐、烟不分!

金俊雄: 确实是这样。

文　丽: 俊雄说到语音问题,我的麻烦是儿化音。刚到北京的时候,我坐出租车,司机问我:"你要去颐和园的哪个门儿?"我根本不知道他在说什么。在泰国我学过"哪个门",但是没学过"哪个门儿"。最奇怪的是北京人说的英语好像也有儿化音。在王府井,一个商店老板问我"Are you a student*er*?"开始我以为他在说汉语,后来才意识到,他说的是带儿化音的英语。

安　娜: 我第一次见到人民币的时候,非常惊奇,因为我看到人民币上写着"中国人民很行"。我知道这句话的意思是说中国人很棒，可是为什么要在钱币上告诉大家中国人很棒呢？现在明白了，上面写的是"中国人民银行"，我看错了一个字，读错了另一个字。

赵　刚：大卫，在我们几个人中，你在中国学习的时间最长，你有什么故事吗？

5. "拦路虎"是什么意思？

大　卫：我学汉语经常遇到的拦路虎是成语。有一次在动物园，我看见熊猫津津有味地吃着竹叶，突然想到一个成语，就脱口而出："你们看，熊猫已经胸有成竹了！"结果周围的人哈哈大笑。还有一次，我看到一群小孩儿在捉迷藏，大家玩得兴高采烈。可是有一个小朋友找来找去都找不到可藏的地方。我想过去帮他，就问他："小朋友，你是不是无地自容了？"我现在还记得那个小孩儿的表情，他莫名其妙看着我说："应该是你无地自容吧？"

6. 大卫使用"胸有成竹"这个成语时，别人为什么会笑？

7. 大卫使用了"无地自容"，小孩儿为什么生气了？

赵　刚：真有意思！我也觉得从书本上、课堂上学到的汉语，一定要有机会使用，才能成为自己的东西。可是找谁去练自己的汉语呢？与其找辅导老师，不如找出租车司机。每次坐出租车，我都和师傅侃大山，天南海北地随便聊，还能了解一般市民的生活呢。出租车司机的性格和见识各不相同，口音也不同，所以每次和他们聊天儿，都能学到很多东西，还能够提高口语和听力水平。我喜欢学这种马路汉语。

8. 和出租车司机聊天儿有什么好处？你有这样的体会吗？

9. 你理解这里说的"马路汉语"是什么意思吗？

VOCABULARY

副课文 **生词表**

1	淡	dàn	*adj.*	bland; tasteless
2	声调	shēngdiào	*n.*	tone
3	儿化音	érhuà yīn	*n.*	r-sound
4	老板	lǎobǎn	*n.*	boss
5	意识	yìshi	*v.*	to be aware, conscious of; to realize
6	钱币	qiánbì	*n.*	coin
7	拦路虎	lánlùhǔ	*n.*	hindrance, obstacle
8	津津有味	jīnjīnyǒuwèi +地		with great interest; with keen pleasure
9	脱口而出	tuō kǒu ér chū		blurt out
10	胸有成竹	xiōngyǒuchéngzhú		have a well-thought-out plan in one's mind; confidently
11	捉迷藏	zhuōmícáng		hide and seek; blindman's buff
12	兴高采烈	xìnggāocǎiliè		in high spirits; excited
13	无地自容	wúdìzìróng		feel extremely ashamed
14	辅导	fǔdǎo	*v. & n.*	to tutor
15	侃大山	kǎndàshān		shoot the breeze; chatting, spending time with sb
16	天南海北	tiānnánhǎiběi		talk about a wide range of subjects
17	市民	shìmín	*n.*	urban residents
18	见识	jiànshi	*n.*	knowledge about various things; experiences

My Father, Laoshe

第二课

儿子眼中的父亲

Laoshe

■ 你觉得你的父亲或母亲是怎样一个人？
■ 在一般的美国家庭中，父母和子女的关系是怎样的？

老舍是中国现代著名文学家。舒乙是老舍的儿子，曾任现代文学馆馆长。下面是著名电视节目主持人杨澜对舒乙的采访。

杨　澜：舒乙先生，您父亲为什么给您起这个名字呢？这个"乙"字有什么来历？

舒　乙：这个得从我姐姐说起。她生在济南，所以叫舒济，繁体的"濟"字难写极了。父母两人很后悔，给小孩取了这么麻烦的名字，上小学多困难啊！所以给我起名字时，就简简单单的，一笔……

杨　澜：而且您正巧是老二，甲、乙、丙、丁排队排到乙字。

舒　乙：对。

杨　澜：您是家里唯一的儿子，老舍先生有没有望子成龙的那种期望，或者说从小对您非常严格？

舒　乙：正好相反，他的儿童观非常独特，不主张管得特别严，过早告诉孩子各种行为规范，约束他天性的发展。所以在我们的成长中，他基本上不管我们。

杨　澜：您的学习成绩好和坏他都不管吗？

舒　乙：不管。像我小妹妹上高中的时候，有一天突然哭着回家，父亲感到很纳闷儿，说："怎么了？"她说："我今天数学考了六十分。""考六十分又怎么样？我小时候净不及格。"

杨　澜：他反而安慰你们。

舒　乙：她说："那我怎么考大学？" "考不取大学在家，我教你英文。"你瞧，他就是这样，向来主张儿童要保持天真，只去发展兴趣和爱好。

杨　澜：老舍先生1947年只身到美国去了，1956年母亲才带着你们全家离开重庆迁回北京，那时您已经是十五岁的半大小子了。父亲和您久别重逢，怎么打招呼？

舒　乙：这个也很有意思。他拄着手杖在站台上接我们，看见我，马上把手<u>伸</u>过来："你好，舒乙！"把我吓坏了，因为那么小，从来没有人和我握过手，何况是自己的父亲。

杨　澜：他完全把您当作一个平辈的朋友了。

舒　乙：他一见面就郑重其事地给我传递了一个<u>信息</u>：当儿子长到一定的年龄，父子就是平等的朋友了。

杨　澜：一般来说，他<u>专心</u>工作，可能生活这一边都撒给您母亲，由她来照顾一家人。他有没有照管过您的衣食住行？

舒　乙：他实际上是一个很温情和蔼的人，表示爱的方式也非常特别。比如说我已经工作，出差前去跟他告别。他说："你过来。"我以为他有什么事，可是他说："你把车票给我看看。"我掏出来给他看。然后他突然又说："你带了几根皮带？"我就<u>琢磨</u>皮带还要带几根吗？"就一根。"他说："那不行。"我说："怎么了？"他说："万一这根断了呢？"

杨　澜：他在很<u>细致</u>的地方用一种很含蓄的方式来表现他的关爱。

舒　乙：是啊。

（摘自杨澜《渴望生活》，因课文需要有删改。）

VOCABULARY
生词表

| 1 | 文学家 | wénxuéjiā | ~~great~~ writer |

【名】古代文学家 | 一位伟大的文学家 | 文学家很受人尊敬。 | 丁小姐爱写小说，希望成为一名文学家。 图家：具有某种专门知识或从事某种专门活动的人。 图作家 | 画家 | 音乐家 | 书法家。

| 2 | 文学馆 | wénxuéguǎn | hall of writers |

【名】一位文学馆工作人员 | 在文学馆举办书画展览 | 请问去中国现代文学馆怎么走？ 图馆：收藏、展览或进行文化体育活动的地方。 图美术馆 | 博物馆 | 展览馆 | 图书馆。

| 3 | 馆长 | guǎnzhǎng | curator |

【名】副馆长 | 一位中国国家博物馆馆长 | 他做图书馆馆长二十年了。 图长：负责人，领导人。 图厂长 | 省长 | 部长 | 班长。

| 4 | 主持人 | zhǔchírén | presenter |

【名】会议主持人 | 一位电视节目主持人 | 春节晚会通常有四个以上的主持人。 图介绍人 | 经纪人 | 代理人 | 负责人。

| 5 | 来历 | láilì | origin |

【名】有来历 | 查明来历 | 这笔钱来历不明，不能接受。 | 说起这支笔，可是大有来历。

| 6 | 繁体 | fántǐ | traditional Chinese character |

【名】繁体字 | 繁体形式 | 这本书是繁体印刷的。 | 简体字比繁体的更容易学习。 "车"这个字的繁体形式是"車"。 图体：文字的书写形式。 图简体 | 草体 | 楷体。

| 7 | 正巧 | zhèngqiǎo | by chance |

【副】事情发生的时候，我正巧在场。 | 老师叫我找你去，正巧你来了。 | 他打电话来时，我正巧不在家。

| 8 | 甲、乙、丙、丁 | jiǎ、yǐ、bǐng、dīng | first, second, third, fourth |

【名】甲、乙、丙、丁四种 | 甲、乙、丙、丁四级 | 甲、乙、丙、丁四类中，甲是第一类。 | 这段对话里有甲、乙、丙、丁四个人物。

| 9 | 唯一 | wéiyī | only, sole |

【形】唯一的心愿 | 唯一的遗憾 | 他是我唯一的亲人。 | 这是唯一一条上山的公路。

| 10 | 望子成龙 | wàngzǐ-chénglóng | to have high expectations for your children |

哪个父母不是望子成龙呢？ | 望子成龙的愿望是好的，但有时会给孩子带来过大的压力。 | 家长们望子成龙的心情可以理解。

| 11 | 期望 | qīwàng | hope, expectation |

【名】美好的期望 | 人民的期望 | 过高的期望 | 社会在发展，人们也不断提出了新的期望和要求。 图期：等待。 图希望 | 愿望 | 盼望。

| 12 | 儿童观 | értóngguān | philosophy toward childraising |

【名】父母的儿童观对孩子的成长有很大影响。 | 要树立正确的儿童观。 图观：观点，看法。 图世界观 | 人生观 | 价值观。

| 13 | 管 | guǎn | to discipline |

【动】管孩子可不是一件容易的事。 | 现在的学生管起来比较难。 | 这件事你管不管？

| 14 | 规范 | guīfàn | standard, the norm |

【名】道德规范 | 语言规范 | 学生要遵守行为规范。 | 一定要按照规范服务。 图范：模范；好榜样。 图典范 | 示范 | 模范 | 范例。

15	约束	yuēshù	to restrict, restrain

【动】严加约束 | 约束自己的行为 | 这种规定约束不了他们。

16	天性	tiānxìng	natural disposition

【名】孩子的天性 | 人类的天性 | 这个孩子天性善良。 | 他天性不爱说话。 | 互相帮助是人类的天性。📖性：性格。📖个性 | 耐性。

17	纳闷儿	nàmènr	to feel puzzled

【动】这事儿太让人纳闷儿了。 | 他心里纳闷儿，但嘴上没说出来。 | 我一直很纳闷儿昨天是谁找我。 | 这有什么好纳闷儿的！

18	<u>安慰</u>	ānwèi	to comfort, console

【动】安慰家属 | 安慰病人 | 谢谢你安慰我。 | 人在伤心的时候特别需要别人安慰。 | 你要多安慰安慰他，叫他别太难过。📖抚慰 | 劝慰 | 告慰 | 慰问 | 慰劳。

19	向来	xiànglái	always

【副】向来如此 | 向来很认真 | 他向来不喜欢热闹。 | 妈妈起床向来很早。 | 他说话向来简洁明了。📖近来 | 从来。

20	主张	zhǔzhāng	to advocate, recommend

【动】主张和谈 | 主张和平解决问题 | 他主张立刻出发。 | 我主张大家先去看电影。

21	天真	tiānzhēn	innocent

【形】天真活泼 | 天真烂漫 | 孩子的笑容是最天真的。 | 你的看法太天真了。

22	只身	zhīshēn	solitarily, alone

【副】只身前往 | 只身一人在国外 | 他只身一人来到香港。 | 我每年暑假都去看望只身在外打工的父亲。

23	迁	qiān	to move

【动】迁移 | 迁居 | 搬迁 | 当这里不再适合古人类生存时，他们就不得不迁往别处。 | 公司已经迁到新办公地点了。

24	半大小子	bàn dà xiǎozi	teenager

她有个儿子，如今已长成半大小子了。 | 都半大小子了，还得让父母操心。 | 楼下常有一群半大小子吵吵闹闹，让人无法安静。

25	久别重逢	jiǔbié-chóngféng	to reunite after a long time

老朋友久别重逢，大家格外高兴。 | 我们久别重逢，可得好好聊聊。 | 和亲人久别重逢的喜悦是难以用言语形容的。

26	打招呼	dǎzhāohu	to greet somebody

【动】互相打个招呼 | 随便打个招呼 | 见到我来，大家都过来打招呼。 | 他很热情，总是主动和别人打招呼。📖打手势 | 打哈欠 | 打滚儿。

27	拄	zhǔ	to lean on (a stick)

【动】拄拐杖 | 拄着棍子走 | 手拄着地做俯卧撑。

28	手杖	shǒuzhàng	walking stick

【名】一根手杖 | 老爷爷手里拄着手杖，走得很慢。

29	站台	zhàntái	platform

【名】站台票 | 长长的站台 | 我到站台接你。📖台：某些高而平的建筑、设备。📖讲台 | 舞台 | 主席台。

30	<u>伸</u>	shēn	to stretch, extend

【动】伸展 | 伸直 | 伸头 | 伸胳膊伸腿 | 把你的五指伸开。 | 这架照相机的镜头可伸可缩，真棒！

31	平辈	píngbèi	person of the same generation

【名】我和他是平辈。 | 他比我大很多，可是我们是平辈，因为他是我父亲的学生。📖晚辈 | 长辈 | 同辈。

32	郑重其事	zhèngzhòng-qíshì	to take something seriously

*郑重其事*地说 | 大家随便说说自己的想法就可以了，不必太*郑重其事*。| 虽然只是个小聚会，但大家都穿得*郑重其事*。| 六岁的小女儿*郑重其事*地宣布，今天的家庭会议将由她来主持。

33	传递	chuándì	to pass, hand something down

【动】*传递*火炬 | *传递*爱心 | *传递*信件 | 他负责*传递*消息。

34	专心	zhuānxīn	to concentrate hard

【副】*专心*研究 | 不*专心*学习，是无法取得好成绩的。| 他在课堂上*专心*听讲，认真记笔记，所以课后很轻松。◧专：集中在一件事上。◧专注 | 专车 | 专刊。

35	撇	piē	to cast aside, neglect

【动】他把我们都*撇*在一边，自己去玩了。| 别把大家的话*撇*在脑后。| 孩子都*撇*给我，我一个人照顾不过来。

36	衣食住行	yī shí zhù xíng	basic necessities

*衣食住行*是生活的基本需要。| 政府十分关心老百姓的*衣食住行*问题。| 随着经济的发展，人们的*衣食住行*水平明显改善。

37	温情	wēnqíng	tender

【形】*温情*的呵护 | *温情*的目光 | 她是个很*温情*、善良的女人。◧情：感情。◧亲情 | 人情 | 爱情 | 豪情。

38	和蔼	hé'ǎi	amiable

【形】亲切*和蔼* | 态度*和蔼* | *和蔼*的笑容 | 在大家的印象中，他永远都是一副*和蔼*可亲的样子。

39	方式	fāngshì	way

【名】工作*方式* | 行为*方式* | 做事情要注意*方式*。| 你的*方式*方法有问题。

40	出差	chūchāi	to go on a business trip

【动】*出差*期间 | 去北京*出差* | *出差*到深圳 | 他*出差*去了。| 前两天，我*出*了一次*差*。◧差：公务。

41	皮带	pídài	leather belt

【名】一根*皮带* | 一条宽*皮带* | 军用*皮带* | 我去买根*皮带*。◧裤带 | 腰带 | 背带 | 鞋带。

42	琢磨	zuómo	to ponder, think over

【动】<口> 仔细*琢磨* | 这件事让我*琢磨*了很久。| 我不会做这道题，你帮我*琢磨琢磨*。

43	细致	xìzhì	attentive to detail

【形】非常*细致* | 他做事认真，多*细致*的地方都能想得到。

44	含蓄	hánxù	implicit

【形】性格*含蓄* | *含蓄*的目光 | *含蓄*地笑了笑 | 这个人说话向来都很*含蓄*。| 你太*含蓄*了，别人不懂你的意思。

45	关爱	guān'ài	care and concern

【名】父母的*关爱* | 无限的*关爱*和同情 | 深切的*关爱* | 是老师和同学们的*关爱*让他战胜了困难。

PROPER NOUNS			
46	杨澜	Yáng Lán	Yang Lan, a famous TV presenter of China

中国著名电视节目主持人。

47	济南	Jǐnán	Jinan, in Shandong Province

城市名。山东省省会，中国历史文化名城，自古有"泉城"的美称。南面是泰山，北边是黄河。

48	重庆	Chóngqìng	Chong qing, a city in the west of China

城市名。原属四川省，现在是中国四个直辖市之一。中国历史文化名城。在长江边。

VOCABULARY IN CONTEXT

后悔

麻烦

细致

专心

安慰

琢磨

反而

Fill in the blanks with words from the boxes.

正巧

打招呼

告别

完全

A

WORD PROCESSING PRACTICE
Choose 40 words from the Vocabulary section and type them on your computer using *pinyin* input method.

B

Fill in the blanks with the words from the boxes.

甲：没想到这件事现在这么_____，我特别_____当初没有听你的。

乙：既然已经这样了，就_____把它做完吧，现在说这些也没有用了。

甲：我做错事时，你从来不责怪我，_____总是_____我，我很感谢。

乙：别再_____已经过去的事了，你也没有什么大错，以后考虑事情再_____一些就行了。

C

　　汉语里，在不同场合，和不同对象说的话往往是不一样的。比如，和别人_____，最普通的说法就是"你好"。如果你和他关系比较熟，_____最近又有一段时间没有见面，你可以说"最近怎么样啊"、"最近忙什么呢"。假如是和别人_____，通常的说法就是"再见"。但如果是你邀请的客人，只说"再见"就显得太简单了，人们常常说的是"您慢走"。这个说法的意思不能_____从字面上理解，它并不是真的让客人慢慢走的意思，而是一种表示关心和客气的说法。

LANGUAGE CONNECTION

从⋯⋯说起
is often used to begin a narration.

For example
■ 要说这个柜子的来历，得从我奶奶说起。

⋯⋯极了
follows an adjective and shows a strong degree of emphasis about the thing you are describing.

For example
■ 大家都喜欢张老师，因为她的课讲得好极了。

Ⓐ 从⋯⋯说起

"这个得从我姐姐说起。"

Complete or rewrite the sentences using "从⋯⋯说起."

1. 要说这块手表的来历，_____

   _____。

2. 要问这条狗从哪里来的，_____

   _____。

3. 原　句：关于这件事我有很多话要跟他说，但是不知道怎么开始。

   替换句：_____

   _____。

Ⓑ ⋯⋯极了（extremely）

"繁体的'濟'字难写极了。"

Write sentences using "⋯⋯极了" and the information below.

1. 人人都买的冰激凌

   _____。

2. 2000000000000，这是一个几乎数不清的数字

   _____。

3. 拿到奥斯卡奖的男演员

   _____。

4. 200公斤重的蛋糕

   _____。

5. 她只能穿最小号的鞋

   _____。

正好相反

shows that what is going to be said is quite contrary to the condition or situation just described.

For example
A：你是不是喜欢吃四川菜？
B：正好相反，我不能吃辣的。

净

means "always" and is usually used in spoken Chinese.

For example
■他上课净迟到，老师总批评他。

或者说

"或者" and "说" are used together to connect two sentences with similar meaning.

For example
■你是不是对这个决议有看法？或者说，你有保留意见？

何况

is used to emphasize a further meaning.

For example
■学好母语都要花很大的气力，更何况学习另一种语言。

当……

can be used to describe the time of an event. It is usually used together with "……的时候" and other words that indicate time.

For example
■当我们的飞机到达北京的时候，天已经黑了。

C **正好相反**（on the contrary）

"正好相反，他的儿童观非常独特。"

Complete the dialogs using "正好相反."

1. 甲：听说他这人爱说别人坏话。

   乙：＿＿＿＿＿＿＿＿＿＿＿＿＿＿。

2. 甲：你是不是打算再呆一年？

   乙：＿＿＿＿＿＿＿＿＿＿＿＿＿＿。

3. 甲：据说这部电影非常不错。

   乙：＿＿＿＿＿＿＿＿＿＿＿＿＿＿。

D **净**（always）

"我小时候净不及格。"

E **或者说**（in other words）

"老舍先生有没有望子成龙的那种期望，或者说从小对您非常严格？"

F **何况**（even less; more so）

"从来没有人和我握过手，何况是自己的父亲。"

G **当……**（when...）

"当儿子长到一定的年龄，父子就是平等的朋友了。"

万一

is used to describe a situation that is unlikely to happen.

For example

- 万一天气变冷，衣服带得不够就麻烦了。

或者说	
何况	
当……	
净	

H **万一**（in case）

"万一这根断了呢？"

Complete the sentences using "万一."

1. _____ 你的签下去的份_____,

被狗咬了怎么办呢？

2. _____ 万一我的东西以后一挂下来 ,

我的东西给谁呢？

3. _____ 万一我的前年早听一个小时 ,

我把他吵醒了也不太好。

RECAP

Fill in the blanks with the words from the boxes.

1. 他球拍都不会拿，_____打球呢。

2. _____夕阳下山的时候，天边火红火红的，漂亮极了。

3. 别_____欺负你姐姐，你这淘气鬼！

4. 这是一个严重的问题，_____，是一个不能轻视的问题。

COMMON EXPRESSIONS

为什么
For example
- 已经是春天了，为什么天气还这么冷？

有什么……
For example
- 你们有什么问题？

怎么了
For example
- 你怎么了？不舒服吗？

怎么 + V
For example
- 你怎么去？
- 你是怎么来美国的？

有没有……
For example
- 你有没有冬天游泳的习惯？

A 为什么（why...）

is used to ask someone for a reason.

"您父亲为什么给您起这个名字呢？"

B 有什么……

is used to ask about the contents or details of something. It requires a full answer.

"这个'乙'字有什么来历？"

C 怎么了（what's wrong/up？）

You can ask how a person is feeling with "怎么了."

"父亲感到很纳闷儿，说：'怎么了？'"

D 怎么 + V（how...）

is often used to ask for the way or the method to do something.

"那我怎么考大学？"

E 有没有……

is a selective question. It requires an answer that is either positive or negative.

"老舍先生有没有望子成龙的那种期望？"

RECAP

Role play the following situations using the words from the boxes.

为什么

有什么……

怎么 + V

有没有……

Situation 1 : Your classmate comes into the classroom, waving his arms and saying, "Fantastic! Great!" You want to know why he is so happy. Role play the conversation with your classmate.

Situation 2 : After a conversation on the phone, Lingling goes into her room without saying a word. After a long time, her mother goes into Lingling's room and finds her crying. Role play the conversation between Lingling and her mother.

Situation 3 : Your classmate says he needs your help and wants to borrow some money from you. You want to know the reason. Role play the conversation with your classmate.

COMMUNICATION CORNER

Instructions:

- Conduct research using the Internet, books, magazines, or newspapers for information about Lao She or another famous Chinese writer.

- Work in pairs. Ask your partner questions about the writer they have researched. Then switch roles.

作家的故事

Guidelines:

You can start by asking your partner some background information about the writer, such as which period he/she worked in, his/her most famous work, etc.

◀ 你说的这位作家生活在哪个时代？

◀ 你说的这位文学家的代表作是什么，你是从哪儿了解到他的信息的？你为什么想到要了解他呢？

You can clarify your understanding by restating your partner's answers and asking follow-on questions.

◀ 你是说，他的作品已经有好几部被翻译成英文了吗？

◀ 她不仅是中国那个时代非常突出的女作家，而且个人经历充满传奇色彩，那她的婚姻和家庭有什么特殊的故事吗？

◀ 那后来呢？

Finally, you can express your feelings about what you have learned about the writer.

◀ 是啊，这位作家不仅作品给人带来享受，他富有战斗精神的人生也让人敬佩！

◀ 你说的故事真有意思。

◀ 原来是这样呀。

WRITING TASK

Instructions:

- Conduct a survey on the topic "How parents express their love for their children." Prepare a list of interview questions and interview 3 of your classmates. Take notes during the interviews.

- Write a short report summarizing what you learned from the interviews.

- Keep your writing to about 300 words.

天下父母心

Guidelines:

You may ask questions like these during your interview. 采访

父母怎么给孩子过生日？

如果孩子的期末考试成绩很不好，不同的父母会怎样对待他们的孩子？

孩子生病的时候，父母怎么样对待他？

作为父母，和孩子之间最常用的沟通方式是什么？

Note down the answers to each of your questions during the interviews.

In your report, compare and contrast the ways parents from different cultures express their love for their children.

Raising Children
in a Cross-Cultural
Marriage

副课文

跨国婚姻家庭
中的孩子

Pre-reading

■ 你知道东方和西方在家庭教育方面有哪些不同吗?

■ 你家的家庭教育方式是怎样的?

主持人: 观众朋友,今天我们请来了一位跨国婚姻家庭中的妈妈,还有她的儿子杰西。杰西既接受了中国式教育,也接受了西方式教育。杰西,你喜欢爸爸还是喜欢妈妈?

杰　西: 喜欢妈妈。

主持人: 那你比较怕谁?

杰　西: 妈妈。

主持人: 哦,也是妈妈。杰西听话吗?如果不听话怎么办?

1.杰西生活在怎样的家庭中?

妈　妈: 孩子不听话是经常的事儿。我的脾气比较急,孩子小的时候,我父母帮忙照顾,非常宠爱他。杰西不高兴的时候就会跟我父母叫喊,我特别生气,要惩罚他。

2.杰西不听话的时候,妈妈怎么办?

主持人: 看来妈妈比较厉害。

妈　妈: 我很严厉地骂杰西时,他爸爸坐在旁边,虽然不满意,但是并不说什么。他主张耐心说服教育,一次谈不通,就谈两次,一定要让孩子理解、记住他所犯的错误。但是我们俩有个协议,就是当一个人管教孩子时,另一个人不要提意见。

3.爸爸是什么态度?

4.爸爸妈妈为什么要定一个协议?

主持人: 后来爸爸去跟他谈吗?

妈　妈：是，他会和孩子谈很长时间，有时将近一个小时，然后他们俩手拉着手走出来，孩子跟我和外公、外婆说对不起。

> 5.杰西比较接受怎样的教育方式？

主持人：杰西，跟你说话时，谁的态度好一些？

杰　西：爸爸说话比较耐心。

主持人：看来教育孩子一定要有耐心。

主持人：现在孩子在家庭中，除了得到父母的爱，还有爷爷奶奶、姥姥姥爷的爱，而隔代人更加宠孩子。

> 6.姥姥姥爷怎样对待杰西？

妈　妈：这点在我们家表现得特别明显。爷爷奶奶是外国人，还好些。外公外婆特别宠孩子，杰西要怎样就怎样。

主持人：那怎么办呢？

> 7.妈妈不同意姥姥姥爷的教育方式，怎么办？

妈　妈：真没有办法。我从小离开家，父母把对我的爱加倍地用到孩子身上。所以杰西3岁时，我就把他接到北京来上幼儿园，现在孩子的个性挺独立的。

主持人：你觉得是东方式的教育比较成功还是西方式的教育比较成功？

> 8.在跨国婚姻家庭中孩子教育的难点是什么？

妈　妈：各有利弊，我比较喜欢东方的教育方式。

主持人：杰西的情况比较特殊，他接受了三种不同的教育，妈妈是一种教育，爸爸是一种教育，他的外公外婆又是一种教育，有时他很难确定自己的行为标准。

妈　妈：我对这个问题也特别困惑。

> 9.你喜欢怎样的教育方式？为什么？

主持人：对孩子的教育是一个大问题，需要家长认真研究，通过有效的沟通寻找到共识，在方法上取得一致。谢谢！

VOCABULARY

副课文 生词表

1	跨国	kuàguó	international, transnational
2	婚姻	hūnyīn	marriage
3	脾气	píqi	temper
4	惩罚	chéngfá	to punish
5	厉害	lìhai	strict, stern
6	骂	mà	to scold
7	犯	fàn	to do (something wrong)
8	协议	xiéyì	agreement
9	隔代	gédài	cross-generation
10	宠	chǒng	to spoil
11	独立	dúlì	independent
12	成功	chénggōng	successful
13	利弊	lìbì	pros and cons
14	困惑	kùnhuò	frustration
15	沟通	gōutōng	to communicate
16	共识	gòngshí	consensus
17	一致	yīzhì	in agreement

UNIT SUMMARY
学习小结

一、重点句型

别看……可是……	别看他们说的普通话不太标准，可是跟他们交谈对提高听力是非常有用的。
并	我并没有被吓倒。
"被"字句	我并没有被吓倒。
"把"字句	重要的是把这些知识用在实际的生活中。
从……说起	这个得从我姐姐说起。
……极了	繁体的"濟"字难写极了。
正好相反	正好相反，他的儿童观非常独特。
净	我小时候净不及格。
或者说	老舍先生有没有望子成龙的那种期望，或者说从小对您非常严格？
何况	从来没有人和我握过手，何况是自己的父亲。
当	当儿子长到一定的年龄，父子就是平等的朋友了。
万一	万一这根断了呢？

二、交际功能

陈述喜欢的缘由。
进入话题，并推进谈话。

三、常用表达式

首先……其次……最后……	首先，我爱学中文的原因是非常欣赏它的实用性；其次，我爱学中文，是因为汉语能帮助我了解中国文化；最后，我爱学中文是因为有挑战性。
我爱……是因为……	我爱学中文是因为有挑战性。
非常欣赏它（他）的……	我爱学中文的原因是非常欣赏它的实用性。
在我看来，……	在我看来，中文学习真的是"师傅领进门，修行在个人"。
为什么	您父亲为什么给您起这个名字呢？
有什么	这个"乙"字有什么来历？
怎么了	父亲感到很纳闷，说："怎么了？"
怎么+动词	那我怎么考大学？
有没有	老舍先生有没有望子成龙的那种期望？

UNIT **2**

FESTIVALS AND CUSTOMS

节日与风俗

Communicative goals

- Talk about similarities and differences in the way two festivals are celebrated
- Express agreement, excitement, or approval
- Explain the source or origin of something

Cultural information

- The Chinese lunar calendar and the animal zodiac
- Major Chinese festivals and celebrations
- Festive foods and their symbolic meanings
- Origins and legends of Chinese festivals

Warm up

　　人们每年都要过很多节日，不同国家有不同的节日，每个节日又有不同的习俗，甚至同样的节日在不同国家的习俗也不相同。

1. 请在下表中填上你知道的节日及其习俗。

节日名称	日 期	起 源	国家	习俗		
				活动	吃	其他
万圣节	10月31日	源于古西欧国家。那时人们相信，亡魂会在10月31日回来。	美国	带着可怕的面具聚会。	提着南瓜灯挨家挨户讨糖吃。	

2. 请你向大家介绍一个节日及其习俗。

**Celebrating
Chinese New Year**

第三课
过年

Pre-reading

■ 你最喜欢过什么节？为什么？
■ 你家怎么过新年？

〖一〗

寒假结束了，一开学，张平就去留学生宿舍找他的美国朋友麦克。

麦克：张平，你回来啦？

张平：回来了。你过年去哪儿了？

麦克：我去王露家了，过得特别开心。除夕那天我在他们家学会包饺子了！王露妈妈包的饺子非常好吃，我一口气吃了二十多个，还吃到一个包了硬币的呢。

张平：真的？你今年肯定要交好运了。

麦克：王露的妈妈也这么说。哎，你回广东老家，在农村过年也特别有意思吧？

张平：那当然了！大年三十，家家户户贴对联、贴"福"字、吃团圆饭，饭桌上一定要有年糕和鱼。晚上一家人围着电视看春节联欢晚会、聊天儿。十二点一到，鞭炮声响成一片，热闹极了！

麦克：有意思，那大年初一呢？

张平：大年初一是新年第一天，大人、小孩都穿上新衣服，到亲戚家拜年，长辈会给孩子发红包，里面包着压岁钱。我小时候能得到几毛钱的压岁钱，就开心得不得了，现在红包里少于一百块，有些人都觉得不好意思给呢。

麦克：是吗？这变化太大了。听说城里过春节也跟以前不一样了。

张平：没错。有人觉得在家里准备饭菜太累，就到
餐馆里去吃团圆饭，还有人利用春节长假到
外地旅游。我女朋友一家这回就去海南过
年了。

麦克：真的？可是我在电视里看到，春节期间，还
是有成千上万的人回家过年。

张平：是啊，不管怎样，春节对于中国人来说，最
重要的还是合家团圆，这一点不会变。对
了，明天是元宵节，我们一起去我女朋友家
吧。过完元宵节，春节才算真正结束呢！

麦克：好，我吃过饺子了，还没吃过元宵呢！

〖二〗

正月十五，元宵节到了。这天下午，麦克在宿舍里等张
平，准备和他一起过节。

麦克：你怎么才来啊，真让人着急。

张平：着什么急啊，天还没黑，元宵节的
花灯还没亮呢。

麦克：那咱们现在干什么？

张平：咱们先去我女朋友家吧。

麦克跟着张平到他女朋友家，吃了一顿元宵。然后麦
克、张平、张平的女朋友三人一起去公园看花灯。

麦克：这些花灯太漂亮了！我最喜欢这些动物灯。

张平：这叫十二生肖灯。你是属牛的吧，看到你的
生肖图案了吗？

麦克：看到了！哈哈，真有趣！

张平女友：咱们猜灯谜去吧，猜灯谜有奖品。

麦克：可是我看不懂，怎么猜呀？

张平：没关系，我们猜中的话，奖品分给你一半。

麦克：那还可以，走吧。

VOCABULARY
生词表

1	除夕	chúxī	Chinese New Year's Eve

【名】除夕夜 | 除夕是中国一年中最热闹的时候了。| 除夕夜的钟声响起，全家人共同庆祝新年的到来。📖夕：夜晚。📖前夕。

2	包	bāo	to wrap

【动】包书 | 头上包着一块白毛巾 | 他用纸把钱包好，放进了贴身的衣服口袋里。| 这件衣服我买了，请帮我包起来好吗？📖包饺子 | 包粽子 | 包包子 | 包馄饨。

3	饺子	jiǎozi	Chinese dumpling

【名】一个饺子 | 一盘芹菜馅饺子 | 饺子你喜欢吃蒸的还是煮的？| 除夕夜，北方人都要包饺子吃。

4	一口气	yīkǒuqì	at one go, without a break

【副】一口气跑回家 | 一口气把话说完 | 他太饿了，一口气吃了三碗饭。| 这本书真有意思，我一口气把它全部读完了。

5	交好运	jiāo hǎoyùn	to have a lucky streak

这么看来，我们就要交好运了。| 我祝大家在新的一年里都交好运。| 你看起来这么有精神，是不是最近交了什么好运了？

6	老家	lǎojiā	hometown

【名】回老家一趟 | 老张的老家在福建。| 回农村老家看看。| 今年他不能回老家过年了。

7	对联	duìlián	a Chinese couplet

【名】一副对联 | 春节对联内容不同，大小不一，但都表达了人们美好的愿望。| 对联是中国春节习俗中很有文化内涵的一部分。📖春联 | 挽联 | 楹联 | 寿联。

8	团圆饭	tuányuánfàn	family reunion dinner

【名】一顿团圆饭 | 分别这么多年，吃顿团圆饭吧！| 每当除夕到来，全家人都聚到一起，热热闹闹地吃团圆饭。

9	年糕	niángāo	Chinese New Year cake

【名】打年糕 | 蒸年糕 | 做年糕 | 一块年糕 | 过年吃年糕是中国的传统习俗，因为它的读音像"年高"。📖蛋糕 | 发糕 | 糕点。

10	联欢	liánhuān	to have a get-together, to have a party

【动】联欢活动 | 军民联欢 | 一场大型联欢会 | 为了庆祝国庆，学校举办了师生大联欢。📖联：联合。📖联盟 | 联系 | 联名。

11	晚会	wǎnhuì	an event/party that takes place in the evening

【名】迎新晚会 | 一台歌舞晚会 | 我是在一个晚会上认识她的。| 春节联欢晚会八点钟开始。| 晚会现场气氛十分热烈。📖舞会 | 聚会 | 宴会。

12	鞭炮	biānpào	firecracker

【名】买两挂鞭炮 | 一阵鞭炮声 | 在中国，过年时家家户户都要放鞭炮。

13	亲戚	qīnqi	relative

【名】一门亲戚 | 亲戚关系 | 我们两家是亲戚。| 我们家是个大家族，所以我有很多亲戚。

14	拜年	bàinián	to pay someone a visit during Chinese New Year

【动】给老师拜年 | 向全国人民拜年 | 我给您拜个早年。| 大年初一一大早，大家就都出门互相拜年去了。| 现在，通过电话、电子邮件拜年的人越来越多了。📖拜：见面行礼表示祝贺。

15	长辈	zhǎngbèi	the older generation

【名】他是我的*长辈*。|对*长辈*要尊重。|*长辈*就得有*长辈*的样子，不能和晚辈们一般见识。☞平辈|晚辈|后辈|小辈。

16	毛	máo	10 cents

【量】<口>八*毛*钱|几*毛*钱|一*毛*等于十分钱。|这种笔九*毛*五一支。

17	压岁钱	yāsuìqián	money given to children as a gift during Chinese New Year

【名】攒*压岁钱*|孩子每年都会收到*压岁钱*。

18	开心	kāixīn	happy, joyous

【形】玩得很*开心*|见到你我*开心*得很。|看样子，这些年他过得不太*开心*。|大伙儿在一起说说笑笑，十分*开心*。

19	红包	hóngbāo	a traditional Chinese red packet with money inside

【名】送*红包*|发*红包*|一个*红包*|我已经成年了，所以今年过年没有收到*红包*。|他今年工作做得非常好，年终分到了一个大*红包*。

20	长假	chángjià	long vacation

【名】"十一"*长假*|我想利用这个*长假*好好休息休息。☞暑假|寒假|春假|休假|请假|假期。

21	外地	wàidì	other places

【名】*外地*货|他到*外地*出差去了。|这个城市有数十万来做生意的*外地*人。|听他说话像是*外地*口音。☞本地|当地|产地|出生地。

22	回	huí	a measure word (for number of occasions)

【量】有一*回*|这一*回*|我去过两*回*上海。|长城我去玩过好多*回*了。|我头一*回*见到这么美的风景。|我给他打过好几*回*电话都没人接。|我们下*回*再来吧。

23	成千上万	chéngqiān-shàngwàn	tens of thousands

*成千上万*的用户|他祖父给他留下了*成千上万*的家产。|*成千上万*的人从各地赶来，观看十月一日天安门广场的升旗仪式。

24	合家团圆	héjiā tuányuán	family reunion

祝*合家团圆*|*合家团圆*的心愿|春节是中国人*合家团圆*的喜庆日子。|老人们最高兴的事就是*合家团圆*。☞合：全。

25	变	biàn	to change

【动】*变*天了。|这个城市*变*样儿了。|他一听这话，脸色都*变*了。|情况*变*了，想法也要跟着*变*。

26	元宵节	yuánxiāojié	the Lantern Festival (on the 15th night of the first lunar month)

*元宵节*联欢晚会|过完*元宵节*才算真正过完年。|唐代开始有*元宵节*观灯的风俗。

27	元宵	yuánxiāo	glutinous rice dumplings

【名】一斤*元宵*|一袋*元宵*|*元宵*可以煮着吃，也可以炸着吃。

28	花灯	huādēng	festive lantern

【名】看*花灯*|闹*花灯*|元宵节一到，沿街的店铺都挂上了各式各样的*花灯*。

29	顿	dùn	a measure word (for meals)

【量】一天三*顿*饭|早上那*顿*饭要吃得好一点。|三个人一*顿*饭花了一百多块钱。

30	生肖	shēngxiào	the animals of the Chinese zodic

【名】十二*生肖*|*生肖*邮票|十二*生肖*纪念品|中国人常常用*生肖*来记年龄。

31	属	shǔ	to be born in the year of

【动】*属*狗|他是*属*马的。|*属*羊的今年是本命年。|明明和爷爷都*属*虎，爷爷今年六十，小李十二，祖孙俩正好差四轮。

32	图案	tú'àn	design

【名】漂亮的*图案*|设计*图案*|这张剪纸的*图案*很有中国特色。

33	<u>有趣</u>	yǒuqù	interesting

【形】很*有趣*|特别*有趣*|*有趣*的传说|*有趣*的风俗|只要仔细观察，就会发现生物界有很多有趣的现象。趣：趣味，兴味。

34	<u>猜</u>	cāi	to guess

【动】*猜*谜语|*猜*着了|她的心思我*猜*不透。|快说吧，别让我们*猜*了。|大家*猜*一*猜*谁来了？

35	灯谜	dēngmí	lantern riddle

【名】猜*灯谜*|三条*灯谜*|这个*灯谜*我实在猜不出来了，你快把谜底告诉我吧。

36	<u>中</u>	zhòng	to hit, be just right

【动】相*中*|看*中*|射*中*|考*中*|你选*中*了哪种颜色？|他*中*了头等奖。|这句话正*中*他的要害，他立刻不说话了。

37	奖品	jiǎngpǐn	prize

【名】很多*奖品*|发*奖品*|参加者每人都能得到一份*奖品*。品：东西；物品。商品|用品|产品|战利品。

PROPER NOUNS			
38	广东	Guǎngdōng	Guangdong Province

中国南部沿海的一个省，简称"粤"。是中国经济第一大省。

39	海南	Hǎinán	Hainan Province

中国南部的一个省，简称"琼"。该省为一海岛，是旅游胜地。

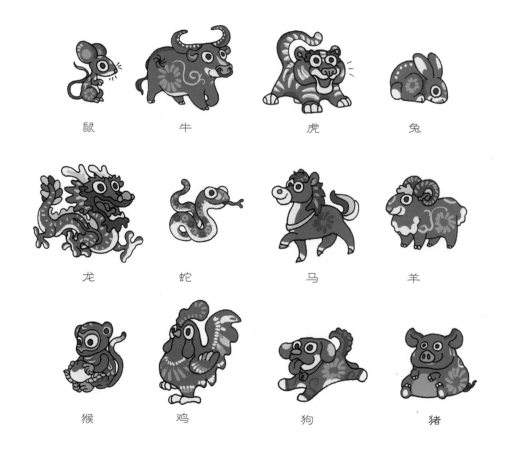

鼠　　牛　　虎　　兔

龙　　蛇　　马　　羊

猴　　鸡　　狗　　猪

VOCABULARY IN CONTEXT

回

毛

顿

遍

开心

外地

一口气

肯定

成千上万

咱们

图案

有趣

中

A Fill in the blanks with measure words.

一_____纸　　　两_____笔　　　三_个_书包

四_____同学　　五_____教师　　六_把_椅子

七_____门　　　八_____马　　　九_____猪

十_____菜

B Fill in the blanks with the measure words from the boxes.

学校门口不远处有一个小面馆，那里面条味道不错，而且特别便宜，一碗西红柿面只要八_____钱。有时我一天连着去那儿好几_回___，早、中、晚三_顿_饭都在那儿吃。不过，在那儿吃饭你不能着急，点了一碗面后，可能要催好几_遍___才能给你端出来，老板说，面条都是现煮的，所以慢。

C Fill in the blanks with the words from the boxes.

1. 甲：你_____吃了八个！你_____特别
　　　爱吃这儿的包子吧！

　　乙：对，每次从_____回来，到这儿吃顿包
　　　子，是最让我_____的事情！

2. 甲：你小时候玩过万花筒吗？几个简单的
　　　_____竟然能变出_____的花样，
　　　你似乎总也猜不_____它下次会是什么
　　　样子。真是太_____了！

　　乙：是啊，它看起来很简单，但是给_____
　　　的童年带来了很多乐趣。

LANGUAGE CONNECTION

学会＋Verb

is used to say that you have learned to do something.

For example
- 我们已经学会用中文打字了。
- 只要有决心，我们就能学会应用这门技术。

Besides "学会," there are other words that have a similar structure and usage. These include "看会," "练会" etc.
- 什么事情都是练会的，而不是看会的。

少于……

means "less than." "于" in this structure introduces the subject of comparison. Similarly, we have "多于"(more than), "晚于"(later than), "低于"(lower than), "慢于"(slower than) etc.

For example
- 如果价钱高于300元，我就不买了。
- 早于八点，商店都不开门。

Complete or rewrite the sentences using the grammar structures listed.

A 学会 + Verb（learned to do something）

"除夕那天我在他们家学会包饺子了。"

1. 只要有决心，_____

   _____。

2. 经过反复尝试，我终于_____

   _____。

3. 我相信_____

   _____。

B 少于……（less than...）

"现在红包里少于一百块，有些人都觉得不好意思给呢。"

1. 我想好了，_____

   _____，我就不买了。

2. 他的学习成绩很棒，_____

   _____。

3. 这个病人的体温_____

   _____。

就

is used to show a connection between two sentences.

For example

- 他等了我半天，我没到，他就走了。
- 小熊猫很胆小，看见有人来，就跑到竹林里去了。

不管（怎样），……还是……

means a situation will not change no matter what happens. "不管" can be followed by "都", "也", "还是".

For example

- 不管怎么忙，他也要抽时间去看望父母。
- 今天不管到几点，都要把这篇文章写完。

C 就（then）

"有人觉得在家里准备饭菜太累，就到餐馆里去吃团圆饭。"

1. 我家小狗 _____ ，_____ ，它就 _____ 。

2. 上个月 _____ ，我和哥哥就 _____ ，_____ 。

3. _____ ，_____ ，就 _____ 。

D 不管（怎样），……还是……（no matter...,still...）

"不管怎样，春节对于中国人来说，最重要的还是合家团圆。"

1. 原　句：无论晚上儿子多晚到家，妈妈都会等着他。

   替换句：_____ 。

2. 原　句：我们列举了种种理由，他仍然不听我们的劝，坚持自己一个人去。

   替换句：_____ 。

3. 原　句：无论如何，我今天一定得写完这个作业。

   替换句：_____ 。

COMMON EXPRESSIONS

肯定

can be used to express opinions when a condition is almost certain.

For example
- 你看，天这么阴，肯定要下雨。
- 这么晚了，他肯定不来了。

那当然了

is usually used when you agree with someone. It means "of course" or "without a doubt."

For example
A：咱们班这回一定会赢的。
B：那当然了！咱们准备得多充分呀！

A：在少林寺学习武功一定会学到很多真功夫。
B：那当然了！少林寺的武僧都有一身过人的本领。

特别……   ……极了
……得＋不得了   太……了

These expressions are all used to indicate very strong emphasis. "特别" should come before the verb/adjective; "极了" should come after the verb/adjective; "……得＋不得了" should also come after the verb/adjective; "太……了" should have the verb/adjective in the middle.

For example
她这个人特别聪明，多难的数学题都能做出来。
最近我忙极了，有时连饭都顾不上吃。
这件衣服实在太漂亮了。

Think of two more situations for each expression given below. Then role play each situation with your partner.

A 肯定（definitely）

"你今年肯定要交好运了。"

Situation 1：你和妈妈准备出门，你发现天很阴……

Situation 2：_____

Situation 3：_____

B 那当然了（of course）

"那当然了！大年三十，家家户户贴对联、贴'福'字、吃团圆饭。"

Situation 1：你请朋友吃你做的蛋糕，朋友觉得很好吃……

Situation 2：_____

Situation 3：_____

C 特别……，……极了   （very; extremely）

……得＋不得了，太……了

"你回广东老家，在农村过年也特别有意思吧？"
"十二点一到，鞭炮声响成一片，热闹极了！"
"我小时候能得到几毛钱的压岁钱，就开心得不得了。"
"这变化太大了。"

Situation 1：朋友请你看电影，可你最近功课很紧，要准备好几门考试……

Situation 2：_____

Situation 3：_____

COMMUNICATION CORNER

Instructions:

- Work in pairs. Imagine your partner has recently bought a new computer and installed a few of the latest games on it.

- Role play a conversation in which one partner invites the other over to play on the new computer.

- Use the expressions we have just learned in the text to express your agreement, admiration or praise.

你的电脑真棒！

Guidelines:

You may start the conversation like this:

甲：最近我刚买了一台电脑，玩……游戏真是棒极了。怎么样，周末去我们家玩一玩？

乙：好主意，这个游戏我平时也常玩儿，可我的电脑速度太慢了，周末就到你们家去玩吧。

You can accept an invitation by saying:

◁ 到你们家玩……游戏？没问题，我很喜欢，就在这个周末吧。

◁ 那好啊！我本来就喜欢玩……游戏。明天怎么样？

◁ 可以啊，这个周末我正好有空，你在家等我好了，我肯定去。

You can express your admiration for the new computer using one of the following sentences.

甲：你的电脑真棒！画面真清晰，哇！看起来特别真实！

乙：那当然了。这是现在市场上最好的电脑。

甲：那一定不便宜吧？

乙：还可以，贵是有一点贵，不过我真是特别喜欢。

Besides the computer, you may also express praise or admiration for other items in your friend's house, such as his book or music collection, his travel photos, etc.

◁ 还可以、还不错、还行（一般程度）

◁ 好极了、太棒了、太帅了、太精彩了、真有意思、真有趣、……是最好的、……是最漂亮的、……是最优秀的……（最高程度）

◁ 没有比这更好的了！（最高程度）

WRITING TASK

Instructions:

- Write about Western festivals that are celebrated in China, and Chinese festivals that are celebrated in America.

- Keep your writing to about 300 words.

东西方节日的相互影响

Guidelines:

You may start by introducing Chinese festivals that are celebrated in America, incorporating details such as who celebrates them, where many people celebrate them, and how they are celebrated.

Correspondingly, write about Western festivals that are celebrated in China.

Western festivals such as Christmas Day and Valentine's Day are becoming more popular among the younger generation in China today. Include your thoughts on this modern development.

Reference Materials

上海

今天是2006年平安夜，据说商场里销售额特别高，而且各个酒吧都坐满了人。因为天气不够冷，所以快12点时街边还有很多人在闲逛。我嫌酒吧人太挤，约了两个朋友到家里聊天，一起等待圣诞节的到来。

——一个中国人的网络日记

休斯顿

由于人们把农历的正月十五看作中国人的传统佳节春节的最后一天，加上今年元宵节又是周末，休斯顿华人社区的各种庆祝活动就显得格外热闹。3月4日全天，整个华人社区喜气洋洋、龙飞狮舞，到处是过年的景象。休斯顿市市长比尔·怀特发布通告：把2007年3月4日命名为休斯顿今年的"中国元宵节"。

——一则新闻报道

The Origin of Chinese Valentine's Day

副课文

七夕节的传说

Pre-reading

■ 你知道西方情人节的来历吗？
■ 很多中国人把传统的七夕节看作中国的情人节，你知道它的传说吗？

1.为什么说七夕节是最具浪漫色彩的节日？

2.牛郎是怎样一个小伙子？

3.牛郎和织女结婚后生活怎样？

七夕是中国传统节日中最具浪漫色彩的节日。相传每年农历七月初七的夜晚，天上的"织女"与"牛郎"都在银河的鹊桥上相会。这里有一个流传千古的美丽爱情故事。

很早以前，有一个聪明、老实的小伙子，跟着哥哥嫂子一起生活，但是哥哥嫂子对他很不好。他白天放牛，晚上就和牛住在一起，大家都叫他牛郎。牛郎一年一年长大了，哥哥嫂子就把他赶出家门。牛郎便带着一头老牛，开始了自己的生活。

一天，天上的七个仙女一起来到人间，牛郎在老牛的帮助下认识了其中最漂亮的织女，他们之间产生了爱情。织女决心不再回到天上，就做了牛郎的妻子。结婚以后，牛郎种地，织女织布，他们生了一儿一女两个孩子，一家人生活得很幸福。但是好景不长，这事让掌管仙女的王母娘娘知道了。她认为，仙女是不可以和地上的人结婚的，于是，亲自来到人间，要强行拆散这对恩爱夫妻，把织女带回天上。

4.王母娘娘是怎样拆散牛郎和织女的？

5.牛郎织女每年七月初七怎样会面？

6.中国青年男女怎么过七夕节？

7.你觉得这个传说有意思吗？为什么？

牛郎知道后，非常着急，又是在老牛的帮助下，带着两个孩子飞上天。眼看牛郎就要追上织女了，谁知王母娘娘拔下头上的金簪一挥，天上就出现了一道天河，牛郎和织女被隔在了河的两岸，只能相对哭泣流泪。他们的爱情感动了喜鹊，千万只喜鹊飞来，在河上搭成了鹊桥，让牛郎织女走上鹊桥相会。王母娘娘也没有办法，只好允许牛郎织女每年七月七日晚上在鹊桥上见一次面。

现在人们把七夕称作中国的情人节，青年男女很喜欢在这一天晚上约会。另外，因为织女是心灵手巧的天仙，所以，七夕的晚上，姑娘们都在室外摆上好吃的瓜果点心，抬头仰望星空，寻找银河两边的牛郎星和织女星，希望能看到他们一年一度的相会，并且请求上天让自己能像织女那样心灵手巧，祈祷自己能有称心如意的美满婚姻。

VOCABULARY
副课文 **生词表**

1	七夕	qīxī	the seventh evening of the seventh month of the Chinese Lunar Year
2	浪漫	làngmàn	romantic
3	相传	xiāngchuán	to pass from generation to generation
4	农历	nónglì	the Chinese lunar calendar
5	鹊桥	quèqiáo	the Magpie Bridge
6	放牛	fàngniú	to graze cattle
7	仙女	xiānnǚ	the Chinese fairy
8	种地	zhòngdì	to cultivate the land
9	织布	zhībù	to weave cloth
10	隔	gé	to be separated (by distance or time)
11	喜鹊	xǐquè	magpie
12	搭	dā	to build
13	情人节	qíngrénjié	Valentine's Day
14	心灵手巧	xīnlíng‑shǒuqiǎo	clever and capable (with one's hands)
15	祈祷	qídǎo	to pray
16	称心如意	chènxīn‑rúyì	perfectly matching expectations

PROPER NOUNS			
17	织女	Zhīnǚ	the weaver fairy from Chinese legend
18	牛郎	Niúláng	Zhīnǚ's husband, a cowherd
19	银河	Yínhé	the Milky Way
20	王母娘娘	Wángmǔ niángniang	the Queen Mother of Heaven

Moon Festival

第四课
中秋节

Pre-reading

■ 你知道现代载人登月飞船吗？知道月球的情况吗？

■ 古代有很多关于月亮的传说，你知道哪些？

农历八月十五日是中国的传统节日——中秋节。那时正好是秋季的中间，所以叫作中秋节。中秋节的夜晚，月亮又圆又大。古人把圆月看作团圆的<u>象征</u>，因此，中秋节又叫"团圆节"。人们过这个节有哪些习俗呢？

赏月

中秋节人们有赏月的习惯。农历十五日的月亮是满满的圆月，<u>洁白</u>、明亮。节日的夜晚，一家人围坐在<u>院子</u>里，一边看月亮，一边聊天儿。老人们喜欢指着月亮告诉孩子们关于月亮的传说，什么嫦娥啦，玉兔啦，吴刚啦……

人们更希望他们的生活像圆月一样永远美好，团团圆圆。但是生活就像月亮一样，有时候圆，有时候缺。比如出门在外的人，中秋节不能和家人团圆，就是一种<u>遗憾</u>，他们只能对着圆月来<u>想念</u>家人。唐代诗人李白的"举头望明月，低头思故乡"，宋代苏轼的"但愿人长久，千里共婵娟"等诗句，都是表达这种心情的千古绝唱。

吃月饼

　　中秋节最重要的习俗是吃月饼。月饼是一种<u>特制</u>的有馅儿的点心。月饼的大小和形状不完全一样，不过大多像中秋的月亮一样，是圆形的。月饼的表面印有各种图案：嫦娥奔月、月中玉兔，还有吉庆的文字，像"花好月圆"、"合家团圆"等等。月饼馅儿的<u>品种</u>就更多了，有果仁的、豆沙的、火腿的、蛋黄的……中秋节之夜，一家人围坐在一起，一边赏月，一边吃团圆月饼，觉得非常幸福。亲朋好友也互相<u>赠</u>送月饼，表达美好的<u>祝愿</u>。

舞火龙

　　舞火龙是香港中秋节最有传统特色的习俗。从每年农历八月十四日的晚上开始，铜锣湾的大坑地区就一连三个晚上举行大型的舞火龙活动。火龙是用草做的，长几十米，身上插满了<u>点燃</u>的香。到了晚上，一条条长长的火龙随着鼓乐欢腾起舞，非常热闹。

　　传说很早以前，香港大坑地区在一次大风灾以后，出现了一条蟒蛇，因为它到处做坏事，后来村民们把它打死了。但是，几天以后，这个地区却出现了传染病。据说人们在菩萨的帮助下，中秋佳节时舞动火龙，便把病魔赶跑了。

　　香港中秋舞火龙的习俗流传至今，已有一百多年的历史了。

跳托球舞

每到中秋之夜，台湾高山族人都要穿起美丽的民族服装，来到日月潭边，在银色的月光下，男男女女一起跳起托球舞。

相传古代有一对青年夫妇，生活在一个水潭边，靠捕鱼度日。一天，太阳和月亮突然都不见了，天地间一片黑暗，禾苗死了，花果不长了，虫鸟也哭起来了。青年夫妇决定要把太阳和月亮找回来。他们发现太阳和月亮是被两条大龙吃到肚子里了，于是他们杀死了那两条龙，还用大树枝把太阳和月亮托上了天空。他们变成了两座山，永远守护在潭边。这个大潭，就是今天的日月潭。

后来每逢中秋，高山族人都要来到日月潭边，模仿那对夫妇的样子，托起象征太阳、月亮的彩球跳舞，以求风调雨顺，五谷丰登。

VOCABULARY
生词表

1	象征[1]	xiàngzhēng	symbol, token

【名】天安门广场是北京的象征。| 火炬是光明的象征。| 鸽子是和平的象征。

2	赏月	shǎngyuè	to enjoy looking at the moon

【动】中秋赏月 | 中秋节的晚上，我们全家人一边吃月饼一边赏月。🔲赏：欣赏；观赏。月：月亮。

3	洁白	jiébái	pure white

【形】洁白的牙齿 | 洁白的上衣 | 🔲洁：干净。

4	院子	yuànzi	courtyard

【名】大院子 | 院子里 | 走出院子 | 打扫院子。

5	遗憾[2]	yíhàn	regret

【名】留下遗憾 | 最大的遗憾 | 终生的遗憾 | 他去过北京，但是没有爬过长城，这真是一个遗憾。🔲遗：留，留下。

6	想念	xiǎngniàn	to miss

【动】想念亲人 | 想念故乡 | 特别想念 | 深深地想念 | 他们在国外，常常想念着祖国。🔲念：想，惦记。🔲想念 | 思念 | 挂念。

7	举	jǔ	to lift, raise

【动】举步 | 举目 | 举手之劳。

8	故乡	gùxiāng	hometown

【名】我的故乡 | 回到故乡 | 离开故乡 | 热爱故乡 | 故乡的朋友 | 故乡的山水。🔲故：原来的；过去的。

9	婵娟	chánjuān	the moon

【名】千里共婵娟。| 婵娟是月亮的代名词。

10	绝唱	juéchàng	unsurpassed masterpiece

【名】千年绝唱 | 人间绝唱 | 文学史上的绝唱。🔲绝：水平、程度等达到顶点的。🔲绝招 | 绝技 | 绝活儿。

11	特制	tèzhì	specially made (for a specific purpose or by a special process)

【动】特制香烟 | 特制的信封 | 特制的卡片 | 这种车是为残疾人特制的。

12	馅儿	xiànr	filling

【名】饺子馅儿 | 肉馅儿 | 素馅儿 | 今天包子的馅儿有点儿咸。

13	嫦娥奔月	Cháng'é bēn yuè	a legend about Chang'e who flew to the moon

嫦娥奔月是中国最著名的神话故事之一。

14	吉庆	jíqìng	auspicious occasion

【形】吉庆话 | 吉庆图案 | 吉庆的日子 | 充满吉庆欢乐的气氛 | 这幅画有吉庆的意义。

15	花好月圆	huāhǎo-yuèyuán	a wish for family happiness

花好月圆的时刻。

16	品种	pǐnzhǒng	breed, kind

【名】品种齐全 | 品种繁多 | 水果的品种 | 货物的品种 | 增加新品种。

| 17 | 果仁 | guǒrén | kernel |

【名】一粒果仁 | 果仁面包 | 果仁巧克力。▣仁：果实或果核里的东西。▣桃仁 | 杏仁。

| 18 | 豆沙 | dòushā | sweetened bean paste |

【名】豆沙包 | 豆沙馅儿 | 豆沙月饼 | 豆沙面包。

| 19 | 火腿 | huǒtuǐ | ham |

【名】火腿肉 | 火腿肠 | 火腿面包。

| 20 | 蛋黄 | dànhuáng | yolk |

【名】咸蛋黄 | 蛋黄月饼。

| 21 | 祝愿 | zhùyuàn | wish |

【名】接受祝愿 | 朋友的祝愿 | 美好的祝愿 | 真诚的祝愿。

| 22 | 点燃 | diǎnrán | to ignite |

【动】点燃蜡烛 | 点燃火炬 | 每人手里都拿着一个点燃的火把。

| 23 | 鼓乐 | gǔyuè | drumbeats |

【名】欢快的鼓乐 | 鼓乐急促 | 鼓乐震天 | 鼓乐喧天 | 鼓乐齐鸣。

| 24 | 欢腾 | huānténg | to be elated |

【动】一片欢腾 | 欢腾的气氛 | 欢腾的人群 | 欢腾的景象 | 好消息传来，人们立刻欢腾起来。

| 25 | 起舞 | qǐwǔ | to dance (poetic) |

【动】随风起舞 | 翩翩起舞 | 缓缓起舞 | 跟着音乐起舞。

| 26 | 风灾 | fēngzāi | typhoon, violent storm |

【名】大风灾 | 严重的风灾 | 抵御风灾 | 这次风灾造成了严重损失。▣火灾 | 水灾 | 旱灾。

| 27 | 蟒蛇 | mǎngshé | python |

【名】一条蟒蛇 | 粗大的蟒蛇 | 蟒蛇是无毒的。

| 28 | 传染病 | chuánrǎnbìng | contagious disease |

【名】急性传染病 | 传染病医院 | 预防传染病 | 控制传染病。

| 29 | 菩萨 | púsa | Bodhisattva |

【名】观音菩萨 | 拜菩萨 | 求菩萨保佑！

| 30 | 病魔 | bìngmó | serious illness |

【名】可怕的病魔 | 病魔缠身 | 战胜病魔 | 摆脱病魔。

| 31 | 托 | tuō | to hold up, support by hand |

【动】托着下巴 | 服务员手托茶盘走过来。 | 请你把病人的头托起来。

| 32 | 捕鱼 | bǔyú | to catch fish |

【动】渔民们都出海捕鱼去了。 | 爷爷以捕鱼为生。 | 江边的小孩从小就学会了捕鱼捉虾。 | 昨天一天时间我只捕到几条小鱼。▣捕：捉；逮。

| 33 | 度日 | dùrì | to make a living |

【动】老两口无儿无女，相依度日。 | 一家人靠一点土地艰难度日。

| 34 | 禾苗 | hémiáo | rice or wheat seedlings |

【名】禾苗干枯 | 绿油油的禾苗 | 由于气候干旱，地里的禾苗都枯死了。▣苗：初生的种子植物或幼小的动物。▣树苗 | 麦苗 | 鱼苗 | 火苗。

35	肚子	dùzi	belly, stomach

【名】肚子疼 | 拉肚子 | 肚子饿了。

36	<u>守护</u>	shǒuhù	to guard, defend

【动】日夜守护 | 共同守护 | 妈妈在病床前守护着孩子。▣守卫 | 守候 | 守门。

37	彩球	cǎiqiú	colored ball

【名】一串彩球 | 联欢会现场装饰着彩球。▣彩：彩色。

38	风调雨顺	fēngtiáo-yǔshùn	favorable weather (for agriculture)

风调雨顺的日子 | 盼望风调雨顺 | 但愿新的一年风调雨顺。 | 今年这里风调雨顺，粮食大丰收。

39	五谷丰登	wǔgǔ-fēngdēng	a good harvest

五谷丰登的景象 | 神保佑今年五谷丰登。

PROPER NOUNS			
40	嫦娥	Cháng'é	Chang'e, the Moon Goddess

传说中住在月亮里的一个美女。

41	玉兔	Yùtù	Yutu, the jade hare on the moon

传说中住在月亮里的一只捣药的小白兔。

42	吴刚	Wú Gāng	Wu Gang, the woodcutter on the moon

传说中一个在月亮里不停地砍树的人。

43	李白	Lǐ Bái	Li Bai, a famous poet from the Tang Dynasty

唐代著名诗人。

44	苏轼	Sū Shì	Su Shi, a famous writer from the Song Dynasty

宋代著名文学家。

45	铜锣湾	Tóngluówān	Causeway Bay, a district in Hong Kong

香港地名。

46	大坑	Dàkēng	Tai Hang, a district in Hong Kong

香港地名。

47	高山族	Gāoshānzú	Gaoshan ethnic minority group, in Taiwan

中国少数民族之一，主要分布在台湾。

48	日月潭	Rìyuètán	Sun Moon Lake, in Taiwan

台湾一个有名的风景区。

VOCABULARY IN CONTEXT

Dictate the paragraphs to your partner in the turn. Pay attention to the words colored.

A

1. 他的演唱非常有特色，一般人根本无法模仿。

2. 为了照顾那些不能吃糖的病人，工厂为他们准备了一种特制的月饼，这种月饼就是后来的"无糖月饼"。

3. 传说，这种洁白的小花象征着姑娘对远方恋人的想念。所以，每年花开的时候，姑娘们都喜欢把它戴在头上，表达自己对拥有美好爱情的祝愿。

4. 农历七月十五是中元节，又称"鬼节"。在农村，这一天有一种特殊的习俗，家家都会在房子周围、院子内外点燃灯笼和蜡烛，以寄托对亲人的思念，并期望亲人能在另一个世界里继续守护着家人。

Make a paragraph using the words from the boxes.

B

洁白

想念

表达

到处

LANGUAGE CONNECTION

把A看作B
is used when relating one word to another.

For example
- 人们把动物看作自己的朋友。
- 中国人把红色看作喜庆的标志。

一边……一边……
is used when two actions are taking place at the same time.

For example
- 他一边吃饭，一边看电视。

Look at the pictures and write sentences using the grammar structures listed.

A 把A看作B（to regard A as B）

"古人把圆月看作团圆的象征。"

1. 许多人把长城看作中国的象征。

2. _____ 女神 ____ 美国的象征。

B 一边……一边……（while...）

"一家人围坐在院子里，一边看月亮，一边聊天儿。"

1. _____ 一边倒水，一边烤面包。

2. _____ 一边喝茶，一边跟他聊天儿。

什么……啦……啦……啦……
is used to list different things.

For example

■ 他的兴趣很广泛，什么音乐啦，美术啦，体育啦，都是他感兴趣的。

C 什么……啦……啦……啦……

"什么嫦娥啦，玉兔啦，吴刚啦……"

1. _____

2. _____

每到……
is usually followed by "都" or "就."
It refers to an action or a situation that happens regularly.

For example

■ 每到日落的时候，那个男孩就到村子外边等他的爸爸回来。

D 每到……（every time that...）

"每到中秋之夜，台湾高山族人都要穿起美丽的民族服装……"

1. _____

2. _____

COMMON EXPRESSIONS

……所以称作……

For example

■ 农历的新年一般在立春前后，所以称作春节。

……因此……又叫……

For example

■ 人们在端午节的时候一般要吃粽子，因此端午节在有些地方又叫粽子节。

据说……

For example

■ 据说那个球队已经解散了。

相传……

For example

■ 相传嫦娥本来是后羿的妻子，后来偷吃了长生不老药，就飞到月亮上去了。

……所以称作……

……因此……又叫……

据说……

相传……

A ……所以称作……（therefore known as…）

is used to explain the origin of a name or term.

"那时正好是秋季的中间，所以称作中秋节。"

B ……因此……又叫……（therefore it's also known as…）

is used to explain that something is known by more than one name or term.

"古人把圆月看作团圆的象征，因此，中秋节又叫'团圆节'。"

C 据说……（it is said that…）

"据说人们在菩萨的帮助下，中秋佳节时舞动火龙，便把病魔赶跑了。"

D 相传……（legend has it that…）

"相传古代有一对青年夫妇……"

RECAP

Fill in the blanks with the expressions from the boxes.

很久以前，这儿附近有一条小河，小河的两侧都是陡峭的山崖，山石林立，＿＿＿＿＿＿只有这块地方隐隐约约地露出一线天空，＿＿＿＿＿＿这个地方＿＿＿＿＿＿"一线天"，而那条小河因为从山石间流过，一直流出大山，＿＿＿＿＿＿"见天河"。后来，由于各种自然因素，比如地震啦、泥石流啦、山崩啦，那条河干了，山也没了，这儿变成了现在的一片沙地。

COMMUNICATION CORNER

Instructions:

- Individually, think of ideas for a new festival.

- Work in groups. Take turns to describe your ideas and explain the source or origin of them. Get your partner's suggestions on how to improve them.

- Choose one of your festivals, and give a presentation to your class on the topic "A New Festival."

- Keep your presentation to about 3-5 minutes.

一个新的节日

Guidelines:

🗣 You can introduce your idea of a new festival by giving details such as its name, its features, why it is celebrated, how it is celebrated, who celebrates it, and what other aspects of the festival appeal to you.

◀ 这个节日的名称是什么，你为什么要设计这个节日？

◀ 这个节日有什么突出的特点？

◀ 大家怎么过这个节日？需要做哪些准备？

◀ 哪些人会喜欢过这个节日？

🗣 Here are some useful expressions you could use in your introduction.

◀ 我想设计一个……节，因为……。这个节日最大的特点是……。过节的时候，大家首先……，然后……，另外要……，最后……

◀ ……人比较喜欢过这个节日，这是因为……。过这个节要做一些准备，比如……

🗣 To get your partner's feedback and suggestions on your idea, you can say:

甲：我最喜欢运动，因此我要设计一个和运动有关的节日，比如"棒球节"。因为美国是棒球大国，喜欢打棒球的人太多了。我相信要是有"棒球节"，一定有不少人感兴趣。你愿意过"棒球节"吗？

乙：可以考虑，但是我要了解一下你打算怎么来庆祝"棒球节"……

甲：我觉得应该……，也可以……

WRITING TASK

Instructions:

- Look at the two pictures opposite showing how people in America celebrate New Year's Eve in Times Square, and the Chinese New Year Festival in Chinatown.

- Describe what you see in the pictures and discuss the similarities and differences in the way the two festivals are celebrated.

- Keep your writing to about 300 words.

欢乐时光

Guidelines:

You can start by stating common themes in the two pictures.

> 这两幅图都表现了过节的场面，画面都很生动。

Next, describe in detail what you see in the two pictures: the location, the mood, the people, what they are doing, and their facial expressions.

> 第一幅图表现美国人过新年的场面。在图画中，左边是……，右边是……，近处是……，远处有……，另外，中间是……。人们有的……有的……还有的……，……跑来跑去……

> 第二幅图表现了在美国的中国人如何过传统的春节。其中……

Finally, you can sum up the similarities and differences in the way the two festivals are celebrated.

> 两幅图展现的场面，共同点是画面上的人们都……，区别是……

Making *Zongzi* during the Dragon Boat Festival

副课文
端午节
包粽子

Pre-reading

■ 过不同的节日要吃不同的食物，你能举一些例子吗？
■ 你可以介绍一种节日食品的做法吗？

端午节前夕，在汉语课上，老师教同学们包粽子。

老　师：同学们，我们今天这节课教大家包粽子。你们知道这个时候为什么要包粽子吗？

田　静：我知道，明天是中国农历的五月初五——端午节，端午节要吃粽子。

麦　克：端午节是什么节？

田　静：我听爷爷说，端午节是中国的传统节日。大概在2000多年前，中国分为很多小的国家，其中秦国想要消灭楚国，楚国的屈原看穿了秦王的阴谋，他劝说楚国国王不要相信秦国，但是楚国国王不但不听他的意见，反而把他赶出了首都。秦国的军队很快攻占了楚国首都。屈原在外地，不断听到楚国的坏消息，非常伤心，于是跳进了江里。大家听到屈原自杀的消息，都划着船来到江上打捞屈原。人们还包了粽子投入江中，希望鱼吃了粽子就不会去咬屈原的身体了。

安　娜：啊！这是真的吗？

1.端午节是一个怎样的节日？

2.你知道屈原是哪个时代的人物吗？你知道那个历史时期的情况吗？

3.端午节为什么要吃粽子、赛龙舟？

老　师：田静讲得对，这就是端午节的来历。后来人们在过端午节时有各种活动，比如划龙舟、吃粽子。划龙舟是一种划船比赛，它是从人们在江上划船找屈原发展来的。粽子本来是扔到江里喂鱼的，后来变成人们在这个节日里吃的一种食品了。

莉　莉：老师，越南人也吃粽子，可是和这个故事没关系。

老　师：对，亚洲许多国家都吃粽子，各国有各国的习俗和传说。好，现在我们包粽子。你们知道怎么包吗？

4.包粽子先要做哪些准备工作？

我为同学们准备了糯米、红枣和包粽子的叶子。糯米已经泡了一个晚上，叶子用的是苇叶，也可以用竹叶。现在大家跟着我做。

5.第一步怎么做

第一步：先把粽子叶折成漏斗的形状，一定要用手握紧；

第二步：在最底部放一颗枣，米就不会跑出来了，然后放糯米，中间适当放几颗枣；

6.第二步怎么做

7.第三步怎么做 ?

第三步：把米加满整个漏斗；

8.第四步怎么做 ?

第四步：把多出来的叶子盖住漏斗的口，然后用线捆住。一定要捆得结实一点，不然煮的时候就会散了。

9.怎么煮粽子 ?

10.说说你做粽子的体会。

好，同学们，粽子已经包好了。请把自己包的粽子拿回家去煮。煮的时候要注意，放的水要漫过粽子。先用大火，水开以后改为小火慢慢煮，煮一个小时。希望你们和爸爸妈妈一起过一个快乐的端午节。下课！

VOCABULARY
副课文 **生词表**

1	前夕	qiánxī	eve
2	粽子	zòngzi	steamed rice dumpling
3	看穿	kànchuān	to see through
4	阴谋	yīnmóu	conspiracy
5	自杀	zìshā	to commit suicide
6	打捞	dǎlāo	to pull something out of the water
7	龙舟	lóngzhōu	dragon boat
8	糯米	nuòmǐ	glutinous rice
9	红枣	hóngzǎo	red date
10	泡	pào	to soak
11	苇叶	wěiyè	reed leaf
12	竹叶	zhúyè	bamboo leaf
13	漏斗	lòudǒu	funnel
14	捆	kǔn	to tie, to bundle up
15	漫	màn	to overflow

PROPER NOUNS			
16	端午节	Duānwǔjié	Dragon Boat Festival
17	秦国	Qínguó	the State of Qin during the Warring States Period (475B.C.-221B.C.)
18	楚国	Chǔguó	the State of Chu during the Warring States Period
19	屈原	Qū Yuán	a minister from the State of Chu during the Warring States Period
20	越南	Yuènán	Vietnam

UNIT SUMMARY
学习小结

一、重点句型

学会＋V	除夕那天我在他们家学会包饺子了。
少于……	红包里少于一百块，有些人都觉得不好意思给呢。
就	有些人觉得在家里准备饭菜太累，就到餐馆里去吃团圆饭。
不管(怎样)，……还是……	不管怎样，春节对于中国人来说，最重要的还是合家团圆。
把A看作B	古人把圆月看作团圆的象征。
一边……一边……	一家人围坐在院子里，一边看月亮，一边聊天儿。
什么……啦……啦……啦……	什么嫦娥啦，玉兔啦，吴刚啦……
每到……	每到中秋之夜，台湾高山族人都要穿起美丽的民族服装……

二、交际功能

肯定和称赞。
解释与说明。

三、常用表达式

肯定	你今年肯定要交好运了。
那当然了	那当然了！大年三十，家家户户贴对联、贴"福"字、吃团圆饭。
特别……/……极了/……得＋不得了/太……了	你回广东老家，在农村过年也特别有意思吧？ 我开心得不得了。变化太大了。
……所以称作……	八月十五正好在秋季的中间，所以称作中秋节。
……因此……又叫……	古人把圆月看作团圆的象征，因此，中秋节又叫"团圆节"。
据说……	据说人们在菩萨的指点下，中秋佳节时舞动火龙，便把病魔赶跑了。
相传……	相传古代有一对青年夫妇……

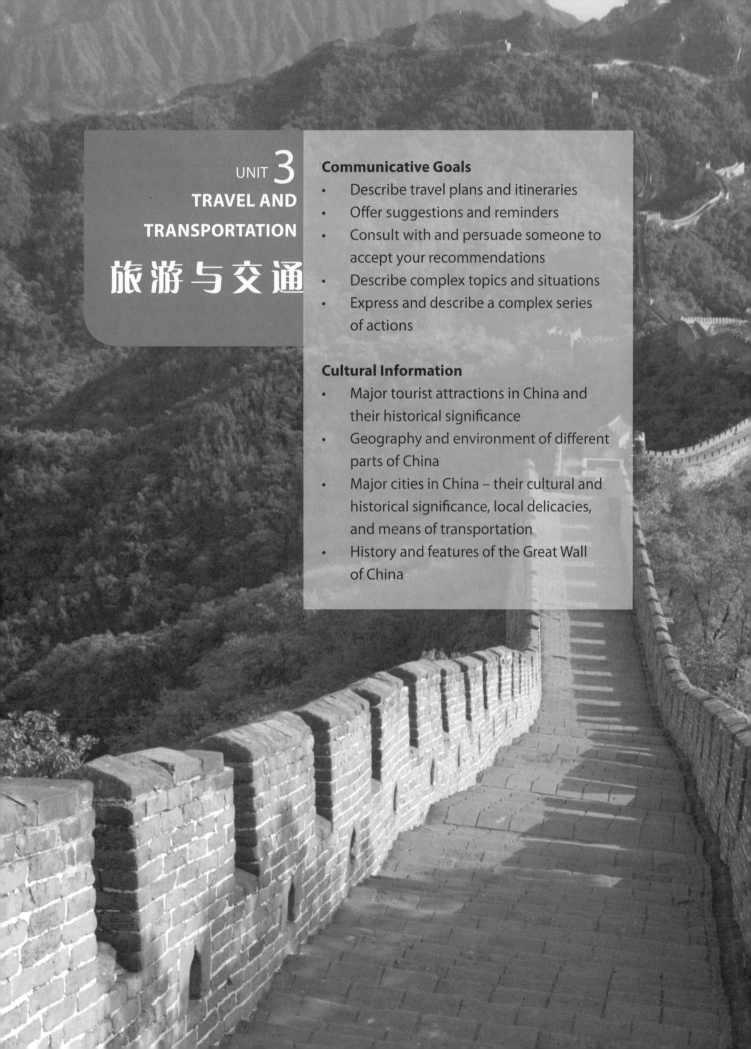

UNIT 3
TRAVEL AND TRANSPORTATION
旅游与交通

Communicative Goals
- Describe travel plans and itineraries
- Offer suggestions and reminders
- Consult with and persuade someone to accept your recommendations
- Describe complex topics and situations
- Express and describe a complex series of actions

Cultural Information
- Major tourist attractions in China and their historical significance
- Geography and environment of different parts of China
- Major cities in China – their cultural and historical significance, local delicacies, and means of transportation
- History and features of the Great Wall of China

Warm up

1. 你去中国旅游过吗？去过哪些地方？能利用你在旅游途中拍下的照片给大家做个简单的介绍吗？能在中国地图上标出你的旅游路线吗？

地图来源：中国国家测绘局

2. 根据下面的描述，你能猜出它们都是什么地方吗？你想到这些地方旅游吗？

〖一〗

中国最著名的旅游胜地之一。它已经有三千年的历史，外形像一堵长长的墙，中国有一句非常有名的话："不到_____非好汉"。

〖二〗

这个景点在中国古老的城市西安。这个地方有中国第一个皇帝——秦始皇的墓地，墓地里有许多古代士兵的塑像。

〖三〗

它是中国明朝和清朝皇帝居住和生活的地方，是中国乃至世界现存最大、最完整的古代宫殿建筑群，快有600年的历史了。在中国古代，一般老百姓都不能去这个地方，所以，它还有一个名字，叫"紫禁城"。

〖四〗

它们是位于中国南方的两个城市，一个有景色秀丽的"西湖"，一个有巧夺天工的园林，有人说"上有天堂，下有苏杭"，说的就是它们。

Planning a Trip to China

第五课

我要去中国旅游

Pre-reading

■ 你想去中国旅游吗？

■ 如果你去中国，最想去什么地方？

美国的林晓明同学和中国的林晓强同学是堂兄弟，他们经常通过网络进行联系。下面是寒假前他们在网上聊天的记录。

晓　明：嗨！晓强哥哥，你现在有时间吗？咱们聊聊？

晓　强：你好！没问题，聊吧！

晓　明：这个寒假我想去中国旅游。

晓　强：太好了！是和叔叔婶婶一起来吗？

晓　明：不，是我一个人来。你能陪我一起旅游吗？

晓　强：当然可以。

晓　明：会不会影响你的学习？

晓　强："读万卷书，行万里路"嘛，旅游也是学习。你想去哪里旅游？

晓　明：以前和父母一起去中国，总是去香港、广东。这次我想去北京、西安、敦煌、新疆、上海、苏州、杭州，还有……

Summer Palace, Beijing

Shanghai　东方真 zhū tǎ

晓　强：哎、哎！你的假期有多长时间呀？

晓　明：二十多天。

晓　强：二十多天怎么能去那么多地方？你不是想坐着飞机到处飞吧？

晓　明：我不想坐飞机，只想坐火车、汽车。要不咱们<u>租</u>一辆汽车，自驾游也行。

晓　强：我说晓明啊，你最好先从网上找一张中国地图，再根据你的时间决定去几个地方，然后咱们再来商量<u>具体</u>的计划。

晓　明：那好吧，过几天我再和你联系。

（几天后）

晓　明：晓强哥哥，现在<u>商量</u>旅行的事，可以吗？

晓　强：可以。你<u>考虑</u>好了？

晓　明：我想去的地方太多了，有些在南方，<u>有些</u>在北方。咱们这次就在北方旅游吧。你看北京、西安、敦煌、新疆怎么样？

晓　强：这几天我在网上<u>查</u>了查，每个地方都有很多可以参观的景点。我觉得四个地方也太多，这次不要去新疆了，暑假再去吧。

晓　明：好，就听你的。那咱们<u>具体</u>计划一下吧。

Beijing

晓　强：你坐飞机<u>直接</u>飞到北京，我去<u>机场</u>接你，旅游就从北京开始。北京的旅游景点很多，我们<u>安排</u>一周的时间吧。

晓　明：我们租一辆汽车好不好？我最近拿到汽车<u>驾驶执照</u>了，我开车，又省钱又省时间。

晓　强：那可不行。在中国开车的司机必须有中国的驾照，你又不懂中国的<u>交通规则</u>，<u>出事</u>怎么办？

晓　明：<u>真倒霉</u>。那我们在北京<u>只能</u>坐公共汽车了？

晓　强：不一定。我们去远的景点，比如长城、十三陵，就乘坐专线旅游大巴；去城里的景点，像天安门、故宫、北海、天坛等地方，就乘轻轨、地铁、公共汽车；去北京的胡同，或者去找一些有北京特色的饭店、小吃店的时候，就坐出租车或骑自行车。如果你想试试北京的人力三轮车，我们在游圆明园、颐和园的时候也可以坐一坐。

晓　明：太好了！

晓　强：第二个星期去西安，我们乘火车去，<u>可以</u>经过河北、山西、河南、陕西四个省，沿路看看风景。火车经过黄河大桥，咱们还可以看到黄河。

晓　明：真棒！到了西安我们先看秦始皇兵马俑吧。

晓　强：我们的火车是早上到西安，我们必须先去旅馆，安排住宿。第一天就逛西安城吧。可以参观钟楼、鼓楼、清真大寺、回民街，去吃点儿有陕西特色的小吃，像羊肉泡馍、麻辣粉什么的。第二天坐专线旅游车去华清池和兵马俑。第三天在城里参观博物馆、大雁塔、小雁塔，最后吃一顿饺子宴，就上火车去敦煌。

Beijing

晓　明：从西安可以<u>直接</u>到敦煌吗？

晓　强：不行。我们得先到兰州，然后再换一趟火
　　　　车，坐十几个小时才能到敦煌。在敦煌要参
　　　　观佛教名胜莫高窟，里面有许多珍贵的壁
　　　　画，还要去风景名胜区鸣沙山和月牙泉。我
　　　　要再查查，还有什么地方可以参观。

晓　明：你把咱们的计划发给我，我得给爸爸妈妈
　　　　看看。

晓　强：行，我尽快发给你吧。我们赶快把计划确定
　　　　下来，好早点儿订票。寒假的车票很紧张。

晓　明：好的。下次再聊。

Summer Palace, Beijing

VOCABULARY
生词表

1	堂兄弟	tángxiōngdì	paternal cousins

我有两个堂兄弟。| 他对堂兄弟的感情和亲兄弟一样。| 爸爸的兄弟生的男孩是我的堂兄弟。

2	记录	jìlù	note, record

【名】一本完整的地震记录 | 把两份记录比较一下 | 关于他出生的记录。 ▣ 录：记下的资料的名称。▣ 附录 | 目录 | 语录 | 同学录 | 通讯录 | 回忆录。

3	嗨	hēi	hi, hey

【叹】嗨，王明，最近在忙什么？ | 嗨，上课了，赶快进教室吧！

4	婶婶	shěnshen	aunt, the wife of someone's father's younger brother

【名】我的两个婶婶都是老师。| 叔叔、婶婶和堂弟，一家三口过得很幸福。

5	读万卷书，行万里路	dú wàn juàn shū, xíng wàn lǐ lù	Read ten thousand books and travel ten thousand miles

"读万卷书，行万里路"是中国的一句古话。|"读万卷书，行万里路"告诉我们读书和实践对人都非常重要。

6	租	zū	to rent

【动】租赁 | 租借 | 租用 | 租房子 | 这么贵我租不起。| 这条船租一个小时多少钱？

7	自驾游	zìjiàyóu	to go on a road trip

自驾游既方便又刺激，所以年轻人很喜欢。| 现在在中国，自驾游很流行。

8	具体	jùtǐ	concrete

【形】具体的办法 | 他具体地介绍了事情的经过。| 请把问题说得更具体一些。| 她介绍得够具体的了。

9	考虑	kǎolǜ	to consider, ponder

【动】考虑问题 | 优先考虑 | 考虑清楚 | 仔细考虑了半天也没做出决定。| 我觉得这件事考虑得不够全面。▣ 虑：思考。▣ 思虑 | 多虑 | 深思熟虑。

10	景点	jǐngdiǎn	scenic spot

【名】旅游景点 | 雕塑景点 | 自然景点 | 人文景点 | 游览景点 | 开发了一个新的观光景点 | 这里是游客最喜欢的一处景点。

11	机场	jīchǎng	airport

【名】新建了一个国际机场 | 到机场接朋友 | 一架客机安全地降落在北京首都机场的跑道上。

12	安排	ānpái	to arrange

【动】安排食宿 | 安排工作 | 安排座位 | 服从安排 | 合理安排 | 他安排得非常周到，每个人都很满意。| 每年暑假学校都安排我们去旅游。

13	驾驶执照	jiàshǐ zhízhào	driver's license

出示驾驶执照 | 驾驶执照过期了。| 没有驾驶执照，开车是违法的。| 他的驾驶执照被没收了。

14	交通规则	jiāotōng guīzé	traffic rules

学习交通规则 | 了解交通规则 | 交通规则是维持交通秩序的重要保障。| 我从来没有违反过交通规则。

| 15 | 出事 | chūshì | to have an accident |

【动】出事地点 | 出事后，司机赶快给医院打电话。| 那个十字路口车来车往，常常出事。| 那里好像出了什么事。

| 16 | 倒霉 | dǎoméi | to be unlucky |

【形】倒霉透了 | 倒了大霉 | 倒霉的事尽让他遇上了。| 今天特别倒霉，一出门就摔了一跤。

| 17 | 专线 | zhuānxiàn | special route |

【名】运输专线 | 增开公共汽车旅游专线 | 共有两条铁路专线通往山里。

| 18 | 大巴 | dàbā | bus |

【名】双层大巴 | 一辆豪华大巴 | 坐大巴到火车站。▣中巴 | 小巴。

| 19 | 乘 | chéng | to take (a bus, car, train, etc.) |

【动】乘客 | 乘电梯 | 我每天乘公共汽车上班。| 请问去天安门乘几路车？| 没赶上这个航班，可以乘下一个。| 今天乘错车了，所以迟到了。

| 20 | 轻轨 | qīngguǐ | light rail |

【名】这个城市准备修建两条轻轨。| 他每天回家都坐轻轨。| 轻轨很方便，可以作为一个城市主要的交通工具。

| 21 | 地铁 | dìtiě | subway |

【名】坐地铁从不堵车。| 连接市区和郊区的地铁驶出了市区。▣城铁。

| 22 | 胡同 | hútòng | alley, lane |

【名】孩子们在一条胡同里玩耍。| 那条胡同非常长。| 北京的胡同很有特点。

| 23 | 人力三轮车 | rénlì sānlúnchē | trishaw |

他买了一辆人力三轮车。| 骑人力三轮车，不用担心它会东倒西歪。| 坐人力三轮车游北京的胡同很有意思。

| 24 | 兵马俑 | bīngmǎyǒng | terracotta |

【名】秦始皇兵马俑在西安。| 他想买一个兵马俑模型作纪念。

| 25 | 羊肉泡馍 | yángròupàomó | a Xi'an specialty made with lamb and dough |

冬天吃一碗羊肉泡馍，浑身上下都暖暖和和的。| 羊肉泡馍是西安的特色食品。| 他很擅长做羊肉泡馍。

| 26 | 麻辣粉 | málàfěn | a spicy vegetable and noodle dish |

我喜欢吃麻辣粉。| 这碗麻辣粉够麻够辣，吃了真过瘾。

| 27 | 饺子宴 | jiǎoziyàn | dumpling feast |

西安饺子宴非常有名。| 饺子宴中的饺子有许多种制作方法。| 昨天的晚饭是饺子宴，大家吃得很开心。▣鱼宴 | 豆腐宴。

| 28 | 佛教 | fójiào | Buddhism |

【名】佛教圣地 | 少林寺是一个著名的佛教寺庙。| 五台山、峨眉山、普陀山、九华山是中国的四大佛教名山。

| 29 | 名胜 | míngshèng | place of interest |

【名】那里有几处风景名胜 | 北京的名胜古迹我几乎都游览过了。

| 30 | 壁画 | bìhuà | mural, wall painting |

【名】大型壁画 | 欣赏壁画 | 创作了一幅精美的壁画 | 敦煌壁画是中国佛教绘画艺术的宝库。▣版画 | 油画 | 国画。

| 31 | 订票 | dìngpiào | to book tickets |

电话订票 | 网上订票 | 集体订票 | 我要订三张音乐会的票。

PROPER NOUNS			
32	敦煌	Dūnhuáng	Dunhuang, a place in Gansu Province
		地名。在甘肃省。以佛教壁画闻名于世。	
33	新疆	Xīnjiāng	the Xinjiang Uygur Autonomous Region
		自治区名。在中国西北部。	
34	苏州	Sūzhōu	Suzhou, a city, in Jiangsu Province
		城市名。在江苏省。是著名的历史文化名城，也是江南水乡的代表。	
35	杭州	Hángzhōu	Hangzhou, a city, in Zhejiang Province
		城市名。在浙江省。著名的西湖在城中心。	
36	十三陵	Shísānlíng	the Ming Dynasty Tombs, in Beijing
		景点名。在北京郊区，是明朝皇家陵园。	
37	天安门	Tiān'ānmén	Tiananmen, in Beijing
		景点名。在北京市中心。	
38	故宫	Gùgōng	the Forbidden City, in Beijing
		景点名。在北京市中心，是世界最大、保存最完好的古宫殿建筑群。	
39	北海	Běihǎi	Beihai Park, in Beijing
		景点名。在北京城内，是清朝皇家花园。	
40	天坛	Tiāntán	the Temple of Heaven, in Beijing
		景点名。在北京城南，是中国古代帝王祭祀天的地方。	
41	圆明园	Yuánmíngyuán	ruins of the Old Summer Palace, in Beijing
		景点名。在北京西北郊，是清代皇家园林。后被八国联军焚毁。	
42	颐和园	Yíhéyuán	the Summer Palace, in Beijing
		景点名。在北京西北郊，是清代皇家园林。	
43	黄河	Huánghé	the Yellow River
		河流名。在中国北部黄土高原，是中国第二大河流，也是中华文明的主要发源地。	
44	秦始皇	Qínshǐhuáng	Qinshihuang, the first emperor of a united China
		秦朝（221B.C.–206B.C.）开国皇帝，中国历史上第一个封建帝王。	
45	华清池	Huàqīngchí	Huaqing Hot Spring, in Shaanxi Province
		景点名。在陕西省临潼。	
46	大雁塔	Dàyàntǎ	the Big Wild Goose Pagoda, in Xi'an
		景点名。在西安市内。	
47	小雁塔	Xiǎoyàntǎ	the Small Wild Goose Pagoda, in Xi'an
		景点名。在西安市内。	
48	兰州	Lánzhōu	Lanzhou, a city in Gansu Province
		城市名。在甘肃省。	
49	莫高窟	Mògāokū	the Mogao Caves, in Gansu Province
		景点名。在甘肃省敦煌。	
50	鸣沙山	Míngshāshān	Mingsha Mountain, in Gansu Province
		景点名。在甘肃省敦煌。	
51	月牙泉	Yuèyáquán	Crescent Lake, in Gansu Province
		景点名。在甘肃省敦煌。	

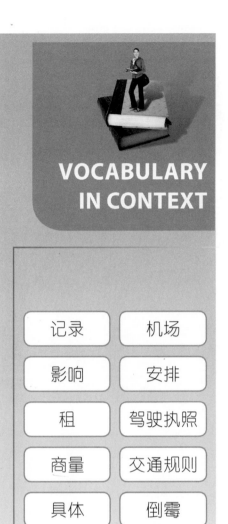

VOCABULARY IN CONTEXT

记录	机场
影响	安排
租	驾驶执照
商量	交通规则
具体	倒霉
考虑	乘
景点	

Complete the dialog with words from the boxes. Then practise the dialog with your partner.

A

During the winter vacation, Xiao Zhang is going to Hangzhou for a vacation. His good friend Xiao Wang takes him to the airport. On the way to the airport, they are caught in a traffic jam.

小张：这是什么人？这么不遵守_____，真_____。

小王：别着急，_____离这里很近，晚一点出发关系不大。

小张：你大概什么时候再来？和你的女朋友_____一下，最好两个人一起来。

小王：_____的时间我也说不清楚。最好不要_____你的工作。要是我有_____就好了，可以自己_____车，不过_____坐专线公共汽车也不错。

小张：你别那么客气，陪你是应该的。下次过来，早一点儿告诉我，我把时间_____好，这里还有一些_____值得去。

小王：当然，这里这么多好玩的地方，我还有很多没玩过呢，应该提前好好_____一下。下次我一定不能忘了带摄像机，这么多有趣的画面，的确应该记录下来。

小张：没关系，用我的也一样。

B Type out the dialog above on your computer using *pinyin* input method.

C Write dialogs using words from the boxes.

寒假	租
景点	名胜

机场	驾驶执照
交通规则	倒霉

1. 甲：_____

   乙：_____

2. 甲：_____

   乙：_____

LANGUAGE CONNECTION

疑问句及疑问语气词
An interrogative sentence proposes a question. Questions can be asked with or without interrogatives. "吗" "呢" "吧" "呀" are examples of Chinese interrogatives. However, there are some differences in what they express.

For example
Without interrogatives:
- 咱们聊聊？
- 会不会影响你的学习？

With interrogatives.
- 你现在有时间吗？
- 你的假期有多长时间呀？
- 从西安可以直接到敦煌吗？
- 他不喜欢吃辣椒吗？

……怎么办
is used to ask a rhetorical question. It shows that you do not agree with the decision of the person to whom you are speaking. It can also be used when you are warning or alerting somebody. "你说" can be placed before "怎么办" for more emphasis.

For example
- 去那么远的地方，咱们都不认识路，迷了路怎么办？
- 你总是这么马虎，万一把护照弄丢了，你说怎么办？（警告）

A 疑问句及疑问语气词（interrogatives）

"……吗？" "……呀？" "……吧？"

Choose the correct question for each group.

1. 你是想早点儿回去，还是想继续留在这里吗？ (　　)

   你是想早点儿回去，还是想继续留在这里呢？ (✓)

2. 你不是现在就想离开吧？　　　　　　　　(✓)

   你不是现在就想离开呢？　　　　　　　　(　　)

3. 你再好好考虑考虑吗？　　　　　　　　　(　　)

   你再好好考虑考虑吧？　　　　　　　　　(✓)

B ……怎么办（what if...）

"你又不懂中国的交通规则，出事怎么办？"

Role play the following situations using "……怎么办."

Situation 1: You want to arrange a date with a girl/boy, but you don't know what to do. You ask your friend for advice. Role play the conversation with your friend.

Situation 2: You are at a shopping center with your friend. You told your friend to keep an eye on your bag while you go to the bathroom. When you return, you find that your bag is gone. Role play the conversation with your friend.

Situation 3: You want to organize a debating competition, but you're afraid that no one will want to participate. Role play the conversation between you and a classmate.

先……再……然后……
is used to describe a series of actions.

For example

- 咱们今天先吃饭，再收拾一下房间，然后出去看电影，怎么样？
- 你先看看天气预报，再决定去不去爬山，决定去了，然后再准备行装也不迟。

c 先……再……然后……（first..., next..., then...）

"你最好先从网上找一张中国地图，再跟据你的时间决定去几个地方，然后咱们再来商量具体的计划。"

Look at the pictures and write sentences using"先……再……然后……"

1. ___先 ___他 ___先 ___洗脸 ___再刷口 ___然后 ___穿睡衣。___

___

2. ___把 ___子口 ___用 ___开了门 ___再看了 ___些电视___
___ ___ ___

3. ___ ___ ___ ___ ___一个 ___ ___ ___家___
___ ___了计算，人 ___ ___ ___

经过……

can be used before a place, a point in time, or an action.

For example

■ 新修的高速公路正好经过我们的小镇。

D 经过……（to pass by...）

"我们乘火车去，可以经过河北、山西、河南、陕西四个省，沿路看看风景。"

Look at the pictures and write sentences using "经过……"

1. _____

_____

2. _____

_____

3. _____

_____

……才能……

is used to explain that something can happen only if certain conditions are met.

For example

■ 只有多听多说，才能学好中文。

■ 我们必须计划好旅游的线路，才能不走冤枉路。

E ……才能……（only if...）

"我们得先到兰州，然后再换一趟火车，坐十几个小时才能到敦煌。"

Look at the pictures and write sentences using "……才能……"

1. _____

_____

2. _____

_____

3. _____

_____

COMMON EXPRESSIONS

怎么能……
For example

- 你怎么能穿这样的衣服参加毕业典礼？
- 我们怎么能不参加这次活动呢？

要不……，……也行
For example

- 要不咱们今天不在家吃饭了，出去随便找个地方吃顿饭也行。
- 你要不就别回家了，在学校里和同学们一起过感恩节也行。

最好 + V
For example

- 今天的晚会非常有意思，你最好参加。
- 为了赶时间，咱们最好别吃饭了。

……怎么样
For example

- 咱们就在这家饭店吃怎么样？
- 我们明天去看场电影，怎么样？

……好不好
For example

- 我们明天去打网球好不好？
- 你去报名参加北京的汉语短训班吧，好不好？

A 怎么能……（how could you possibly...）

is used to express dissatisfaction and annoyance.

"二十多天怎么能去那么多地方？"

B 要不……，……也行（alternatively...）

is used to give an alternative suggestion."也行" means your suggestion is also workable.

"要不咱们租一辆汽车，自驾游也行。"

C 最好 + V（you'd better...）

is used to give a suggestion.

"你最好先从网上找一张中国地图。"

D ……怎么样（what do you think of...）

is used to ask for someone's opinion.

"咱们这次就在北方旅游吧。你看北京、西安、敦煌、新疆怎么样？"

E ……好不好

is used to give a suggestion and to ask for someone's opinion by asking a "yes/no" question.

"我们租一辆汽车好不好？"

RECAP

Role play the following situations using the expressions from the boxes.

怎么能……

要不……，……也行

最好 + V

……怎么样

……好不好

Situation 1 : You want to rent an apartment near your college. You go to a property agent to ask for help. Role play the conversation with the property agent.

Situation 2 : You have been on a lucky streak recently. Your friend would like you to take him out to dinner. Role play the conversation with your friend.

Situation 3 : You would like your mother to celebrate your birthday with you by going out for a meal. However, your mother is very busy. Role play the conversation with your mother.

COMMUNICATION CORNER

Instructions:

- For this activity, you will design a holiday itinerary based on the three places of interest shown in the pictures.

- Research online for information about these places: what to do, where to stay, where to eat, how to get there, and estimated costs.

- In pairs, discuss your trip plan. Revise your plan as necessary to fit each other's specific preferences, budget, and schedule.

告诉你一个很精彩的地方

1.  美丽的三亚，这里有蓝蓝的海水、温暖的阳光；有清新的空气、高大的树木，还有好吃的水果和各种海鲜。

2.  神秘的西藏阿里，山高路险，气候干旱。可是它让无数人向往，因为这里有美丽的神山圣湖，这里的阳光特别灿烂。

3. 一直觉得北京是个奇妙的城市，有着千年的历史，又有时代的辉煌。穿过重重的高楼和宽阔的马路，来到后海酒吧坐一坐，好像回到了安静祥和的老北京。

Guidelines:

You may start off by introducing the places of interest in your trip plan, highlighting major attractions.

这个地方最大的特色是……。特别是……，非常有意思。我建议你去……

Next, you can ask your partner if he has any constraints in terms of budget or schedule.

你打算花多少钱呢？另外，你的假期有多长时间？

Customize your itinerary to fit your partner's needs and constraints, and seek their approval.

这样吧，我们安排……时间。你最好……再……。如果……你可以乘坐……。我们先……，第二天……，第三天……，最后……。这样算下来，一共需要花……钱，和你的要求差不多。

WRITING TASK

Instructions:

- Write a diary entry about a trip you took recently.
- Keep your entry to about 300 words.

我的旅行日记

Guidelines:

- Think about your experiences on a recent trip. Was the experience pleasant, interesting, educational? Were there unforgettable encounters with the weather, accommodation, traffic, local food, and the people there? Did you make any new friends? Did you bring back any special souvenirs?

For example

2月15日   晴

    今天天气真好，早上一直睡到十点才起来，打开窗帘，窗外阳光灿烂，好舒服啊。这个宾馆便宜是便宜，就是不太方便。早上不提供热水，晚上才有热水洗澡。我打开电视看了一会儿，没什么意思，再打开地图……

Old China,
Modern China

副课文

中国不是
博物馆

> **Pre-reading**

■ 你想像中的中国是什么样子？

■ 如果去中国旅游，你最想看什么？吃什么？

1.为什么美国学生看到现代化的北京会失望？

2.人们头脑中对中国和美国的印象是从哪里来的？

3.作者批评了"博物馆"心理，你同意他的观点吗？为什么？

　　许多洋人和海外华人来到中国，为看不到旧中国、老北京而感到遗憾。有个美国学生曾跟我说："我到了北京，可是并没有看到北京，我觉得很失望。"

　　我急忙问道："是怎么回事？"

　　美国学生说："我以为北京是个古老的城市，没想到竟那么现代化！北京到哪儿去了？"

　　听了他的回答，我有些同情，也有些困惑；有些难过，也有些自豪。我突然灵机一动，回答道："我第一次到美国的时候，也很失望。"

　　美国学生关切地问道："为什么？"

　　我一脸严肃地回答说："因为我没有看到牛仔挂着双枪，骑在马背上，我也没有看到印第安人拿着弓箭与白人打仗。真正的古老的美国到哪儿去了？"

　　用这种"博物馆"心理来看待中国的人可能并不止他一个。在许多人的脑海里，似乎中国人仍穿着长袍马褂、拉着洋车。在他们的观念里，凡是"中国的"，必须是"古老的"，而且也只有古老的，才是中国的。如果用这样的心理来看中国近些年的发展，当然要失望了。

其实只要对北京、上海稍有了解的人都能同意：在这两个城市里，吃到麦当劳和肯德基炸鸡是非常容易的事情，而星巴克咖啡也跟茶馆一样受到人们的欢迎。在北京，有穿旗袍的人，也有穿西装的人；有传统的四合院，也有更多的高楼大厦。中国人在保留传统的同时，也进入了现代化的生活。

中国不是博物馆，中国人也不是博物馆里的活标本。洋人到中国来，除了参观长城和兵马俑，也不妨看看三峡大坝和青藏铁路。这些工程一样是人类文明史上的奇迹，很"现代"，也很"中国"！

4.中国的大城市是传统与现代的结合，你对这种现状有什么看法？

5.你会抱着怎样的一个心态去了解现代的中国？

（作者：美国普林斯顿大学，周质平。选自北美《世界日报》，有删改。）

VOCABULARY
副课文 生词表

1	洋人	yángrén		foreigner
2	海外	hǎiwài		overseas
3	自豪	zìháo		proud
4	灵机一动	língjī-yīdòng		a brainwave
5	关切	guānqiè		deeply concerned
6	弓箭	gōngjiàn		bow and arrow
7	看待	kàndài		to look upon, regard
8	脑海	nǎohǎi		brain, mind
9	长袍	chángpáo		long gown
10	马褂	mǎguàr		mandarin jacket
11	洋车	yángchē		rickshaw
12	四合院	sìhéyuàn		a chinese courtyard, quadrangle
13	大厦	dàshà		mansion
14	标本	biāoběn		specimen, sample
15	不妨	bùfáng		might as well, there is no harm
16	奇迹	qíjì		miracle

PROPER NOUNS			
17	印第安人	Yìndì'ānrén	American Indians
18	星巴克	Xīngbākè	Starbucks
19	三峡大坝	Sānxiá dàbà	the Three Gorges Dam
20	青藏铁路	Qīng-Zàng tiělù	the Qinghai-Tibet railway

I Climbed the
Great Wall

第六课
我登上了
长城

Photo: Xinhua News Agency

Pre-reading

■ 你听说过中国的长城吗？关于长城你知道些什么？
■ 为什么去中国旅游的人都要去长城？

施瓦辛格率队跑上了长城

　　2000年5月20日，中国在居庸关长城举办了一次"特殊奥林匹克运动"的宣传活动。这是一次长跑活动，有3000多人参加，包括中国有关方面的领导人、部分国家驻华使节、学生代表、武警代表及运动员代表等。美国的施瓦辛格也参加了这次活动。他站在五个火炬队和志愿者队伍的最前面，手举火炬，率领着人们向长城高处的烽火台跑去。活动以后，施瓦辛格表示，这是一次不平常的活动，它象征着全中国对有特殊需求人士的关心，也表现出为他们平等参与社会活动所作的努力。

VOCABULARY
生词表

| 1 | 驻华使节 | zhùhuá shǐjié | diplomats stationed in China |

【名】一名驻华使节 | 英国驻华使节。

| 2 | 武警 | wǔjǐng | armed police |

【名】一名武警 | 一队武警 | 武警战士 | 武警部队。

| 3 | 火炬 | huǒjù | torch |

【名】一支火炬 | 点燃火炬 | 传递火炬。

| 4 | 率领 | shuàilǐng | to lead |

【动】率领部队 | 率领代表团 | 率领大家前进 | 他亲自率领足球队参加了全国比赛。

| 5 | 烽火台 | fēnghuǒtái | beacon tower on the Great Wall |

【名】一座烽火台 | 明代的烽火台 | 登上烽火台 | 烽火台上浓烟滚滚。📖台：平而高的建筑物。

| 6 | 象征[2] | xiàngzhēng | to symbolize |

【动】玫瑰花象征着爱情。 | 火炬象征着光明。 | 白鸽象征着和平。

PROPER NOUNS

| 7 | 施瓦辛格 | Shīwǎxīngé | (Arnold) Schwarzenegger |

人名。

| 8 | 居庸关 | Jūyōngguān | Juyong Pass on the Great Wall |

长城的一个十分著名的关口。位于北京西北，距离北京城区 50 公里，以地势险要闻名。

| 9 | 特殊奥林匹克运动 | Tèshū Àolínpǐkè Yùndòng | the Special Olympics |

世界三大奥林匹克运动之一，是为全世界有特殊需求者参与体育活动而设立的。国际特殊奥林匹克委员会是美国人尤妮斯 · 肯尼迪 · 施莱佛 1968 年创立的。

Photo: Getty Images

Pre-reading

■ 你喜欢乔丹吗？为什么？

■ 你知道乔丹除了擅长打篮球，还有什么爱好吗？

乔丹登长城做"好汉"

　　2004年5月19日下午，"飞人"麦克尔·乔丹游览了北京八达岭水关长城。此前也曾有几位NBA球星到过长城，这一次，乔丹也像他们一样，登长城做了一回好汉。

　　水关长城的山路很陡，每一级台阶都将近五十厘米高，连续上台阶很费劲。乔丹走在爬长城队伍的前头，走着走着，跟在他身后的媒体记者和球迷就被他落下了一大段距离。

　　乔丹站在"不到长城非好汉"的标语牌前，望着绵延在山峰之间的长城，兴致勃勃地听取了工作人员对水关长城的介绍。乔丹问了关于长城修建年代等几个问题，并问长城到底有多长，工作人员一一作了解答。他在长城上拍了照，还手扶着垛口探出身子张望了一会儿。

　　在烽火台上，上百名球迷一边举着自制的欢迎标语，一边不停地高声尖叫，热闹极了。显然，看到自己最喜欢的篮球明星，大家都非常激动。

VOCABULARY 生词表

10	陡	dǒu	steep

【形】非常*陡* | 山路很*陡*，很难爬。| 楼梯有点*陡*，小心一点儿。

11	厘米	límǐ	centimeter

【量】100*厘米*等于1*米*。| 我的身高是170*厘米*。🔲毫米 | 分米 | 米 | 千米。

12	费劲	fèijìn	to require a lot of effort

【动】挺*费劲* | 毫不*费劲* | 这门课有点难，学习起来比较*费劲*。| *费*了半天*劲*，也没有找到那本书。

13	媒体	méitǐ	media

【名】一家*媒体* | 多家*媒体* | 新闻*媒体* | *媒体*宣传 | 在*媒体*上做广告。

14	落	là	to leave behind

【动】他走路总*落*在别人后面。| 小王走得太快了，把我*落*下了一大段路。| 不努力学习就会被同学们*落*下。

15	距离	jùlí	distance

【名】这两段*距离*相等。| 两座楼之间有二十多米的*距离*。| 我们两个人的看法有*距离*。

16	标语牌	biāoyǔpái	placard, sign

【名】一个*标语牌* | 巨大的*标语牌* | *标语牌*上的字是红色的。🔲广告牌 | 布告牌 | 公告牌。

17	绵延	miányán	to stretch/reach for

【动】*绵延*不绝 | *绵延*千年 | 思绪*绵延* | 那座山*绵延*三百里。

18	兴致勃勃	xìngzhì – bóbó	with great interest

*兴致勃勃*地交谈 | 周末我们班的同学一起*兴致勃勃*地参观了美术馆。| 说到体育运动，他总是*兴致勃勃*的。🔲兴致：兴趣。勃勃：精神旺盛或欲望强烈的样子。

19	到底	dàodǐ	on the earth, exactly

【副】*到底*发生了什么事？| 他的病*到底*怎么样了？| 我们*到底*什么时候出发？

20	解答	jiědá	to answer

【动】*解答*清楚 | 详细地*解答* | 老师*解答*了同学们提出的问题。| 我的疑惑得到了*解答*。

21	垛口	duǒkǒu	battlement

【名】几个*垛口* | 长城*垛口* | 砌成*垛口*。

22	探	tàn	to crane, stretch forward

【动】*探*出头 | *探*头*探*脑 | 坐车的时候不要把身体*探*出窗外。

23	张望	zhāngwàng	to look out

【动】四处*张望* | 向外*张望* | 你到处*张望*，在找什么东西吗？| 在山顶上*张望*了一会儿，大家就都下山了。

24	标语	biāoyǔ	slogan

【名】一幅*标语* | 宣传*标语* | 路边立着一个巨幅*标语*，上面写着"北京欢迎您！"

25	显然	xiǎnrán	obviously

【形】你这么做*显然*不对。| *显然*，他根本不知道发生了什么事情。| 问题的答案很*显然*。

PROPER NOUNS

26	麦克尔·乔丹	Màikèěr · Qiáodān	Michael Jordan

人名。

Pre-reading

■ 你听说过踩高跷这种民间艺术吗?
■ 你喜欢自己国家的哪些民间艺术?

踩着高跷登长城

　　前天上午,65 岁的河北老汉刘德才在一群中外游客的簇拥下,踩着三尺高跷登上了北京八达岭长城。

　　在长城上,所有看到刘老汉绝活儿的中外游客都被惊呆了。有的游客一边打量着刘老汉一边猜测着:"看过了开汽车飞越黄河的,也听说了骑摩托车飞越长城的,这老汉也是来创纪录的吧?"外国游客看到刘老汉居然还能一边走一边做着各种高难度动作,连连惊呼:"中国功夫!中国功夫!"

　　刘老汉告诉记者,他来自河北农村。1999 年 9 月的一天,他踩着高跷走了 15 里山路,登上了海拔 1105 米的狼牙山山顶。

　　"明年我要踩着这 7 斤重的三尺高跷上泰山。"在实现了登长城的愿望之后,刘老汉又有了新的目标。

（《北京青年报》2002 年 10 月 28 日,作者耿振淞,有改动。)

VOCABULARY
生词表

27	老汉	lǎohàn	old man

【名】一位老汉 | 和蔼的老汉 | 老汉今年八十三岁。

28	簇拥	cùyōng	to gather around

【动】观众簇拥在冠军身边。| 几十个小朋友簇拥着老师，听老师讲故事。

29	高跷	gāoqiāo	stilts

【名】高跷演员 | 表演踩高跷 | 我们村有个高跷队。

30	惊呆	jīngdāi	to be startled

【动】眼前的景象把我惊呆了。| 在场的人被这突然的变故惊呆了。

31	打量	dǎliang	to assess, estimate

【动】仔细地打量 | 打量了一番 | 打量着客人 | 他上下打量着我。| 打量了半天，也没有看出这个人有什么问题。

32	猜测	cāicè	to guess, conjecture

【动】无法猜测 | 互相猜测一番 | 大家都在猜测，到底哪一个队能取得这次比赛的胜利。| 事情的结果很难猜测。圖猜：推想；怀疑。圖猜谜 | 猜疑 | 猜忌。圖测：料想，猜想。圖预测 | 推测。

33	创纪录	chuàngjìlù	to set a record

【动】创纪录的成绩 | 他的100米跑又创新纪录了。| 这次运动会创下三项世界纪录。圖创：开始做，开创。

34	居然	jūrán	actually, even

【副】这么简单的问题他居然答错了！| 他居然把蛇放在书包里。| 她居然只有十五岁，我以为超过二十了呢。圖竟然。

35	难度	nándù	level of difficulty

【名】难度很大 | 难度增加 | 试题的难度不大。| 这件事情做起来有一定难度。

36	惊呼	jīnghū	to exclaim (with admiration), to cry out in alarm

【动】大声惊呼 | 惊呼救命 | 他们不由得惊呼："真高呀！" 圖惊叹 | 惊呆 | 惊叫。

37	海拔	hǎibá	above sea level

【名】海拔3000米 | 平均海拔 | 这里海拔比较高。

PROPER NOUNS			
38	狼牙山	Lángyáshān	Langya Mountain, in Hebei Province

山名。在中国河北省易县。山势险要，风景美丽。

VOCABULARY IN CONTEXT

有关	厘米
费劲	兴致勃勃

解答	张望
打量	猜测

距离	象征
记录	影响
经过	倾向

A Fill in the blanks with words from the boxes.

早上起来，他_____地推开门，发现地上积了好几十_____的雪。他_____地在雪地里跑来跑去。_____工作的那些烦心事，他已经忘得一干二净。

B Fill in the blanks with words from the boxes.

老人每天在家门口不停地_____，_____着每一个路过的人，盼望儿子的出现。但是儿子始终没有回来。他_____儿子可能碰到了意外。他问村里的人应该怎么办，但是没有人能够_____老人的难题。

C Write two sentences for each word from the boxes. Use each word as a noun and a verb.

For example

我家距离学校有一公里的路程。*(verb)*
这棵树和那棵的距离大约是十米。*(noun)*

_____

_____

_____

_____

_____

_____

_____

_____

LANGUAGE CONNECTION

缩略语

Abbreviations are often used in Chinese to shorten long words to a word of two or three characters.

For example
- 驻中华人民共和国使节 (驻华使节)
- 全国人民代表大会 (全国人大)
- 奥林匹克运动会 (奥运会)
- 北京师范大学 (北师大)

V₁着V₁着 + V₂

is used to show that a second action has started as the first action is taking place. The first verb (V₁) is usually a word made up of one character.

For example
- 他说着说着就笑了起来。

A 缩略语 （Abbreviations）

" ……包括中国有关方面的领导人、部分国家驻华使节、学生代表、武警代表及运动员代表等。"

Write the abbreviations for the following words.

环境保护（　　　）　　经济贸易（　　　）

民用航空（　　　）　　空中小姐（　　　）

家用电器（　　　）　　邮政编码（　　　）

彩色照片（　　　）　　驾驶执照（　　　）

B V₁着V₁着 + V₂

" 走着走着，跟在他身后的媒体记者和球迷就被他落下了一大段距离。"

Rewrite the sentences using the structure of "V₁着 V₁着 ＋ V₂."

1. 原　句：小李特别累，他看电视的时候，不知不觉睡着了。

  替换句：＿＿＿＿＿＿＿＿＿＿＿＿＿＿＿。

2. 原　句：他越说越着急，哭了起来。

  替换句：＿＿＿＿＿＿＿＿＿＿＿＿＿＿＿。

3. 原　句：他走路的时候一不心，就摔了一跤。

  替换句：＿＿＿＿＿＿＿＿＿＿＿＿＿＿＿。

连动句

is a sentence with two or more verbs which refer to the same subject. In the example sentence, the "连动" verbs are "扶," "探" and "张望."

For example

■ 妈妈生病了，赶快打电话叫出租车送妈妈去医院。

到底

is used to make a further inquiry.

For example

■ 你到底去过那个地方没有？

C 连动句

" 他在长城上拍了照，还手扶着垛口探出身子张望了一会儿。

Complete the sentences using the structure of "连动句."

1. 他早上起床，_____

   _____ 。

2. 他晚上回到家里，_____

   _____ 。

3. 林林到了办公室，_____

   _____ 。

D 到底（after all, exactly）

" 乔丹问了关于长城修建年代等几个问题，并问长城到底有多长。"

Put the words in the correct order.

1. 想　到底　什么　你　干

   完整句：_____

2. 到底　去　你们　不去　还是

   完整句：_____

3. 没有　了　到底　想　你　好

   完整句：_____

显然……

is used for emphasis and can be placed at the beginning or in the middle of a sentence.

For example
- 对这样的条件，他显然不满意。
- 显然，这个消息来源于广播电台。

居然……

is used to express surprise when something unexpected has happened.

For example
- 这么大的声音，他居然没听见。

E 显然……（obviously...）

"显然，看到自己最喜欢的篮球明星，大家都非常激动。"

Put the words in the correct order.

1. 他 人 不是 要找的 显然 我

   完整句：_____。

2. 不 显然 他 知道 这件事

   完整句：_____。

3. 对 他 游戏 很 显然 感兴趣 这种

   完整句：_____。

F 居然……（unexpectedly...）

"刘老汉居然还能一边走一边做着各种高难度动作。"

Put the words in the correct order.

1. 认识 居然 你 不 他

   完整句：_____。

2. 告诉 没有 他 我 居然

   完整句：_____。

3. 只有 包里 居然 一元钱 他的

   完整句：_____。

COMMUNICATION CORNER

Instructions:

- Read the story opposite.
- Work in pairs. Take turns to retell the story in your own words.
- As one person narrates, your partner can point out which details have been left out, or clarify points that are unclear or have been misunderstood.

事情是这样的……

　　小王是一个出租汽车司机，为了迎接2008年奥运会，他每天都抓紧学习英语。

　　有一天晚上，他开车路过前门，看见远处一个外国人在打车。这个外国人个子特别高，所以小王远远地就看见他了。小王还看到前边连续有两辆出租车停了下来，但是又都开走了。小王有些奇怪，心想这些司机肯定是不懂外语，不知道外国人说什么，而自己学了不少英语，现在可以用上了。小王把车开到外国人面前停下，笑着对外国人说："Get in the car, please."这个外国人高兴地上了出租车，就跟小王说起了英语。小王急了，因为他一句也没有听懂。外国人也看出小王大概没听懂，就把手里的纸条递给小王。小王一看更着急了，上面只写了一句话：请把这位先生带到天怡宾馆。

　　小王从小到大在北京住了三十多年，开出租车也六年多了，但是实在不知道天怡宾馆在哪里。看到小王非常迷惑，外国人又递过来一张纸，这张纸上画了一架飞机，飞机旁边是一条路，路边还有一个黑色的圆圈。小王乐了，心想，天怡宾馆肯定是在首都机场附近。于是他调转车头，向机场高速公路驶去。过高速公路收费站的时候，天已经黑了。小王问收费员有没有听说过天怡宾馆，收费员指了指前边的一条小路，说："就在前边那条小路上。"小王高兴得连"谢谢"都忘了说，就把车开了过去。沿着小路走了好一会儿，他才发现前边有一座高楼，正是这家天怡宾馆。小王高兴地大叫："Here, here! 就是这儿了！"这个外国人也高兴极了，留给小王一句话："Beijing taxi driver, Number One!"

Guidelines:

You can use the following prompts during your narration.

- 小王是……，有一次，他遇到……
- 看到这个情况，小王心想……，于是……
- ……以后，……，小王非常着急，……小王明白了，……，于是……
- 过……的时候，小王……，接着……，最后……

WRITING TASK

Instructions:

- Write a newspaper story about the French train TGV setting a new world record for the fastest train on rails.

- Keep your writing to about 300 words.

新的世界纪录

Guidelines:

- When writing newspaper stories, the basic facts, conclusion, lead etc. come first. As you move through the story, more and more details and background are provided. The main texts of this lesson are examples of news writing styles. Choose an effective headline for your article to get people's attention.

Reference materials for your article:

- 日本、德国和法国竞争
- 新的世界纪录是每小时574.8公里
- 原来的世界纪录是每小时515.3公里
- 法国高速列车创造了最新世界纪录
- 法国可以更好地开拓中国、阿根廷等地的巨大市场
- 原来的世界纪录是由另一列法国列车在1990年创造的
- 2007年4月3日法新社报道

100,000 Miles Long
and 3,000 Years Old

副课文

三千年，
十万里

Pre-reading

- 你知道中国是从什么时候开始修建长城的吗？
- 看到长城的图片，你有什么感想？

谁最早开始修长城

1.古代中国人修建长城的目的是什么？

早在公元前9世纪的周朝时，为防御北方民族的侵袭，修建了连续排列的城堡和烽火台。公元前7世纪，许多诸侯国也都修建了自己的长城，防止邻国的入侵。公元前221年，秦始皇统一全国后，开始把秦、燕、赵等国北部的长城连接起来，建成秦长城。此后汉朝、明朝都曾大规模修建过长城。

在历史上，长城沿线是农牧经济的过渡地区，长城是游牧经济和农耕经济冲突的产物。修筑长城的目的是为了防止战争。只有渴望和平、不想打仗的民族才会投入这么大的人力、物力修筑万里长城。

长城到底有多长

周朝诸侯国修的长城各有数百公里长。秦长城从今天的甘肃东部起，直到鸭绿江，全长5000多公里。汉长城比秦长城还要长，有10000多公里。此后各朝也不断有修筑长城的。明朝修筑长城的工程延续了200多年，初期的长城全长7300多公里。中期以后，经过修整的从山海关到嘉峪关一线的长城比较完好，长度为6700公里，相当于13400里，因此，被称为"万里长城"。

事实上，周朝的春秋、战国时期诸侯国及以后各朝修建的长城总长度加起来超过50000公里，也就是100000里，相当于绕地球赤道$1\frac{1}{4}$（一又四分之一）圈。

2.中国的长城为什么叫"万里长城"？

天下有多少"好汉"

中国有一句名言："不到长城非好汉"，意思是说没登过险要的长城就不算英雄。长城作为"世界上最长的墙"，同时作为"世界文化遗产"，是许多到北京旅游的中外游客必去的地方——他们都希望自己是一名"好汉"。到目前为止，仅八达岭长城一处就已经接待外国元首400多位，接待中国游客1.2亿人次，接待外国游客1500万人次。

3.你想登上长城做"好汉"吗？说说你的计划吧。？

孟姜女的传说

人们只要一提到长城，就一定会说到秦始皇，说他修长城害死了很多人。有一个民间故事，叫"孟姜女哭长城"，说的是秦始皇时期，有一个叫孟姜女的女人，她丈夫被抓去修长城。后来，孟姜女去给丈夫送冬天的衣服，才知道他早就累死了，并被埋在了长城底下。她伤心地痛哭起来，哭得天昏地暗，最后竟把长城哭倒了八百里。

4.在你自己的国家，有什么有意思的传说吗？请你讲一讲。？

后来，人们为了纪念她，就在山海关长城边修建了一座孟姜女庙。

VOCABULARY

副课文 生词表

1	公元前	gōngyuánqián	B.C.
2	防御	fángyù	to defend against
3	侵袭	qīnxí	to invade, attack
4	城堡	chéngbǎo	castle, fortification
5	诸侯	zhūhóu	the nobles, ruling classes
6	入侵	rùqīn	to invade
7	沿线	yánxiàn	along the route
8	农牧	nóngmù	farming
9	过渡	guòdù	to evolve, develop
10	游牧	yóumù	to move about in search of pasture
11	农耕	nónggēng	to grow crops
12	冲突	chōngtū	to clash
13	产物	chǎnwù	outcome
14	渴望	kěwàng	to long for, aspire to
15	延续	yánxù	to extend, to last for
16	修整	xiūzhěng	to repair
17	险要	xiǎnyào	treacherous terrain with strategic value
18	元首	yuánshǒu	head of state
19	人次	réncì	people (number of times)
20	民间故事	mínjiān gùshi	folk tale
21	天昏地暗	tiānhūn-dì'àn	bad weather coupled with strong winds

PROPER NOUNS

22	周朝	Zhōucháo	the Zhou Dynasty (1046 B.C.–256 B.C.)
23	燕	Yān	the State of Yan during the Zhou Dynasty
24	赵	Zhào	the State of Zhao during the Zhou Dynasty
25	汉朝	Hàncháo	the Han Dynasty (206 B.C.–220 A.D.)
26	鸭绿江	Yālùjiāng	the Yalujiang River
27	山海关	Shānhǎiguān	Shanhai Pass on the Great Wall
28	嘉峪关	Jiāyùguān	Jiayu Pass on the Great Wall
29	孟姜女	Mèngjiāngnǚ	Mengjiangnu, a legendary woman from ancient China

UNIT SUMMARY
学习小结

一、重点句型

疑问句及疑问语气词 (……吗? ……呀? ……吧?)	你现在有时间吗?
……怎么办	你不懂中国的交通规则,出了事怎么办?
先……再……然后……	你最好先从网上找一张中国地图,搞清楚中国有多大,再根据你的时间决定去几个地方,然后咱们再来商量具体的计划。
经过……	我们乘火车去,可以经过河北、山西、河南、陕西四个省。
……才能……	我们得先到兰州,然后再换一趟火车,坐十几个小时才能到敦煌。
缩略语	……包括中国有关方面的领导人、部分国家驻华使节、学生代表……
V_1着V_1着 + V_2	他说着说着就笑了起来。
连动句	人们手拿红旗唱着歌大步走着。
到底	你到底去过那个地方没有?
显然……	对这样的条件,他显然不满意。
居然……	这么简单的事情,他居然不知道。

二、交际功能

建议和提醒。

对发生的事件进行叙述和说明。

三、常用表达式

怎么能……	二十多天怎么能去那么多地方?
要不……,……也行	要不咱们租一辆汽车,自驾游也行。
最好+V	你最好先从网上找一张中国地图。
……怎么样	你看去北京、西安、敦煌、新疆怎么样?
……好不好	我们租一辆汽车好不好?

UNIT 4
PEOPLE AND SOCIETY

民族与社会

Communicative Goals
- Express disbelief and surprise
- Relate a different cultural practice or a social phenomenon
- Express regret for things that happened (or didn't happen) in the past

Cultural Information
- Chinese ethnic minorities (e.g. Bai, Dai, Tibetan, Kazak) and their cultural practices
- Types of residences in China: courtyard house, shared dormitory housing and apartment
- "Pushing Hands", a film directed by Ang Lee that explores the clash of eastern and western family values

Ethnic girls of Yao minority, Guangxi

Warm up

1. 中国是一个多民族的国家。在你的想象中，不同民族的人生活在一起会是什么样子？

2. 在你看来，现在最严重的社会问题是什么？

The Three Pagodas of Chongsheng Temple
in Dali, Yunnan

The Hospitable Southwest

第七课

远方的客人请你留下来

Pre-reading

■ 你喜欢旅游吗？什么地方给你留下的印象最深？
■ 你去过中国的少数民族地区吗？请谈谈你的见闻。

杰克一年前从美国来到上海学习中文，现在是上海一所大学的留学生。暑假期间，杰克到中国南方旅游。旅途的见闻让他很兴奋，他便给好友李凡写了一封信。

100083

北京市朝阳区牡丹园6号楼304室

李凡　　收

贴邮票处

云南省西双版纳州景洪市农林南路8号傣园酒店312房间　杰克
邮政编码 666100

李凡：

　　你这次旅行怎么样，回到北京了吗？

　　长期以来，我就有一个愿望，就是到中国的少数民族地区看一看。这次我终于有机会来云南旅游了。在"彩云之南"，少数民族独特的待客方式给我留下了深刻的印象。

　　我参加了一个旅游团，这样吃饭住宿就不用自己操心了。我们首先去的是白族人的故乡——大理。大理是一座很美的古城。朋友告诉我说，大理的风光全写在白族姑娘的头饰上了。我想，这怎么可能呢？如此秀丽多彩的山川，小小的头饰怎么写得下？朋友让我仔细看白族姑娘的头饰，那美丽的绣花头巾、头巾上雪白的绒毛等等，分别代表了大理"风、花、雪、月"四种美景，非常有意思。

在一个白族人的家里，主人热情地用茶水招待了我们。和一般的用茶水招待客人不太相同，主人每次倒好茶水，都会用双手把杯子举得高高的，然后再放到我面前。我本来以为这只是很普通的茶水，端起来尝了尝却感觉与众不同：在主人给我的三杯茶中，每一杯的味道都不一样。第一杯稍有一点苦味，第二杯比较甜，第三杯没有第二杯甜，但是很香，又有一点辣。就在我纳闷的时候，主人跟我说，这就是白族招待客人的"三道茶"，每一道都经过了认真的加工。第一道茶是"清苦之茶"，比喻人生应当吃苦耐劳才能有所作为；第二道茶叫做"甜茶"，象征着生活先苦后甜；最后一道茶是"回味"茶，让人回味无穷。这三道茶，象征着人生的三种境界。

离开大理，我们到了云南西北部的香格里拉——一个梦一般美丽的藏族地区。刚进入村寨，一个年轻的藏族小伙子就把一条雪白的纱巾围在我的脖子上。我一时感到莫名其妙，不知道说什么好。朋友告诉我说，这种纱巾在藏语里叫"哈达"。主人给客人献哈达，表示对客人的热烈欢迎。

Shangri-la, Yunnan

"哈达为什么是白色的呢？"我问朋友。

"藏族人认为白色象征纯洁、吉祥，所以哈达一般是白色的。"

哈达有这么美好的含义，我一定要永远珍藏它。

　　告别了香格里拉热情的藏族朋友，我们到了位于云南南部的西双版纳，去拜访住在那里的傣族朋友。朋友提醒我说，进入傣家竹楼，应该把鞋放在门外，而且在屋里走路一定要轻，不能坐在门槛上，更不能跨过火塘。如果不注意的话，会被认为是不礼貌的。听了这些，我真有点担心，不知道傣族人会不会欢迎我这个"不懂礼貌"的人。

　　我们到了傣家门口，一位少女在门口欢迎我们。她手里端着放有花瓣的水，并用树枝把水轻轻地洒到我们身上，表示对我们的欢迎和祝福。我们上了竹楼，主人热情地请我们坐下，然后家里的老人给我和朋友的手腕拴上红红的丝线，祝福我们吉祥如意，平安幸福。热情的傣族小姑娘还唱起了歌，朋友告诉我，她唱的是云南民歌《远方的客人请你留下来》，邀请我们留下。我想如果能在傣家竹楼住上几天，那一定会特别有意思。

　　我打算在西双版纳再呆几天，然后回上海。假期过得太快，很快又要开学了。上次听你说可能会去上海，大概什么时候去呢？

　　祝

身体健康，生活愉快！

杰克

2007年5月24日

VOCABULARY
生词表

1	见闻	jiànwén	n.	what one sees and hears

【名】*见闻*很广 | 增长*见闻* | 瑞士*见闻* | *见闻*杂记 | 小说生动地描写了一个旅行家的旅途*见闻*。

2	彩云	cǎiyún	n.	colorful clouds

【名】*彩云*朵朵 | 片片*彩云* | 傍晚，天边的*彩云*拥着落日，美得像幅画儿。▣ 彩：多种颜色。
▣ 彩车 | 彩带 | 彩旗 | 彩页 | 五彩。

3	待客	dàikè	v.	to host (a guest)

【动】*待客*热情 | 每个民族都有自己的*待客*传统。 | 水果和点心是节日*待客*不可缺少的食品。▣ 待：
招待。▣ 招待 | 接待 | 款待。

4	印象	yìnxiàng	n.	impression

【名】模糊的*印象* | 没有*印象* | 我对他的*印象*很好。 | 二十几年过去了，这个城市给我的*印象*始终
没变。

5	<u>操心</u>	cāoxīn	v.	to concern oneself with; to worry about

【动】非常*操心* | *操心*国事 | *操*了不少心 | *操*不完的心 | 别太为这件事*操心*了。 | 为了儿女的事
她把心都*操*碎了。▣ 操劳 | 操作。▣ 费心 | 担心。

6	头饰	tóushì	n.	headwear

【名】纯银*头饰* | 设计*头饰* | 美丽的*头饰* | 这次时装展，设计师在模特的*头饰*上下了很大功夫。
▣ 服饰 | 装饰 | 佩饰 | 饰物。

7	秀丽	xiùlì	adj.	beautiful

【形】*秀丽*的山河 | 容貌*秀丽* | 这里山水*秀丽*，风景优美。 | 他的字体*秀丽*，就是缺乏力度。
▣ 秀：清秀；美丽而不俗气。▣ 秀美 | 秀气 | 秀雅 | 秀色。

8	多彩	duōcǎi	adj.	colorful

【形】丰富*多彩* | 生动*多彩* | *多彩*的世界 | 这里有*多彩*的民族风情。

9	绣花	xiùhuā	v. & n.	to embroider; embroidery

【动,名】会*绣花*的巧手 | 小姑娘很擅长*绣花*。 | 过去的女孩子都要学习*绣花*。 | *绣花*不仅要心灵手巧，
更要有足够的耐心。▣ 绣字 | 刺绣 | 绣品 | 苏绣（苏州刺绣）。

10	头巾	tóujīn	n.	headscarf

【名】一块*头巾* | 丝绸*头巾* | 头上包着*头巾* | 那个戴着粉色*头巾*的女人是我们老师。

11	绒毛	róngmáo	n.	fluff, down

【名】*绒毛*玩具 | *绒毛*制品 | 优质*绒毛* | 小鸡长着一身浅黄色的*绒毛*，十分可爱。▣ 羊毛 | 鸡毛
| 毛笔。▣ 羽绒 | 羊绒。

12	道	dào	m.w.	course

【量】上了三*道*菜 | 涂了七*道*漆 | 三*道*手续你才办了一*道*，还差得远呢。

13	比喻	bǐyù	v.	to illustrate the meaning of sth

【动】人们常用园丁来*比喻*教师。 | *比喻*就是打比方。 | 他是那样坚强，人们常把他*比喻*成钢铁战士。
▣ 比方 | 比拟。▣ 明喻 | 暗喻 | 借喻 | 隐喻。

14	吃苦耐劳	chīkǔ nàiláo		be able to endure hardship

吃苦耐劳的精神 | 一个吃苦耐劳的民族 | 吃苦耐劳是中华民族的传统美德。 | 应该培养孩子吃苦耐劳的精神。

15	有所作为	yǒusuǒ zuòwéi		promising, able to accomplish sth

以他的才能，无论到了哪儿，都能有所作为。 | 没有很强的能力是很难真正有所作为的。

16	回味	húiwèi	*v.*	to reminisce

【动】值得回味 | 回味无穷 | 记忆中很多有趣的小事非常耐人回味。

17	境界	jìngjiè	*n.*	state, realm, world

【名】思想境界 | 境界高远 | 这就是他理想的境界。 | 这部电影把我们带入了一个神奇的境界。

18	村寨	cūnzhài	*n.*	village

【名】许多村寨 | 一个少数民族村寨 | 古老的村寨隐藏在长满绿树的山间。

19	纱巾	shājīn	*n.*	scarf

【名】一条洁白的纱巾 | 纱巾不仅可以系在脖子上，还可以包在头上、披在肩上。

20	莫名其妙	mò míng qí miào		baffling

莫名其妙的话 | 他这个人简直莫名其妙。 | 她莫名其妙地哭了起来。 | 大家不明白他这话什么意思，都莫名其妙地看着他。

21	哈达	hǎdá	*n.*	long piece of silk used as greeting gift

【名】哈达是一种纱巾或丝巾。 | 一些少数民族有向贵客献哈达的习俗。

22	纯洁	chúnjié	*adj.*	pure, innocent, chaste

【形】心地纯洁 | 天真纯洁 | 纯洁的友谊 | 这是一种非常纯洁的感情。▣ 纯净 | 纯真 | 纯粹。▣ 圣洁 | 清洁 | 洁净。

23	珍藏	zhēncáng	*v.*	to treasure; to keep or store sth in good condition

【动】珍藏版 | 珍藏多年，完好无损。 | 这些照片很有意义，值得珍藏。 | 这个酒厂有很多陈年好酒，其中有些已经珍藏了三十年以上。

24	告别	gàobié	*v.*	to bid farewell

【动】告别亲友 | 告别过去 | 和妈妈告别 | 他告别故乡，出国留学。 | 他把信交给了队长，就匆匆告别了。

25	提醒	tíxǐng	*v.*	to remind

【动】提醒一下 | 及时地提醒 | 我要是忘了，请你提醒我。 | 到时候请你提个醒儿。▣ 提示 | 提出。▣ 唤醒 | 叫醒 | 睡醒。

26	竹楼	zhúlóu	*n.*	bamboo house

【名】一座竹楼 | 傣族人住竹楼已经有 400 多年的历史了。

27	门槛	ménkǎn	*n.*	threshold

（～儿）【名】一道门槛儿 | 木制门槛儿 | 跨过门槛儿 | 这座学校的门槛儿很高。

28	火塘	huǒtáng	*n.*	fireplace

【名】一个火塘 | 在中国南方亚热带地区的少数民族家庭中通常都有一个或几个火塘，供人们在家中取暖、照明或做饭。

29	礼貌	lǐmào	*n. & adj.*	polite

【名，形】懂礼貌 | 这样做太不礼貌了。 | 这孩子挺有礼貌的。 | 他礼貌地回答了老师提出的所有问题。

30	花瓣	huābàn	n.	petal

【名】一片粉色的*花瓣* | 水池里撒满了玫瑰*花瓣*。| 国画中*花瓣*的画法只有几种，但想把*花瓣*画好很难。

31	手腕	shǒuwàn	n.	wrist

【名】掰*手腕* | 戴在*手腕*上 | 手链是一种套在*手腕*上的饰物。 📖 脚腕 | 护腕 | 腕部。

32	<u>拴</u>	shuān	v.	to fasten

【动】*拴*绳子 | *拴*住了 | *拴*结实 | 他把马*拴*在树上。 | 这件事把他们几个人都*拴*在一起了。

33	<u>邀请</u>	yāoqǐng	v.	to invite

【动】*邀请*客人 | 接受*邀请* | 盛情*邀请* | *邀请*了两次 | 我准备周六*邀请*几个朋友来玩一玩。

34	<u>呆</u>	dāi	v.	to stay

【动】*呆*不住 | *呆*久了 | *呆*烦了 | 一个人在屋里*呆*着太冷了。 | 他在家一*呆*就是十年。

PROPER NOUNS

35	杰克	Jiékè		Jack

人名。

36	景洪	Jǐnghóng		Jinghong, a city in China's Yunnan Province

中国西双版纳著名旅游城市。

37	白族	Báizú		the Bai people, an ethnic minority in Yunnan

民族名。中国西南边疆一个具有悠久历史和文化的少数民族。主要分布在云南省大理白族自治州。

38	大理	Dàlǐ		Dali, a prefecture in Yunnan. The Bai people reside here.

地名。位于云南省中西部，是白族的主要聚居地，保存着浓厚的白族风情。是中国著名的旅游胜地。

39	香格里拉	Xiānggélǐlā		Shangri-la, the Tibetan autonomous area in Yunnan

地名。即迪庆，藏语意为"吉祥如意的地方"，是云南省唯一的藏族自治州，也是全国 10 个藏族自治州之一。该地地理位置和气候条件独特，自然景观优美。

40	西双版纳	Xīshuāngbǎnnà		Xishuangbanna, the Dai autonomous area in Yunnan

地名。西双版纳傣族自治州位于中国云南省南端，是中国的一块热带森林区，也是世界北回归线上仅存的一片绿洲，国家级重点风景名胜区。

41	傣族	Dǎizú		the Dai people, one of China's ethnic minority groups

中国少数民族之一，主要聚居在云南。

VOCABULARY IN CONTEXT

操心

道

比喻

莫名其妙

告别

提醒

礼貌

拴

邀请

呆

Imagine that you are writing a letter to your mother about a trip you took. Read the following sentences and fill in the blanks with appropriate words or phrases.

A

1. 人们都喜欢把这独有的风景线_____成美丽的少数民族姑娘。

2. 这次我在四川、云南一带游览，觉得这里不仅风景秀美，而且有独特的民族风情。也正是这种民族风情，构成了西南地区独有的一_____道_____风景线。

3. 但是，刚开始的时候，有一件事情让我感觉特别纳闷：当我_____歇脚的人家准备离开时，他们却使劲拉住我，一定要在我的背包上系一个_____着红线的苹果。

4. 我的旅途非常顺利，您就别再为我的吃、住、行_____了。

5. 后来才知道，苹果在他们眼中是"平安"的象征，给远行的人送苹果，是祝福一路平安！

6. 这里的人_____而好客，几乎在每个寨子里，我都会受到当地人的_____，在某户人家歇歇脚、喝喝茶，舒服地_____上一两个小时。

7. 我_____，开始时还以为他们拉我的背包是 *提醒* 我落下了什么东西呢。

Next, arrange the sentences in a logical and appropriate order for the letter.

B

妈妈：

　　您好！

_____。

女儿/儿子××
×年×月×日

LANGUAGE CONNECTION

For example

- 你跟他见过面吗？
- 这件事是你的不对，你应该向他道个歉。
- 我能请你跳个舞吗？

A 离合词 (Split Verb)

"热情的傣族小姑娘还唱起了歌。"

Some verbs in Chinese consist of two characters. When necessary, we can insert another element between the two characters. For example, the word "唱歌" in the text is a verb, but between "唱" and "歌", "起了" is added. There are many other similar verbs.

For example

跳舞	跳个舞，跳一会儿舞，跳起舞来，跳过舞
担心	担着心，担什么心
见面	见了面，见一面
道歉	道个歉，道过歉

Complete the following sentences using split verbs.

① 为了我们的友谊，咱们＿＿＿＿＿！（干杯）

② 音乐响起来了，大家高兴地＿＿＿＿＿。（跳舞）

③ 甲：下个星期举行学生会主席选举，你打算选谁？

　乙：＿＿＿＿＿＿＿＿＿。（投票）

④ 甲：马路上怎么有这么多的水？

　乙：＿＿＿＿＿＿＿＿＿。（下雨）

⑤ 甲：你现在就睡觉吗？

　乙：不，我想先＿＿＿＿＿＿＿。（洗澡）

V + 在 + noun of place

"大理的风光全写在白族姑娘的头饰上了。"

"应该把鞋放在门外，而且在屋里走路一定要轻。"

The construction "V + 在 + noun of place" refers to a thing or a person that is now in a different state as a result of an action done to the thing or person. "在" is followed by a noun of place.

For example
- 老师把答案写在黑板上了。
- 他坐在第一排。

Arrange the following words or phrases in the proper order in which they would occur in a complete sentence. Read the sentences.

① 书　所有　放　书包　在　里　的　都

② 把　你　请　行李　放　车　在　上　的

③ 睡　地板　在　我　上　想

④ 站　他　的　我　面前　在

 Writing Conventions on an Envelope

The writing conventions of a formal Chinese letter are different from an English one. On the envelope, the receiver's address is written in the top lefthand corner and the sender's in the lower righthand corner. The receiver's name is written in the center of the envelope. The mailing address is written with the place-name of the bigger region before the smaller one. The receiver's postcode is written before his/her address and the sender's after his/her address.

Write the mailing information on an envelope using the following details.

收信人姓名：王林
收信人地址：北京市新街口
　　　　　　外大街19号
邮政编码：100875

寄信人地址及姓名：
沈阳市幸福街123号 李丽
邮政编码：110000

Next, address an envelope with the mailing information of someone you are writing to.

The construction "V+得+another element" can be used to describe the result of an action. In the given example, the result of the verb "举" is that the cup is "高高的". "得" can be followed by an adjective, a phrase or a clause. The description can be about the action itself, the doer or the recipient of the action.

For example

- 我昨天起得很晚。
  (about the action)
- 看到这个场面，那个小孩儿吓得直哭。(about the doer)

 D   V + 得 + another element

"主人每次倒好茶水，都会用双手把杯子举得高高的……"

Complete the following sentences using the construction "V+得+another element".

① A student asking the teacher if she had answered the question correctly...

学　生：老师，我回答得对吗？

老　师：＿＿＿＿＿＿＿＿＿＿＿＿＿＿＿＿＿＿。

② One student asking another about his reaction to an unpleasant encounter...

学生甲：你当时生气了吗？

学生乙：＿＿＿＿＿＿＿＿＿＿＿＿＿＿＿＿＿＿。

③ How would you describe the joy felt by someone who has been accepted into his preferred university?

当他＿＿＿＿＿＿＿＿＿＿，＿＿＿＿＿＿＿＿＿＿。

COMMUNICATION CORNER

Instructions:

- Look up stories of seemingly strange and amusing persons and/or practices and share them with your partner, e.g., hundreds of people dining together at a long table, girls fetching water with a water jar on their heads.

- Tell what you know of the background to these unusual practices.

- Switch roles with your partner.

这不可能吧

Guidelines:

In this lesson, you learned two very interesting language functions of our daily communication: how to express disbelief and surprise. While both show your disagreement with the proposed idea, the former suggests that you have not expected it and therefore do not believe it at all, whereas the latter suggests that it has turned out to be different from your expectations and therefore you find it hard to accept.

To express disbelief, the most common expression is "怎么可能". Other expressions include:

- 我才不信呢！
- 说得跟真的一样，肯定不会的！
- 我不信 / 这不可能，除非……

To express surprise, the most common expression is "这我可没想到"，"我觉得非常意外". There are other expressions. For example,

- 我原来以为……可是后来发现……
- 我从来没听说过这样的事，那次却突然看到……
- 我简直不敢相信自己的眼睛，因为我看到……

Ethnic Koreans in China

Long-table feast of the Dong minority

WRITING TASK

Instructions:

- Write a formal letter to the city mayor to tell him about a social problem that you have observed and your suggestions on how to address it.

- Keep your writing to about 300 words.

给市长的一封信

Guidelines:

Start your letter with a formal salutation.

尊敬的市长先生：
    我想向您反映关于……的问题。

State the problem clearly and concisely. Highlight the main issues and give examples to illustrate your points.

- 这个问题主要表现在几个方面。一是……二是……

- 关于这个问题，有很多事例可以说明。例如……

Keep your suggestions clear and well-structured.

- 对于这个问题的解决，首先，我认为应该……，其次……

- 我觉得问题的关键是……，所以我建议政府……

The Kazak Girl's Chase

副课文

"姑娘追"

Lake Sayram, largest alpine lake in Xinjiang

Pre-reading

■ 你参加过婚礼吗？婚礼上有哪些特别的习俗？
■ 请你介绍一个特别的娱乐活动。

1.中国有多少个民族？

2."姑娘追"是什么意思？

3.哈萨克小伙子认为他长得壮的原因是什么？

　　中国有五十六个民族，各自都有独特的风俗习惯和娱乐活动，"姑娘追"就是其中的一种。

　　"姑娘追"是中国新疆地区哈萨克族小伙子追求姑娘的一种方式，也是一项体育娱乐活动。在一次哈萨克族青年的婚礼上，笔者就目睹了一次这样的活动。

　　那场婚礼是在美丽的赛里木湖畔举行的，新郎是牧场的放马能手，新娘是牧羊能手。

　　我们一坐下来，新郎就给我们端来了奶茶。看见他上身只穿了件背心，浑身肌肉闪闪发光，大家都夸他健壮。我问他："你吃什么长得这么壮？"没想到他回答说："你们汉族吃草，我们哈萨克是吃肉的，就像公牛一样壮！"翻译赶紧解释："对不起，哈萨克和维吾尔语中'草'和'菜'是一个词，误会了！"大家哈哈大笑起来。

Men riding horses on the grand grassland of Xinjiang

4. "姑娘追"游戏的规则是什么？

5. 在游戏中，姑娘手中的鞭子会抽打怎样的小伙子？

6. "心上人"是什么意思？

7. 你喜欢"姑娘追"这个游戏吗？为什么？

过了一会儿，有许多青年男女参加的"姑娘追"开始了。在宽阔的草原上，一对一对的青年男女骑着马从起点出发，绕过一个中点后再跑回来。在去的路上，姑娘只能绝对顺从。所以，尽管小伙子一路上嬉皮笑脸，不停地和姑娘开着玩笑，姑娘羞得满脸通红，但也不能有所表示，只是一言不发。可是在返回的路上，情况就大不一样了。小伙子调转马头往回跑，姑娘就骑着马紧追小伙子，要给他一点小小的"报复"。姑娘一手抓住马缰绳，一手扬鞭子，把鞭子甩得呼呼作响。姑娘要是对这个小伙子有意，就会把鞭子举得高高的，却只是在小伙子的头上晃来晃去，而不落下。如果姑娘不喜欢这个小伙子，小伙子就会遭到皮鞭抽打。

游戏过程中，场上热闹非凡。参加婚礼的人有的为姑娘叫好，有的为小伙子加油。姑娘们挥鞭追赶，英姿勃勃；小伙子们拼命逃跑，模样狼狈，引来阵阵哄笑。

在"姑娘追"游戏中，最后一对出场的是今天的新郎和新娘，他们才是今夜的主角。只见新娘子的皮鞭举得高高的，在空中转着圈儿，就是不忍心抽打心上人。快到终点了，新娘子只是象征性地甩了几下皮鞭。看来他们是今夜最甜蜜的一对了。

月亮爬上了天空，哈萨克人唱起了欢乐的婚礼歌，一群伴娘举着一块块大方巾在新娘身旁边歌边舞。帐篷四周坐满了参加婚礼的男男女女，帐篷内外充满了爱与温暖。

（选自雅思思《向草原进军——哈萨克的婚礼》，有删改。）

VOCABULARY
副课文 **生词表**

1	牧场	mùchǎng	*n.*	pasture
2	能手	néngshǒu	*n.*	expert
3	奶茶	nǎichá	*n.*	milk tea
4	背心	bèixīn	*n.*	vest
5	浑身	húnshēn	*n.*	all over (the body)
6	健壮	jiànzhuàng	*adj.*	strong, robust
7	误会	wùhuì	*v.*	to misunderstand
8	宽阔	kuānkuò	*adj.*	broad
9	顺从	shùncóng	*v.*	to obey; to submit
10	嬉皮笑脸	xīpíxiàoliǎn		grin cheekily
11	羞	xiū	*v.*	to blush
12	一言不发	yīyánbùfā		without saying a word
13	缰绳	jiāngshéng	*n.*	halter
14	鞭子	biānzi	*n.*	whip
15	英姿勃勃	yīngzībóbó		handsome and spirited
16	狼狈	lángbèi	*adj.*	awkward
17	主角	zhǔjué	*n.*	the lead character
18	帐篷	zhàngpeng	*n.*	tent

PROPER NOUNS

| 19 | 哈萨克族 | Hāsākèzú | | the Kazak people, one of China's ethnic minority groups |
| 20 | 赛里木湖 | Sàilǐmùhú | | Lake Sayram, the largest alpine lake in Xinjiang |

Moving into a Modern Apartment

第八课

搬家手记

Pre-reading

■ 你搬过家吗？你搬家的时候有什么感受？

■ 你知道中国人近些年在居住条件方面有哪些变化吗？

从筒子楼的旧房搬到新家已经两个月了，每天忙这忙那的，家里的东西还没有整理完，主要是那几千册书。我的书很多，原来家里没地方放，不得不打成捆堆在床下，所以一家人常常为找书发愁。现在看着书房里四个巨大的书柜，我心里有说不出的高兴。只是要分门别类地收拾好，还得一些日子。

新家所有房间的光线都很好，每天早晨，拉开客厅的窗帘，看着阳光一点点照进屋里，呼吸呼吸新鲜空气，心情好极了。

新房子让人满意的地方还有卫生间。卫生间很宽敞，我装了一个大号的浴缸，下班回来，在浴缸里舒舒服服地泡一泡，浑身的疲倦就都被赶走了。

这个周末我请几户老邻居来家里吃饭。以前家里房子小，从来没有一次请过那么多客人，所以搞得我手忙脚乱。老伴也说我请的人太多了。其实也没什么关系，吃饭是次要的，主要是老邻居聚一聚。我请的这些老邻居都是以前住四合院时的好朋友，大家说起当年在四合院的生活，就有说不完的话。

当时我们都住在一个有几个院落的大杂院里，里里外外一共住了十四户人家。我家住在第三个院子的东房，从大门到家，要路过住在第二个院子的老张家。记得那时老张家最早买了电视机，是一台十四英寸的黑白电视机。一到晚上，老张就把电视机搬到院子里，于是十多户人家的男男女女、老老少少都聚到那里，大家看电视的

Hutong, ancient city alley or lane typical in Beijing

看电视、聊天儿的聊天儿，那里就成了我们大杂院最热闹、最好玩的地方。但是大杂院的冬天可不好过，因为没有暖气，一到冬天，家家户户都要烧煤炉取暖，房子熏得黑黑的。

后来大家陆陆续续搬进了单位的楼房。住处离办公室很近，而且楼房里装有暖气，冬天比大杂院舒服多了。那时几家人合起来用一个大厨房。邻居们都是在同一个单位工作的同事，大家都很熟悉，所以经常在一起热热闹闹地做饭。谁家没有了盐或醋，只要说一声，就会有好几个人递上自家的给你用。那时候小孩子似乎都觉得自家的饭菜比不上邻居家的好吃。大人们呢，做了好吃的也忘不了把别人家的小孩算上。比如不管谁家包了饺子，全楼道的孩子都有份儿。

现在大家都买了商品房，住进了各种各样的小区，大门一关，谁也不认识谁。每一户人家都有自己的厨房、卫生间，已经不需要和邻居共享了。

人真是奇怪，原来住在大杂院的时候，总是羡慕住在楼房里的人生活方便，住到楼房后，又盼望着有更宽敞的房子。现在生活条件好了，唯一的遗憾是失去了亲密的邻居。我是一个爱热闹、喜欢交朋友的人，但是搬到新家两个月了，也没有机会和新邻居说上几句话。我真怀念曾经在大杂院和单位筒子楼里一起生活过的朋友和邻居。

VOCABULARY
生词表

| 1 | 筒子楼 | tǒngzilóu | n. | tube-shaped dormitory building [with one corridor, public toilets and a kitchen] |

【名】一座*筒子楼* | 我们是住*筒子楼*时的邻居。

| 2 | 整理 | zhěnglǐ | v. | to tidy up |

【动】*整理*房间 | *整理*一下 | *整理*得很清楚 | *整理整理*自己的房间 | 这些材料要及时加以*整理*。
▣整顿 | 整治 | 整修。▣清理 | 治理 | 修理。

| 3 | 册 | cè | m.w. | volume |

【量】几*册*书 | 这套书一共五*册*。 | 我这套书不全，缺两*册*。 | 全书分上、中、下三*册*。

| 4 | 打 | dǎ | v. | to pack |

【动】*打*包 | 他只用了十分钟就把行李*打*好了。 | 这么多麦子*打*成捆儿得多长时间？

| 5 | 捆 | kǔn | n. | bundle |

(~儿)【名】稻草*捆儿* | 扎成*捆儿* | 一家人齐动手，一会儿就把大*捆儿*都改成小*捆儿*了。

| 6 | 发愁 | fāchóu | v. | to worry |

【动】为房子*发愁* | *发*起*愁*来 | 你*发*什么*愁*？钱的问题我来想办法。 | 长这么大他都不知道什么叫*发愁*，这回他可知道了。▣犯愁 | 解愁。▣发困 | 发愣 | 发呆 | 发怒 | 发懒。

| 7 | 书柜 | shūguì | n. | bookcase; book shelf |

【名】新*书柜* | 一个*书柜* | 木制*书柜* | 买*书柜* | 他的房间里摆了四个大*书柜*。▣柜：放衣服、文件等用的器具，一般为木制或铁制。▣衣柜 | 碗柜 | 鞋柜 | 保险柜。

| 8 | 分门别类 | fēnmén biélèi | V. | classify and categorize |

图书要*分门别类*地摆放，找的时候才容易找到。 | 这些问题又多又杂，要*分门别类*地加以处理。

| 9 | 收拾 | shōushi | v. | to pack; to sort out |

【动】*收拾*屋子 | *收拾*干净 | 行李已经*收拾*好了。 | 你今天*收拾收拾*房间吧。

| 10 | 光线 | guāngxiàn | n. | light |

【名】*光线*充足 | 微弱的*光线* | 遮住*光线* | 这儿*光线*太暗了，什么也看不清。 | 现在*光线*不好，等一会儿出了太阳我们再照相吧。

| 11 | 窗帘 | chuānglián | n. | curtain |

(~儿)【名】挂*窗帘* | 花布*窗帘* | 一道*窗帘* | 买的*窗帘*不如做的合适。 | 阳光透过白纱*窗帘*照到屋内的地板上。▣帘：用布、竹子等做成的起遮挡作用的东西。▣布帘 | 竹帘 | 门帘。▣窗口 | 窗台 | 窗花 | 窗户。

| 12 | 宽敞 | kuānchǎng | adj. | spacious |

【形】*宽敞*的教室 | 房间并不*宽敞*。 | 收拾一下，觉得屋里*宽敞*多了。 | 我希望有个*宽敞*的院子种点儿什么。▣宽阔 | 宽大 | 宽广。

| 13 | 装 | zhuāng | v. | to install |

【动】*装*订 | *装*电灯 | *装*空调 | 机器已经*装*好了。 | 门上的锁*装*歪了。

| 14 | 浴缸 | yùgāng | n. | bathtub |

【名】圆形浴缸 | 陶瓷浴缸 | 买一个浴缸 | 浴缸里注满了水。

| 15 | 疲倦 | píjuàn | adj. & n. | tired; fatigue |

【形，名】身体疲倦 | 疲倦的样子 | 不知疲倦 | 两天两夜没睡觉，工人们都极度疲倦。☞疲劳 | 疲惫 | 疲乏。☞困倦 | 倦意。

| 16 | 手忙脚乱 | shǒumáng jiǎoluàn | | (caught) in a flurry (一) |

事先做好充足的准备，做事就不会手忙脚乱了。 | 眼看上课要迟到了，他手忙脚乱地收拾好书包冲出宿舍。 | 第一次做饭手忙脚乱的，做得并不好吃，但我仍然很高兴。

| 17 | 次要 | cìyào | adj. | secondary |

【形】次要地位 | 次要的人物 | 形式是次要的，内容才是主要的。 | 配角看起来都是次要人物，但要演好也不容易。☞主要 | 重要。

| 18 | 聚 | jù | v. | to gather together |

【动】聚会 | 聚餐 | 欢聚一堂 | 大家聚在一起商量商量。 | 明天是星期天，我们找个地方聚聚。

| 19 | 院落 | yuànluò | n. | courtyard |

【名】这个院落是明清时的建筑。 | 整个院落坐北朝南。 | 我喜欢那个布置得很有特色的小院落。 | 他渴望有一个自己的小院落，空闲时可以种花赏月。

| 20 | 大杂院 | dàzáyuàn | n. | residential compound occupied by many households |

（~儿）【名】拥挤的大杂院儿 | 他是我儿时大杂院儿里的好伙伴。 | 这里原先是一片大杂院儿，现在全是高楼大厦。 | 这个大杂院儿共有六个小院，住着上百口人。☞院：房屋及其周围用墙等围起来的空间。☞四合院 | 独门独院 | 深宅大院。

| 21 | 路过 | lùguò | v. | to pass by |

【动】正好路过 | 路过我们家的时候一定要来玩儿。 | 路过商店，顺便买点儿东西。 | 从北京到南京要路过天津。

| 22 | 暖气 | nuǎnqì | n. | central heating |

【名】停暖气了。 | 来暖气了。 | 暖气太热了。 | 我们学校的暖气烧得很好。| 黄河以北的楼房里都有暖气设备。

| 23 | 煤炉 | méilú | n. | coal stove |

【名】生煤炉 | 一只煤炉 | 手提式蜂窝煤炉 | 她每天回家第一件事就是打开煤炉烧开水。☞电炉 | 火炉 | 炉灶 | 炉火纯青。

| 24 | 取暖 | qǔnuǎn | v. | to warm oneself |

【动】生火取暖 | 取暖设备 | 互相取暖 | 我们家烧煤取暖。

| 25 | 熏 | xūn | v. | to be filled with fumes |

【动】熏肉 | 烟熏火燎 | 烟把墙都熏黑了。

| 26 | 陆陆续续 | lùlùxùxù | | one after another |

客人们陆陆续续地到了。 | 这几年，他陆陆续续地写了十几本小说。 | 一到春天，桃花、杏花、梨花等就陆陆续续地开了。 | 快过年了，在外工作的人都陆陆续续地回老家了。

| 27 | 单位 | dānwèi | n. | workplace, work unit |

【名】工作单位 | 先进单位 | 单位的工作人员 | 单位合并了 | 今天有很多单位来参加比赛。| 我们单位明天出去旅游。

| 28 | 楼道 | lóudào | n. | corridor |

【名】一条楼道 | 黑黑的楼道 | 走过楼道 | 楼道里的灯坏了。 | 从楼道的这一头走到那一头，我也没找到朋友的家。

| 29 | 有份儿 | yǒufènr | v. | to have a share |

【动】人人有份儿 | 见者有份儿 | 别着急，大家都有份儿。

| 30 | 商品房 | shāngpǐnfáng | n. | commodity housing |

【名】开发商品房 | 购买商品房 | 高级商品房 | 商品房市场 | 目前,市场上的商品房大都卖得太贵，普通人很难买得起。◉ 房:房子;有墙、门、窗等给人居住或做其他用途的建筑物。◉ 平房 | 楼房 | 房产 | 房主。

| 31 | 小区 | xiǎoqū | n. | housing estate |

【名】住宅小区 | 花园小区 | 小区居民 | 建设小区 | 这个小区虽然不大，但设计很好。◉ 区:地区。◉ 山区 | 风景区 | 工业区 | 居民区。

| 32 | 共享 | gòngxiǎng | v. | to share |

【动】资源共享 | 利益共享 | 共享空间 | 好东西要和大家共享。

| 33 | 羡慕 | xiànmù | v. | to envy; to admire |

【动】羡慕别人 | 令人羡慕 | 羡慕得要命 | 他很羡慕我。 | 大家都羡慕她家庭那么幸福。

| 34 | 怀念 | huáiniàn | v. | to miss; to cherish the memory of sth |

【动】怀念祖国 | 日夜怀念 | 强烈地怀念 | 这是一个值得怀念的地方。 | 节日的时候总是格外怀念家乡和亲人。◉ 想念 | 思念 | 惦念。

VOCABULARY IN CONTEXT

Form two teams - a Red and Blue team. The teams take turns to guess a phrase described by the other team. The team that is providing the description may either explain the meaning of the phrase, or describe a situation in which the phrase is used without giving the actual phrase away.

Take "愤怒" for example. The Red Team can describe it this way: "形容一个人特别生气时的心情，两个字", or "当你发现有人没有经过你的同意就从你的桌上拿走了你心爱的书，而且还胡乱地扔在教室的地上时，你会很……"

Now, let's play the game using the following phrases.

发愁

收拾

疲倦

路过

陆陆续续

聚（一聚）

怀念

羡慕

手忙脚乱

LANGUAGE CONNECTION

Both "从" and "离" can be used with nouns of places in the constructions "从+ noun of place" and "离+noun of place".

The difference is that "从+noun of place" indicates the starting point of an action while "离+noun of place" signifies distance.

For example

- 我刚从学校回来。
- 学校离火车站三公里。

"从+noun of place" can also be used to signify distance. In this case, use the construction "从……到……".

For example

- 从我的家到学校很远。
- 从学校到火车站三公里。

Ⓐ Prepositions "从" and "离"

"从筒子楼的旧房子搬到新家已经两个月了。"

"住处离办公室很近。"

Fill in the blanks with "从"or "离".

① 甲：你是_____哪儿来的？

乙：我是_____上海来的。

甲：上海_____这儿远吗？

乙：上海_____这儿不太远。

② 甲：你家_____学校有多远？

乙：_____我家到学校只有一公里。

甲：你早上几点_____家里出发？

乙：七点半。

A比不上B

"那时候小孩子似乎都觉得自家的饭菜比不上邻居家的好吃。"

The construction "A比不上B" is used to compare two things. It means "A is not as good as B". The construction may be followed by an adjective. If there is an adjective, the adjective is usually positive.

The sentence in the text means that the children thought their neighbors' food tasted better than theirs.

For example

- 这台电脑比不上那台好用。
- 很多人觉得这套新教材比不上旧教材。

Rewrite each of the following dialogs into a sentence using the construction "A比不上B".

① 杰　克：这是你新买的书包吗？

　 大　卫：是。你觉得怎么样？

　 杰　克：我还是觉得以前那个书包更好看。

　 改写：杰克觉得＿＿＿＿＿＿＿＿＿＿＿＿＿＿＿＿＿。

② 杰　克：听说了吗？学校的乒乓球队来了新教练。

　 大　卫：我早就知道了。我觉得这位教练没有以前那位好。

　 改写：大卫觉得＿＿＿＿＿＿＿＿＿＿＿＿＿＿＿＿＿。

③ 汤　姆：你的汉语说得比我流利多了。

　 麦　克：哪里，哪里。其实你的发音也不错。

　 改写：汤姆＿＿＿＿＿＿＿＿＿＿＿＿＿＿＿＿＿＿＿。

In the first sentence, "老邻居" is both the object of the verb "请" and the notional subject of the complement "来家里吃饭".

In the second sentence, "住在楼房里的人" is both the object of "羡慕" and the notional subject of the complement "生活方便".

This kind of construction is called "兼语句" in Chinese grammar.

For example
- 你的朋友让我把这本书带给你。
- 我喜欢他聪明好学。
- 谢谢你帮助我。

 C 兼语句 ("Object + Complement" Construction)

"这个周末我请几户老邻居来家里吃饭。"

"原来住在大杂院的时候，总是羡慕住在楼房里的人生活方便。"

Rewrite the given sentences using an "object + complement" construction.

① 王林的自行车坏了，他的朋友杰克会修自行车。

王林想＿＿＿＿＿＿＿＿＿＿＿＿＿＿＿＿＿＿＿＿＿。

② 毛毛的新家很宽敞。她很喜欢她的新家。

毛毛＿＿＿＿＿＿＿＿＿＿＿＿＿＿＿＿＿＿＿＿＿。

③ 大卫上课总是迟到，老师经常批评他。

老师＿＿＿＿＿＿＿＿＿＿＿＿＿＿＿＿＿＿＿＿＿。

④ 杰克上课时突然生病了，老师说必须马上去医院。

老师＿＿＿＿＿＿＿＿＿＿＿＿＿＿＿＿＿＿＿＿＿。

This construction indicates that different people in a group are doing different things.

For example
- 在晚会上，大家跳舞的跳舞，唱歌的唱歌，热闹极了。

 D V_1的V_1，V_2的V_2

"大家看电视的看电视、聊天儿的聊天儿。"

Describe the following situations using the construction "V_1的V_1，V_2的V_2".

① 操场上有很多人，有的人在跑步，有的人在打羽毛球。

＿＿＿＿＿＿＿＿＿＿＿＿＿＿＿＿＿＿＿＿＿＿＿。

② 教室里，同学们在打扫卫生，有的人擦地，有的擦玻璃。

＿＿＿＿＿＿＿＿＿＿＿＿＿＿＿＿＿＿＿＿＿＿＿。

③ 动物园里有许多可爱的猴子，有的在吃东西，有的在睡觉，对参观的人视而不见。

＿＿＿＿＿＿＿＿＿＿＿＿＿＿＿＿＿＿＿＿＿＿＿。

指示代词 (Demonstrative Pronoun)

> "老朱凭着他的太极功夫成为当地的名人,在一家中国会馆做太极教练,整天忙这忙那,生活丰富多彩。"（副课文例句）

Say what the underlined words in the following sentences refer to and then read the sentences aloud.

① 在玩具店里,他<u>这</u>也想摸摸,<u>那</u>也想动动。

② 小明指着一个玩具问:"<u>这</u>是新的吗?"

③ 他最近心情不好,总是觉得<u>这儿</u>也不满意,<u>那儿</u>也不满意。

④ 你先仔细地看,别老是问<u>这</u>问<u>那</u>的。

"这","那","这儿","那儿" can be used to indicate a specific thing or place, or a non-specific thing or place. When referring to non-specific things or places, "这" and "那", and "这儿" and "那儿" appear side by side in a sentence.

In the text, for example, "这" and "那" appear together and both refer to non-specific things.

For example

- 他走进新家,看看这儿,看看那儿,感觉很满意。
- 他们俩见了面,说说这,说说那,高兴极了。

 前缀和后缀 (Prefix and Suffix)

Think of words with the following affixes. How many can you think of?

老　小　子　儿　头　者

The affix is an important component of a word. In a word with two or more syllables, the "stem" has a specific lexical meaning while the "affix" is added to the stem to denote an additional meaning. The prefix and suffix are commonly used affixes.

For example, in "老张" and "房子", "老" is a prefix and "子" a suffix.

In Chinese, the following characters are common prefixes: "阿" (as in "阿爸", "阿姨", "阿明"), "老" (as in "老王", "老虎", "老汉", "老板", "老乡"), and "小" (as in "小王", "小姐", "小孩儿").

And the following characters are common suffixes: "子"(as in "桌子", "瓶子", "裙子", "筷子"), "头"(as in "石头", "骨头", "念头"), "儿"(as in "鸟儿", "花儿", "盖儿"), and "者"(as in "记者", "读者", "学者", "演唱者").

COMMUNICATION CORNER

Instructions:

- Do you have any regrets in your life? For everything you gain, you lose something else; it could be your favorite stuffed animal, a book or a good friend. Do you regret any decision that you've made (or not made) while growing up?

- Describe and explain what you most regret to your partner.

- Listen to your partner's advice and consider if it will help alleviate your feelings of regret.

- Switch roles with your partner.

我成长，我失去

Guidelines:

In this lesson, the writer expressed some regrets although his living conditions have improved over time. What were his regrets and how did he express them?

🗣 Here are some other ways of expressing regrets:

◀ ……我真/很/非常遗憾……，因为那是……

◀ ……太可惜了/……实在令人惋惜，如果能够再有一次机会，我一定……

◀ ……让我感到特别遗憾，我总想……

🗣 When someone shares his or her regrets about the past, we would typically soothe him or her and offer some practical advice.

◀ 好了，别想了，事情已经过去了，现在……

◀ 没关系，也许……，这样也不错。

◀ 噢，也许你现在还可以……，只要你……就能……

◀ 我倒有个建议，你看行不行？如果……，那么你就……，也许事情就不一样了。

WRITING TASK

Instructions:

- Design a poster for a movie you have seen.

- Include details such as the director(s), actors, synopsis of the plot and a brief commentary on the movie.

- Include pictures and an eye-catching tagline.

制作一张电影海报

Guidelines:

Highlight the most important features of the movie, e.g., award-winning director, strong cast, major awards won by the film, etc.

- 本片由著名导演……执导，著名演员……主演。
- 本片曾获得……大奖。

Keep the film synopsis brief and clear. If you can include an element of suspense or anticipation, the effect may be better.

- 这个电影说的是一个……的故事。
- 故事发生在……
- 故事的主人公是……
- 他们最后的结局会怎样呢？

You could add a brief commentary on the plot, the performance of the cast and other aspects. The commentary should inform and excite movie-goers.

- 本片故事情节曲折，演员的表演……尤其在……方面，这是一部最……的电影。

You may use images from the film or your own drawings for your poster.

Look at other movie posters for inspiration.

"Pushing Hands"

副课文

老年人的烦恼

——电影《推手》观后感

Pre-reading

■ 你觉得生活在你身边的老人有哪些烦恼？

■ 我们应该怎样帮助老人？

> 1.老朱到美国以后，最大的烦恼是什么？

> 2.老朱在什么地方可以找到快乐？

> 3.儿子的想法为什么会伤害老朱？

> 4.老朱怎样独立生活？

　　如果你看过电影《推手》，那你一定还记得老朱这个传统的中国老人的形象。

　　老朱77岁时，从北京来到美国，和独生子晓生一家生活在一起。老朱不会说英语，美国儿媳玛莎呢，又不会说汉语，所以他们根本无法交流。他们的年龄、文化背景以及生活习惯差异太大了。因为在家里无法和儿媳交流，老朱只有在中国会馆才能找到一些快乐。在这里，他是众多学生崇拜的太极拳教练，而且还和台湾来的陈太太成了朋友。由于无法化解父亲和妻子的矛盾，儿子晓生便希望父亲和这位陈太太的感情尽快发展，这样父亲就可以搬出去和陈太太一起生活了。老朱发现儿子的真实想法后，自尊心受到很大伤害，他一个人离家出走了。

　　影片中最让人伤感的是老朱离开儿子家时，给儿子留下了一封信，信中说："天下之大，岂无安身之地？"世界这么大，怎么会找不到一个小小的地方呆着呢？老朱来到中国城，做了一名高龄洗碗工，开始独立生活。

5.老朱和儿媳的矛盾反映了怎样的文化冲突？

6.电影中的老朱是怎样解决孤独寂寞问题的？

7.你对中国传统的几代同堂的生活方式有什么看法？

老朱的儿子其实是很有孝心的，儿媳玛莎人也不坏，但他们和老朱为什么很难生活在一起呢？主要是东西方文化差异带来的冲突。老朱辛苦一生，把儿子抚养长大，希望和儿子一家住在一起，共享天伦之乐，这是中国家庭生活的传统模式。但是对于很多美国年轻人来说，是难以接受的。晓生痛苦地对妻子玛莎说："在我的文化里，一个人关照父母，就应该像父母关照他一样。父亲是我生命的一部分，你为什么不能接受他呢？"

世上每个人都有变老的一天，如果一个人老了，身边没有儿女陪伴，怎么面对孤独寂寞的生活呢？在《推手》中，导演给老朱安排了一个美好的结局，老朱凭着他的太极功夫成为当地的名人，在一家中国会馆做太极教练，整天忙这忙那，生活丰富多彩。这时，他和陈太太再次相遇了。陈太太的情况和老朱相似，她刚从女儿家搬出来，一个人住在公寓里。两位老人和儿女的生活既保持了一定距离，又都留有一份亲情，而自己的老年生活也有了新的希望。

虽然《推手》的故事发生在美国，但是老年人的生活、老年人和年轻人如何相处等问题，在当今中国，也是现实的社会问题。和玛莎一样，如今中国的年轻人也难以接受几代同堂的传统生活方式。老年人怎样才能找到幸福、保持自己内心的快乐，这是一个具有普遍意义的社会问题。

VOCABULARY
副课文 **生词表**

1	独生子	dúshēngzǐ	n.	only son
2	差异	chāyì	n.	difference
3	会馆	huìguǎn	n.	club, association
4	崇拜	chóngbài	v.	to adore
5	化解	huàjiě	v.	to resolve
6	自尊心	zìzūnxīn	n.	self-esteem
7	出走	chūzǒu	v.	to leave; to run away from (home)
8	伤感	shānggǎn	v.	to feel sad, emotional
9	岂	qǐ	adv.	used in formal Chinese to achieve the effect of a <u>rhetorical question</u>
10	安身	ānshēn	v.	to settle oneself down in a place
11	高龄	gāolíng	adj.	elderly, aged
12	天伦之乐	tiānlún zhī lè		the happiness of family life
13	陪伴	péibàn	v.	to accompany
14	孤独	gūdú	adj.	being alone
15	寂寞	jìmò	adj.	lonely
16	结局	jiéjú	n.	ending
17	亲情	qīnqíng	n.	feelings of kinship
18	几代同堂	jǐdàitóngtáng		several generations living under the same roof

UNIT SUMMARY
学习小结

一、语言点

1. 离合词
   热情的傣族小姑娘还唱起了歌。

2. V+在+处所名词
   大理的风光全写在白族姑娘的头饰上了。

3. 信封格式

4. V+得+其他成分
   主人每次倒好茶水，都会用双手把杯子举得高高的……

5. 介词"从"和"离"
   从筒子楼的旧房子搬到新家已经两个月了。

6. A比不上B
   那时候小孩子似乎都觉得自家的饭菜比不上邻居家的好吃。

7. 兼语式
   这个周末我请几户老邻居来家里吃饭。

8. V_1的V_1，V_2的V_2
   大家看电视的看电视、聊天儿的聊天儿。

9. 指示代词
   老朱成天忙这忙那，生活丰富多彩。

10. 前缀、后缀
    老张、房子

二、功能项目

1. 不相信
   这怎么可能呢？如此秀丽多彩的山川，小小的头饰怎么写得下？

2. 意外
   我本来以为这只是很普通的茶水，端起来尝了尝却感觉与众不同。

3. 遗憾
   现在生活条件好了，我唯一的遗憾是失去了亲密的邻居。

UNIT **5**

FAMOUS PEOPLE AND HISTORY

名人与历史

Communicative Goals
- Explain an idea by including examples and relevant details
- Describe admirable characteristics of a person
- Summarize key points

Cultural Information
- Confucius, the famous Chinese thinker and social philosopher
- Dr Sun Yat-Sen, the founder of modern China
- China's two major rivers and five sacred mountains
- China's seven ancient capitals
- The Silk Road and trade in Chinese history during the Han and Tang dynasties
- Fuwa, the official mascots of the Beijing 2008 Olympic Games

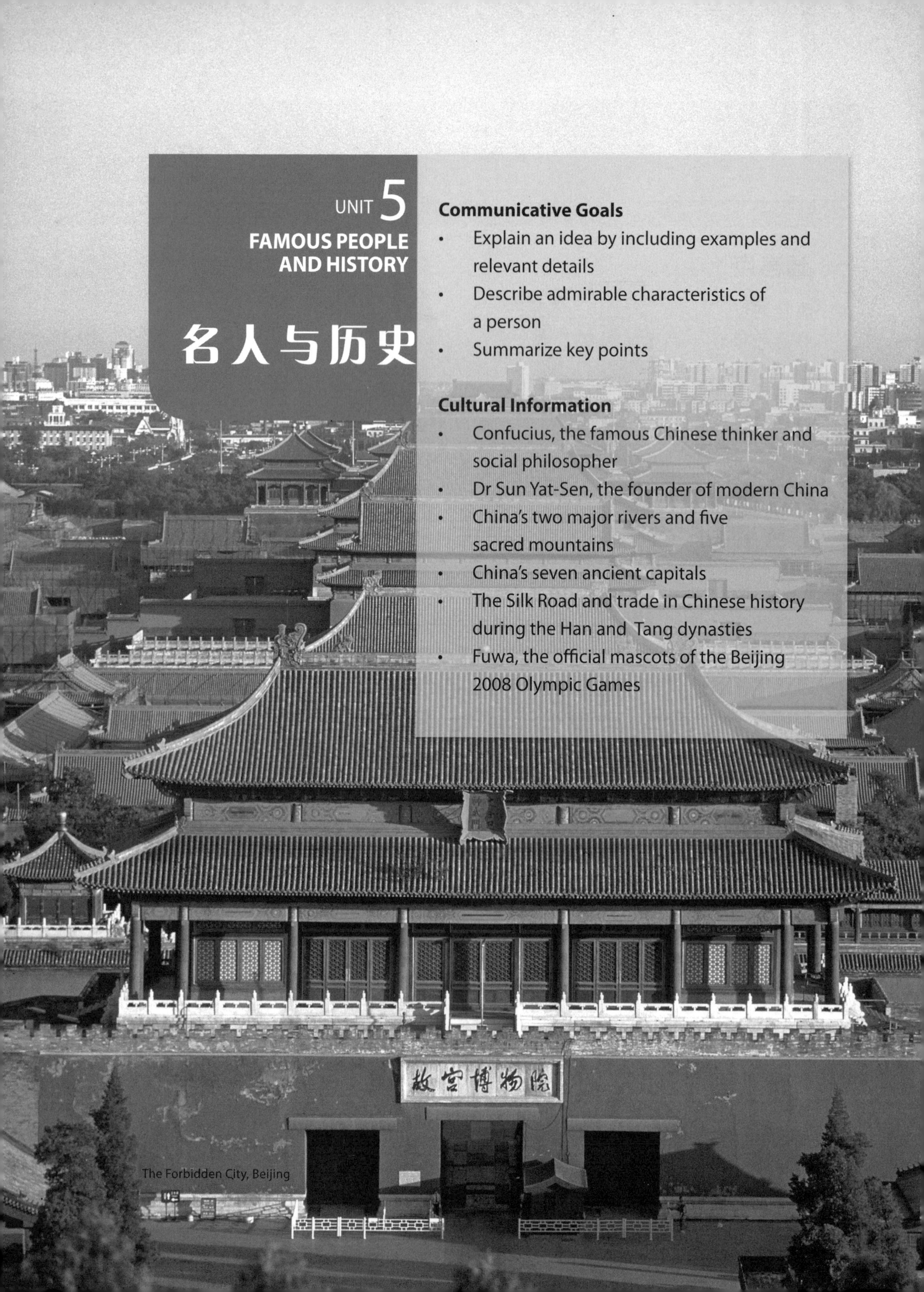

故宫博物院

The Forbidden City, Beijing

Warm up

请同学们辨认下列名人，分组讨论，说明他们的身份和他们对历史的贡献，然后填写表格。

姓名	国籍	时代	历史贡献
马丁·路德·金	美国	20世纪	争取人权的斗争
林肯	美国	19世纪	解放黑奴的方式。
爱迪生 (Edison)	美国	19世纪	发明留声机，爱迪生发明史的灯泡。
马克·吐温 (Twain)	美国	19世纪	用自己的笔名打造出的写成，应用美国的独特主义方式完成。
孔子	中国	公元前65世纪	中国儒家的思想家、教育家。
孙中山	中国	十20世纪	推翻封建制度，建立了中国第一个民主国。
李白	中国	唐代 (世纪)	唐朝诗人之一，被称为诗仙。
wǔ zé 武则天	中国	唐代 (7世纪)	中国历史上第一位女皇帝。

Who Was Confucius?

第九课

孔子是谁？

■ 你的国家有哪些有名的教育家？请说说他们的事迹。
■ 中国人很尊敬孔子，你知道为什么吗？

如果你问中国人孔子是谁，人们也许会回答，他是一位伟大的思想家，或者说是一位教育家；也可能有人回答说，他是中国历史上的圣人。这些回答都没有错，但似乎都离我们太远。我更愿意把孔子看作是一位富有智慧的、和蔼可亲的长者。《论语》这部书记录了许多他说过的话，还有他生活中的一些细节，即使在两千多年后的今天，我们仍然可以感受到他的亲切。

孔子是一位老师。那时候普通人一般是没有办法读书学习的，可是在孔子这里，只要想学习，他都会教他们，所以许多人从很远的地方来向他学习。据说他的学生先后有三千人，最优秀的有七十二人。孔子曾说过一句很有名的话，"学而时习之，不亦说（悦）乎？"意思是学了一门知识，要不断地复习，在实践中掌握它，这是一件很快乐的事情。就像我们学习汉语，在教室里学习后，要反复练习、使用，才会觉得有意思。

孔子很注意教学方法。有一次，有两个学生先后问了孔子同样一个问题："听到什么建议就马上去做吗？"孔子对第一个学生说："你的父亲和哥哥都在，怎么能听到就去做呢？"意思是在做以前还应该征求一下父亲和哥哥的意见。孔子对第二个学生说："对，应该马上去做。"同样的问题，孔子给了完全相反的回答，这使其他的学生感到很困惑。孔子解释说："他们俩一个性格很急躁，所以就要让他在做事之前多考虑考虑，多听听别人的意见；而另一个性格很内向，所以要鼓励他。"

孔子常常说到"仁"这个词。简单地说,"仁"就是爱,就是对别人的关心。那么在人与人的交往中,"仁"的最基本的原则是什么呢?有一次,一个学生问孔子,有没有一句话可以一辈子都照着它去做呢?孔子说:"己所不欲,勿施于人。"意思是自己不想要的东西或不想遇到的事情,不要强迫别人接受。我理解这句话的意思,就是当我们要对别人做一件事情的时候,要先换一个位置想一想,看看自己愿意不愿意接受这样的事情。

在这个世界上,可能每个人都希望自己很富有。孔子说,如果能够使自己富有的话,即使很辛苦的工作他也愿意去做。如果做不到呢?孔子说,那他就做他喜欢的事情。如果一个人为了得到钱,使用不正当的手段,那么即使他很富有,他的生活也不可能快乐;而一个有修养、有爱心的人,即使家里很穷,他的心里也永远是快乐的。这是不是很有道理?

孔子就是这样一个人,富有智慧,心中充满了仁爱,充满了快乐。《论语》中描述孔子,说他神态安详,温和而严肃,有威严但又很亲切。难怪他的学生都那么热爱他、尊敬他呢。

孔子是一位很博学的人,他的学生认为他"学无常师",也就是说没有固定的老师。据说孔子曾向老子请教过,但他所创立的儒家学说与老子的思想却有很大的不同。

VOCABULARY
生词表

1	思想家	sīxiǎngjiā	n.	thinker

【名】一个著名的思想家 | 中国古代思想家很多。⊙家：掌握某种专门学识或从事某种专门活动的人。 📖画家 | 专家 | 音乐家 | 科学家 | 艺术家 | 政治家。

2	教育家	jiàoyùjiā	n.	educator

【名】一位伟大的教育家 | 一个儿童教育家 | 一位教育家来作报告。

3	圣人	shèngrén	n.	sage

【名】一位受人尊敬的圣人 | 圣人的话有很大的影响力。 | 成为圣人不是一件容易的事。

4	智慧	zhìhuì	n.	wisdom

【名】获得智慧 | 智慧来自学习和实践。 | 这本书里充满了智慧的语言。 | 这个孩子有让人吃惊的智慧。

5	长者	zhǎngzhě	n.	venerable elder

【名】一位头发花白的长者 | 以长者的身份说话 | 他很有长者的风范。

6	部	bù	m.w.	a classifier used with a numeral to modify nouns denoting books, film, etc

【量】一部著作 | 一部电视剧 | 一部电影 | 一部手机 | 我买了一部词典。

7	细节	xìjié	n.	details

【名】忽视细节 | 观察细节 | 故事细节 | 他平时不太注意生活细节。 | 这篇小说的每个细节都写得十分感人。

8	感受	gǎnshòu	v.	to feel

【动】感受家庭的温暖 | 我们感受到了成功的快乐。 | 很多人一到中国就能感受到中国人的热情。 | 这位画家对美的感受能力很强。

9	亲切	qīnqiè	adj.	kind; amiable

【形】亲切的笑容 | 亲切的问候 | 显得亲切 | 亲切得很 | 她待人很亲切。 | 他的声音让我感到特别亲切。 | 校长亲切地跟学生们交谈。

10	先后	xiānhòu	adv.	successively; one after another

【副】我先后收到他五封信。 | 他先后游览了故宫、天坛、长城等。 | 这个月，老板先后出过三次差。

11	实践	shíjiàn	n.	practice

【名】实践经验 | 缺乏实践 | 实践证明，他的想法是错误的。 | 年轻人应该多参加社会实践。 | 那是一次成功的实践。

12	征求	zhēngqiú	v.	to solicit; seek; ask for

【动】去中国留学，我想先征求一下爸爸的意见。 | 还是向大家征求征求意见再决定。

13	相反	xiāngfǎn	adj.	opposite; on the contrary

【形】相反的结果 | 意见相反 | 态度相反 | 他俩对这件事的看法完全相反。 | 两辆车朝着相反的方向开走了。

14	困惑	kùnhuò	adj.	perplexed; puzzled; confused

【形】十分困惑 | 困惑的目光 | 这是让他们感到困惑的问题。

15	急躁	jízào	adj.	irritable; impatient

【形】急躁的小伙子 | 性格急躁 | 一听到事情弄糟了，他就急躁起来。| 做事不能急躁，要有耐心。| 事情虽然处理得有些急躁，但总算没出问题。| 他显得非常急躁，不知道遇到了什么事。

16	内向	nèixiàng	adj.	introvert / extrovert

【形】这个人有点儿内向。| 小王内向得很。| 内向的人一般不喜欢说话。

17	鼓励	gǔlì	v.	to encourage

【动】鼓励孩子 | 值得鼓励 | 鼓励一下 | 热情地鼓励 | 互相鼓励 | 口语课上，老师应该鼓励学生多说。| 对于孩子的每一点进步，父母都应该及时给予鼓励。

18	交往	jiāowǎng	n.	interactions

【名】交往多 | 交往深 | 有交往 | 正常的交往 | 他们之间交往比较密切。| 他们两家没有什么交往。| 到了国外，要入乡随俗，注意交往的方式。

19	原则	yuánzé	n.	principle

【名】制定一条原则 | 提出一项原则 | 这个原则大家都要遵守。| 无论什么时候，都要坚持原则。| 你怎么这么没有原则？| 在一些原则问题上，我们不能让步。

20	一辈子	yībèizi		all one's life

他当了一辈子医生。| 两位老人在一起生活了一辈子。| 老师的鼓励和帮助，我一辈子忘不了。

21	强迫	qiǎngpò	v.	to force; to compel

【动】这家公司强迫我们接受他们的条件。| 老师不能强迫学生学习。| 强迫小孩子做事，会引起他的反感。

22	位置	wèizhì	n.	position; place

【名】调换位置 | 位置改变了 | 他在公司里找到了一个合适的位置。| 有时候说话时应该考虑自己的位置。

23	手段	shǒuduàn	n.	means

【名】这个手段 | 手段不高明。| 他们想采取强迫的手段达到目的。| 这件事要通过法律手段才能解决。

24	修养	xiūyǎng	n.	self-cultivation

【名】有修养 | 修养好 | 那个人一点儿修养也没有。| 这个服务员的修养很差。| 每个人都要不断提高自己的修养。

25	爱心	àixīn	n.	loving care; thoughtfulness

【名】大家的爱心让她很感动。| 老人对孩子们充满了爱心。| 帮助残疾人，每个人都要献出一份爱心。

26	神态	shéntài	n.	expression; manner

【名】神态自若 | 神态各异 | 他神态严肃地走了进来。| 那人的神态有些不自然。| 小姑娘显出不好意思的神态。

27	安详	ānxiáng	adj.	composed; calm; serene

【形】面容安详 | 举止安详 | 父母安详地坐在椅子上交谈着。| 看见他安详的样子，我的心也安静下来。

28	严肃	yánsù	adj.	serious; solemn; earnest

【形】大家严肃一点。| 他的样子严肃极了。| 他严肃地对我说："我不是开玩笑。" | 他说得很严肃，我们都相信了。| 爸爸工作起来一向严肃、认真。

29	威严	wēiyán	n.	authority; dignity

【名】摆出了长者的威严 | 表现出一种威严 | 他认识到了法律的威严和无情。| 父亲的话使我感受到他的威严。

30	博学	bóxué	*adj.*	learned

【形】*博学多才* | 这个人很*博学*。| 我的汉语老师是一位*博学*的长者。

31	学无常师	xué wú cháng shī		One can treat anyone with more knowledge than oneself as a teacher

她*学无常师*，认真地向各种人请教。

32	固定	gùdìng	*adj.*	fixed; regular

【形】*固定*的时间 | *固定*的位置 | 我还没有*固定*的工作。| 房子还没有找好，所以现在住的地方很不*固定*。|

33	请教	qǐngjiào	*v.*	to ask for advice

【动】*请教*问题 | 向人*请教* | *请教*一下 | 老师，我想*请教*您一个问题。| 这个问题最好去*请教请教*王老师。

34	创立	chuànglì	*v.*	to found; to create

【动】经过一辈子的努力，这位教育家*创立*了一种新的教育理论体系。| 一个新的学科很难一下子*创立*起来。| 他所*创立*的学说后来又有了新的发展。

35	学说	xuéshuō	*n.*	theory; doctrine

【名】经济*学说* | 创立*学说* | 一种*学说* | 进化论*学说*影响很大。| 近年来出现了很多新的*学说*。

PROPER NOUNS			
36	《论语》	Lúnyǔ	*The Analects of Confucius*

儒家的重要经典，记录了孔子和他的弟子们的言行。

37	老子	Lǎozǐ	a great philosopher in ancient China and the founder of Taoism

人名。姓李，名耳，又叫老聃，著有《道德经》，是道家学派的创始人。主张"清静""无为"。

38	儒家	Rújiā	Confucian school (of thought)

先秦时期创立的一个思想流派，以孔子为代表，主张礼治，强调传统的伦常关系等，对中国社会有很大的影响。

Fill in the blanks with the words in the list. Note that not all the words will be used.

VOCABULARY IN CONTEXT

- 智慧
- 感受
- 先后
- 征求
- 困惑
- 急躁
- 鼓励
- 交往
- 强迫
- 手段

A

　　有一年夏天，曹操带领部队去打仗，天气热得出奇，天空中一丝云彩也没有。部队在弯弯曲曲的山道上行走着，到了中午时分，士兵的衣服都湿透了，行军的速度也慢了下来，好几个体弱的士兵竟然_____晕倒在路边。

　　曹操看到行军的速度越来越慢，十分着急。可是，几万人马连水都喝不上，大家怎么能加快速度呢？曹操叫来向导，_____他的意见，问他有什么办法。可是向导摇摇头说没有办法，因为泉水在山谷的另一边，太远了。曹操想了想，说："不行，时间来不及。"可是怎么样才能_____士兵们尽快前进呢？他知道用_____的_____是不行的。曹操抬头看了看前边的树林，灵机一动，对向导说："你什么也别说，我有办法了。"他骑马赶到队伍前面，用马鞭指着前方对士兵们说："前面有一大片梅林，那里的梅子又甜又酸，好吃极了。我们快点赶路，绕过这个小山就到梅林了！"士兵们听后，大家都好像_____到了梅子吃在嘴里的滋味，也不觉得口渴了，精神也一下子也变好了，脚步也大大加快了。

　　就这样，曹操用自己的_____，解决了难题。

B　Write down the idiom that originated from this story. Then, discuss the meaning of this idiom with your partner.

LANGUAGE CONNECTION

A rhetorical question is a question posed without expectation of an answer but merely as a way of making a point. When the question is expressed in a negative form with words such as "难道", "怎么", or "哪儿", the speaker expects or assumes an affirmative answer from the listener.

For example

- 你不是已经知道了吗？（你已经知道了。）
- 难道这样的电影不值得看吗？（这样的电影值得看。）
- 她怎么会说这种糊涂话？（她不会说这种糊涂话。）
- 他哪儿有钱？（他没钱。）

A 反问句 (Rhetorical Question)

"你的父亲和哥哥都在，怎么能听到就去做呢？"

Form groups. Each student from each group comes up with three different situations. Students from each group are to suggest rhetorical questions based on the different situations given by students from another group. The whole class then comments on the rhetorical questions.

Situation : You know very well that Xiao Li dislikes a particular style of clothes but Mary thinks otherwise. Use a rhetorical question to express your opinion.

The rhetorical question: 他怎么会喜欢这种样式的衣服呢?

Situation 1 : _____ 。

The rhetorical question: _____ 。

Situation 2 : _____ 。

The rhetorical question: _____ 。

Situation 3 : _____ 。

The rhetorical question: _____ 。

B   难怪 (no wonder)

"难怪他的学生都那么热爱他、尊敬他呢。"

Use "难怪" when you realize the reason behind something. There is usually another clause stating the reason before or after the clause containing "难怪".

For example
- 难怪这蔬菜这么新鲜，原来是刚刚摘下来的。
- 他生病住医院了，难怪没参加毕业典礼呢。
- 外面下大雪了，难怪天这么冷。

In groups, think up as many sentences as possible using "难怪" based on the given contexts. The group that can come up with the most number of coherent sentences wins.

Situation: He didn't come to the party.

The sentence: 难怪他没来参加晚会，原来他妈妈生病了。

Situation 1: He didn't come to class.

The sentence: _____。

Situation 2: He has gone to Shanghai.

The sentence: _____。

Situation 3: Xiao Wang took part in the contest yesterday.

The sentence: _____。

Situation 4: I didn't tell him about it.

The sentence: _____。

Situation 5: Yesterday was Valentine's Day.

The sentence: _____。

Situation 6: Our class emerged champion in the basketball competition.

The sentence: _____。

As prefix, a quasi-prefix is placed before a monosyllable or a disyllable. It can be the first syllable of a compound word and can be attached to words to form other words.

For example

- 可——可爱、可亲、可笑、可怜……
- 不——不科学、不道德、不文明、不礼貌……

C 类前缀 (Quasi-Prefix)

"我更愿意把孔子看作是一位富有智慧的、和蔼可亲的长者。"

Form two groups. The teacher writes a quasi-prefix on both the left- and righthand sides of the blackboard. Students from each group then write on their side of the blackboard as many words as possible that contain the given quasi-prefix. The group with more words wins.

D 连词"而"

"他们俩一个性格很急躁，……而另一个性格很内向，所以要鼓励他。"

"而" is a conjunction connecting two words, phrases or clauses. The two parts that are connected by "而" may be in a parallel relationship, a continuous or progressive relationship, a modifier-head relationship or an adversative relationship.

For example

- 她的文笔简练而生动。(parallel)
- 各组的成绩都很好，而三组的成绩最突出。(progressive)
- 我为了进一步了解中国文化而努力学习汉语。(modifier-head)
- 这里已经是春暖花开，而北方还是寒冷的冬天。(adversative)

Form two groups. Each student in the first group is to think of two different situations and describe them to a student from the other group. The latter student then has to construct a sentence using the conjunction "而" to represent each of the situations. The class comment on whether the sentences are accurate.

Situation : We made an appointment to go to the cinema in the afternoon. I was there but he wasn't.

The sentence: 昨天我去看电影了，而他却没去。

Situation 1 : _____

The sentence: _____ 。

Situation 2 : _____

The sentence: _____ 。

Situation 3 : _____

The sentence: _____ 。

Situation 4 : _____

The sentence: _____ 。

Situation 5 : _____

The sentence: _____ 。

Situation 6 : _____

The sentence: _____ 。

COMMUNICATION CORNER

Instructions:

- The class is divided into two teams. Each team prepares two or three stories of Chinese idioms.

- Appoint a representative in your team to present one of the stories to the class. Members of the other team have to guess the idiom and explain its meaning. The class determines if the given answer is correct.

- The two teams take turns to present until all the stories have been told.

- Write down the idioms that have been guessed correctly. The team with the most number of correct answers wins.

这是什么意思呢?

Guidelines:

In this lesson, you learned several expressions used to explain a point of view, a famous quote or words of wisdom, or the characteristics of a person. Now try to apply these expressions in this activity.

🗣 Choose stories of idioms that you are familiar with or have studied in the past. For example,

在古时候，矛和盾都是打仗用的武器。矛是用来刺杀敌人的，盾是用来保护身体避免被对方的矛刺中的。传说很久以前，楚国有个卖兵器的人，在市场上卖矛和盾。为了让别人买他的东西，他先举起盾向大家夸口："你们看，我的盾是世上最坚固的盾，任何锋利的东西都不能刺穿它。"接着，又举起他的矛，吹牛说："你们再看看我的矛，它锋利无比，无论多么坚硬的盾，都挡不住它，一刺就穿！"围观的人听了他的话都觉得很好笑，人群中有人问道："按照你的说法，你的矛能够刺穿任何坚硬的盾，而你的盾又能阻挡任何锋利的矛，那拿你的矛来刺你的盾的话，结果会怎么样？"卖兵器的人听了，一下子说不出话来，只好拿着矛和盾匆匆离开了。

The idiom is 自相矛盾。

🗣 You could use the following expressions to explain the meaning of an idiom.

◀ 这个成语的意思是说……
◀ 这个成语本来的意思是……，后来，人们用这个成语比喻……

🗣 If you disagree with someone else's explanation, you could use the following expressions:

◀ 我们认为应该把这个成语解释为……，因为……
◀ 其实，这个成语的意思是……，而不是……
◀ 我理解这个成语故事的意思，就是……
◀ 这个成语其实是用来比喻……

WRITING TASK

Instructions:

- Describe a person who has qualities that you admire or like.

- Keep your writing to about 300 words.

我的××／我所熟悉的××

Guidelines:

First, choose a person to talk about. It could be somebody you know personally or a famous person.

Start by introducing him/her. How did you get to know him or her? If you do not know this person personally, would you like to meet him or her?

- 我的××，是一个……的人。
- ××是我非常崇拜的一个明星，他（她）……

Explain why you admire this person. Describe the qualities that you most admire about this person. Include examples, reasons, and other details that will develop your points. You may quote things that he or she has said or what others have said about him or her.

- 他是一个非常认真的人，有一次……
- 她非常爱我，对我的一切都非常关心，比如……
- 他的歌唱得非常好，他的演唱会……

In your conclusion, remind your reader of the admirable qualities the person possesses.

- ××就是这样一个人，他……
- 我非常喜欢××，因为她……
- 总的来讲，××……

Father of Modern China

副课文

参观中山陵

天下为公

Pre-reading

■ 你知道中国是从什么时候开始有皇帝的吗？什么时候最终推翻了皇帝统治？

■ 你知道孙中山吗？知道他的哪些事情？

暑假，美国夏威夷某中学的汤姆到中国旅游，他的中国笔友小明陪他在南京参观。

小　明：汤姆，今天你想去哪儿参观？

汤　姆：到了南京一定要看看孙中山的陵墓。

小　明：好，那就去中山陵吧。

（在中山陵）

小　明：汤姆，你看那座有三个门的石牌坊，咱们过去看看吧。

汤　姆：牌坊上"博爱"这两个字是谁写的？

小　明：是孙中山写的，陵墓的正门上刻的"天下为公"也是孙中山的亲笔字。这些正是孙中山一辈子的奋斗目标和理想。

汤　姆：哎！你看碑文上说孙中山先生就葬在这里。

小　明：这是一个纪念碑。孙中山先生在19世纪末开展革命活动，组织起义，1911年推翻了清朝政府，后来做了中华民国大总统，1925年3月12日在北京逝世。为了纪念他，特地修了这个陵墓。1929年6月才把孙中山的灵柩从北京香山运到这里。墓穴在山顶上。

1.中山陵是什么地方？

2."博爱"是什么意思？

3.为什么说"天下为公"是孙中山一辈子追求的目标？

4.孙中山在历史上的最大功绩是什么？

5.孙中山是什么时候葬到中山陵的？

汤　姆：山顶？哎呀，还要爬这么多台阶吗？

小　明：是呀，从广场到祭堂一共有392级台阶，这个数字代表当时中国有三亿九千二百万人。顺着台阶上去，就可以看见祭堂。咱们俩比赛吧，看谁先爬上去。

（到了陵墓最高处）

小　明：这就是祭堂，门上刻的六个字你认识吗？

汤　姆：怎么会不认识？"民族""民生""民权"，孙中山的三民主义嘛。

6. "三民主义"的内容是什么？

小　明：你知道得还挺多。

汤　姆：我在美国学过中国历史。我在中国参观的时候发现，用孙中山的名字命名的地方特别多。

7. 为什么会有很多地方用"中山"命名？

小　明：是呀，在中国和世界各地用"中山"命名的公园就有四十多个，还有道路、学校、图书馆什么的。

汤　姆：小明你知道吗？孙中山以前在我们中学读过书。

8. 孙中山是什么时候去美国的？去做什么？

小　明：真的吗？我只知道孙中山12岁的时候去了美国的檀香山，本来他哥哥只想让他帮忙做生意，可是他坚决要求上学，没想到就是在你们学校读的书。

汤　姆：我们学校里有一座房子就是孙中山当年读书的地方，现在我们还在里面学习呢。

9. "不虚此行"是什么意思？

小　明：有机会我一定去看看。汤姆，今天参观感觉怎么样？

汤　姆：不虚此行！孙中山领导辛亥革命推翻了封建皇帝，真是一位伟人！

10. 你认为什么样的人可以称为伟人？

Background:
The school building where Dr. Sun attended classes at Oahu College, now Punahou School, in Hawaii

VOCABULARY
副课文 **生词表**

1	陵墓	língmù	n.	mausoleum; tomb
2	牌坊	páifāng	n.	archway
3	博爱	bó'ài	v.	to have universal love
4	埋葬	zàng	v.	to bury
5	推翻	tuīfān	v.	to overthrow; to overturn
6	总统	zǒngtǒng	n.	president
7	逝世	shìshì	v.	to die; to pass away
8	灵柩	língjiù	n.	coffin containing the remains of the deceased
9	墓穴	mùxué	n.	burial pit
10	祭堂	jìtáng	n.	memorial hall
11	不虚此行	bù xū cǐ xíng		It's been a worthwhile trip

PROPER NOUNS			
12	夏威夷	Xiàwēiyí	Hawaii
13	孙中山	Sūn Zhōngshān	Dr. Sun Yat-sen (1866-1925), leader of modern China's democratic revolution
14	中山陵	Zhōngshān Líng	Dr. Sun Yat-sen's Mausoleum
15	天下为公	tiānxiàwéigōng	the world or country for all; the whole world or country as one community
16	中华民国	Zhōnghuá Mínguó	Republic of China
17	民生	mínshēng	the principle of people's livelihood
18	民权	mínquán	the principle of democracy
19	檀香山	Tánxiāngshān	Honolulu
20	辛亥革命	Xīnhài Gémìng	the Republican Revolution of 1911

China Highlights

第十课
我知道的中国
历史和文化

■ 关于中国的历史与文化，你记忆最深刻的是什么？
■ 你在上历史文化课时，一般用什么方法进行记忆？

🎧 我认为，对于一个外国留学生来说，学习中国5000年的历史和文化是一个很大的挑战！夏、商、西周、春秋、战国、秦、汉、三国、两晋、南北朝、隋、唐、宋、元、明、清——别说对历史事件一无所知，就是这些朝代名称也记不过来。实在太困难了，最好减去十个朝代。

可既然我们来到中国，就应该对中国的历史和文化有些了解。我慢慢地发现了一个方法可以更好地学习这方面的知识。我们可以通过数数的方法，从一数到七，来记中国的历史和文化，这样也许更方便。

一统天下

秦始皇统一了中国，建立了强大的封建国家。从那时起，中国开始形成了一整套封建制度。同时，秦朝也扩大了中国的领土面积，并统一了汉字、货币。秦始皇是中国历史上的第一个皇帝。

两★河

我们要是跟中国人说话，提起黄河和长江，他们大都会觉得我们对中国有所了解。我告诉你们一个秘密，如果你知道黄河是中国的母亲河，是中国文化的摇篮，他们会更喜欢你。你先别管是什么意思，学会说就可以了。

《三字经》

"人之初，性本善，性相近，习相远……"这是过去中国小孩子几乎人人都会背的识字课本，你知道这本书吗？学习中国历史文化，如果连《三字经》都没听说过，那可就得加油啦！

四大菜系

"四"可以让我们联想到许多中国的文化，如四大菜系，四大发明，文房四宝……我比较喜欢四大菜系，谁不喜欢吃好吃的饭菜呀？鲁菜、苏菜、川菜、粤菜，你最喜欢哪一种？这些菜早就通过各种途径传到了美国，现在你想吃什么都很方便的。

五岳

"五"在中国文化里也是一个重要的数字。五岳、五帝、五霸……对我来说，还是五岳最有趣。所谓的五岳原本是中国传说中神仙居住的地方，后来被道教继承了，用来指中国人崇拜的五座名山，分别是泰山、华山、衡山、恒山和嵩山。什么？黄山？那不是！不过人们常说"五岳归来不看山，黄山归来不看岳"，就是说从五座大山回来就不想看其他的山了，但是黄山的风景更好，从黄山回来连五岳都不想看了。但遗憾的是，这几座名山我都没去过。

The Yellow Mountain, Anhui

六艺

你知道在孔子的时代，学生在学校都学习哪些课程吗？我来告诉你，他们要学习礼仪、音乐、射箭、驾车、识字写字、算术，这叫做"六艺"。够全面的吧？

七大古都

北京、西安、洛阳、安阳、开封、杭州、南京都曾经做过中国的首都。我们最喜爱哪一个？当然是北京！为什么？因为我们在北京学习！

以上用数数的方法简单介绍了中国的历史和文化，希望对大家的学习有帮助。谢谢大家，我的演讲完了。

（作者：方爱，北京大学美国留学生。文章有改动。）

VOCABULARY
生词表

1	挑战	tiǎozhàn	v.	to challenge

【动】*挑战*书 | *挑战*者 | 提出*挑战* | 面对*挑战* | *挑战*和机遇并存 | 巨大的*挑战* | 我们有信心迎接各种*挑战*。| 他们在学习上互相*挑战*。

2	一无所知	yī wú suǒ zhī		to know nothing

昨天发生的事，他*一无所知*。| *一无所知*的人是最大胆的。| 我对他的情况*一无所知*。

3	朝代	cháodài	n.	dynasty

【名】不同的*朝代* | 每一个*朝代*都有自己的特点。| 中国古代经历过很多*朝代*。| 西安做过好几个*朝代*的国都。| 北京故宫是明、清两个*朝代*的皇帝住过的地方。

4	减	jiǎn	v.	to reduce; to subtract

【动】*减*价 | *减*产 | 五*减*三等于二。| 试题如果做错了就会被*减*分。

5	数	shǔ	v.	to count

【动】*数*鸡蛋 | *数*了两遍，我的衣服还是少一件。| 请*数数*今天有多少人参加这个晚会。| 这个三岁的小孩儿可以从一*数*到一千。

6	一统天下	yītǒng tiānxià		to unify the whole country, to monopolize the world

*一统天下*的局面 | *一统天下*的地位 | 传说中，汤圆象征唐朝的*一统天下*。| 在激烈的竞争中，没有哪个品牌可以*一统天下*。

7	封建	fēngjiàn	n.	feudalism

【名】反*封建* | 半*封建* | *封建*王朝 | *封建*帝王 | 中国的*封建*社会有两千多年。

8	领土	lǐngtǔ	n.	territory

【名】一片*领土* | 收回*领土* | 国家的*领土*不可以侵犯。| 每一个人都要保护国家*领土*的完整。

9	面积	miànjī	n.	area; surface area

【名】增加*面积* | 扩大*面积* | 学生宿舍的*面积*不太大。| 中国的陆地*面积*大约有 960 万平方公里。

10	统一	tǒngyī	v.	to unify

【动】*统一*祖国 | *统一*意见 | *统一*着装 | 国家的*统一*、民族的团结是最重要的。| 他俩的看法常常不*统一*。| 咱们一起讨论一下，*统一统一*想法。

11	货币	huòbì	n.	money; currency

【名】各国*货币* | *货币*基金 | 兑换*货币* | 中国现在用的*货币*是人民币。| 用美元可以换别的国家的*货币*。| *货币*制造由政府控制。| 欧元作为一种新的*货币*开始在世界上流通。

12	皇帝	huángdì	n.	emperor

【名】一位*皇帝* | 小*皇帝* | *皇帝*专制 | 古代时，*皇帝*有最高的权力。| 中国唐代最有名的*皇帝*是唐太宗。| 溥仪是中国清代最后一个*皇帝*。| 北京故宫是*皇帝*的"家"。

13	提起	tíqǐ	v.	to mention; to speak of

【动】*提起*一件事 | *提起*王先生，没有一个人不知道。| 一*提起*女儿，母亲就感到非常自豪。

14	有所	yǒusuǒ	v.	to some extent; somewhat

【动】*有所*增加 | *有所*减少 | *有所*改善 | *有所*变化 | *有所*不同 | 他的汉语水平*有所*提高。

15	母亲河	mǔqīnhé	n.	mother river

【名】黄河、长江是中华民族的两条*母亲河*。｜我们要保护我们的*母亲河*。

16	摇篮	yáolán	n.	cradle

【名】学校是培养人才的*摇篮*。｜大海是地球生命的*摇篮*。｜河流被看作人类文明的*摇篮*。

17	管	guǎn	v.	to bother about sth

【动】你别*管*这是谁的自行车，你想骑就骑吧！｜别*管*那么多！｜那个人就是喜欢*管*闲事。

18	《三字经》	sānzìjīng		Three-Character Textbook for children in ancient China

《三字经》是古代儿童读物。

19	人之初，性本善	rén zhī chū, xìng běn shàn		At the beginning people are good by nature.

20	性相近，习相远	xìng xiāng jìn, xí xiāng yuǎn		Their natures are similar, but their habits are different.

21	背	bèi	v.	to recite; to learn by rote

【动】*背*单词｜*背*课文｜倒*背*如流｜他把那首诗*背*错了。｜有人能把上百万字的《红楼梦》*背*下来。

22	识字	shízì	v.	to learn to read; to become literate

【动】*识字*游戏｜看图*识字*｜*识字*不多的人读书会比较慢。｜他说他不*识字*。｜那个老人在教孙子*识字*。

23	加油	jiāyóu	v.	to cheer

【动】大家为运动员鼓掌*加油*。｜朋友们*加油*干哪！｜再*加*一把*油*！

24	五岳	wǔ yuè	n.	five famous high mountains in China

【名】攀登*五岳*｜三山*五岳*｜泰山居*五岳*之首。

25	五帝	wǔdì	n.	five emperors

【名】三皇*五帝*。

26	五霸	wǔbà	n.	five powers; five hegemonic states; five overlords

【名】春秋*五霸*。

27	神仙	shénxiān	n.	supernatural being; celestial being; immortals

【名】相信*神仙*｜没有*神仙*｜"龙王"在中国的传说中是会降雨的*神仙*。｜我不是*神仙*，不能什么事都知道。

28	礼仪	lǐyí	n.	rituals and etiquette; ceremony

【名】*礼仪*小姐｜注重*礼仪*｜西周是一个*礼仪*制度十分严格的朝代。｜献哈达是藏族的一种独特的*礼仪*。｜社会生活和人际关系的各种*礼仪*是不可忽视的。

29	射箭	shèjiàn	n.	archery

【名】*射箭*项目｜学*射箭*｜后羿是一位擅长*射箭*的天神，他*射箭*百发百中。｜他从小练习骑马*射箭*。

30	驾车	jiàchē	n.	chariot driving

【名】*驾车*技术｜在古代战争中，*驾车*的人站在车前中间的位置上。

31	六艺	liùyì	n.	six art forms

【名】五经*六艺*｜学习*六艺*｜儒家用*六艺*教学生。

| 32 | <u>演讲</u> | yǎnjiǎng | v. | to make a public speech |

【动】听演讲 | 喜欢演讲 | 演讲是一门艺术。| 张教授给我们做了一个精彩的演讲。

PROPER NOUNS

| 33 | 夏 | Xià | | Xia Dynasty (ca. 2070-1600 B.C.) |

朝代名。约从公元前 2070 年到公元前 1600 年。启建立的中国历史上的第一个奴隶制国家。

| 34 | 西周 | Xīzhōu | | Western Zhou Dynasty (1046-771 B.C.) |

朝代名。约从公元前 1046 年到公元前 771 年。都城在镐京（现在陕西省西安西南）。

| 35 | 春秋 | Chūnqiū | | Spring and Autumn Period (770-476 B.C.) |

时代名。一般把公元前 770 年到公元前 476 年划为春秋时代，简称春秋。

| 36 | 战国 | Zhànguó | | Warring States Period (475-221 B.C.) |

时代名。从公元前 475 年到公元前 221 年。因为诸侯连年战争，所以称为战国。

| 37 | 两晋 | Liǎngjìn | | Jin Dynasty (265-420) |

朝代名。从公元 265 年到公元 420 年，是西晋和东晋的合称。都城分别在洛阳和建康（现在南京）。

| 38 | 南北朝 | Nán-Běi Cháo | | Northern and Southern Dynasties (420-589) |

时期名。从公元 420 年到公元 589 年，中国形成南北对立的局面，历史上称为南北朝。

| 39 | 隋 | Suí | | Sui Dynasty (581-618) |

朝代名。从公元 581 年到公元 618 年。隋文帝杨坚建立，统治时间很短。都城在长安（现在陕西省西安）。

| 40 | 宋 | Sòng | | Song Dynasty (960-1279) |

朝代名。从公元 960 年到公元 1279 年，是北宋和南宋的合称。都城分别在汴梁（现在河南省开封）和临安（现在浙江省杭州）。

| 41 | 元 | Yuán | | Yuan Dynasty (1206-1368) |

朝代名。从公元 1206 年到 1368 年。都城在大都（现在北京）。

| 42 | 清 | Qīng | | Qing Dynasty (1616-1911) |

朝代名。从公元 1616 年到公元 1911 年。公元 1644 年入关，都城在北京。

| 43 | 道教 | Dàojiào | | Taoism |

中国的一种宗教。由东汉张道陵创立，入道者需出五斗米，所以又称为五斗米教。后又分化为很多派别。道教把老子看作教祖，尊称他为太上老君。

| 44 | 泰山 | Tài Shān | | Mount Tai in Shandong Province |

山名。位于山东省，为五岳中的东岳，被称为"五岳之尊"，以雄伟著名。

| 45 | 华山 | Huà Shān | | Mount Hua in Shaanxi Province |

山名。位于陕西省，为五岳中的西岳，以险著名。

| 46 | 衡山 | Héng Shān | | Mount Heng in Hunan Province |

山名。位于湖南省，为五岳中南岳，以秀美著名。

| 47 | 恒山 | Héng Shān | | Mount Heng in Shanxi Province |

山名。位于山西省，为五岳中北岳，以幽美著名。

| 48 | 黄山 | Huáng Shān | | The Yellow Mountain in Anhui Province |

山名。位于安徽省。以奇松、怪石、云海、温泉著名。

VOCABULARY IN CONTEXT

挑战

一无所知

减（去）

数（数）

统一

提起

管

背

演讲

Complete the following dialogs using the words and phrases given in the list. You may use more than one word for each dialog so as to develop it into a paragraph. Note that not all the words and phrases will be used.

Ⓐ

① 你觉得这次考试怎么样？

_____。

② 毕业以后王兰到哪里去工作了？

_____。

③ 我最近胃口太好了，什么都想吃，体重增加得特别快，你说我该怎么办啊？

_____。

④ 大事儿、小事儿都得告诉我，听明白了吗？

_____。

⑤ 你们餐厅服务员的衣服五花八门，穿什么式样的都有，不太合适吧？

_____。

⑥ 你干嘛那么生气？

_____。

⑦ 最近学校有什么活动？

_____。

⑧ 咱们到底还有多少钱？

_____。

Ⓑ Next, have a conversation with your partner and ask him/her some questions. Your partner is to answer your questions using the words and phrases in the list.

LANGUAGE CONNECTION

The construction "既然…… 就……" consists of two clauses. The first clause introduces a premise that has already been realized or confirmed and the second clause states the conclusion that is reached on the basis of the premise.

For example

- 既然他一定要申请这所大学，我就不提其他的建议了。

 A 既然……就…… (since/as...)

"既然我们来到中国，就应该对中国的历史和文化有些了解。"

Complete the following sentences.

① _____，那我就不客气了。

② 既然大家都知道了，_____。

③ _____已经晚了，_____。

④ _____，_____明天再来吧。

⑤ 既然_____，_____。

⑥ _____，那_____。

B 大都 (almost all)

" 我们要是跟中国人说话，提起黄河和长江，他们大都会觉得我们对中国有所了解。"

"大都" means "almost all" or "the great majority". It is usually placed before a verb or an adjective.

For example

- 我们班的学生大都来自韩国。
- 这个商店的商品大都比较贵。

Make sentences using "大都" based on the given contexts. Refer to the example given. Can you think of other ways to express the same meaning?

Situation : 90% of the teachers in kindergarten are female.

The sentence：幼儿园的老师大都是女老师。

Situation 1 : Our classmates …

The sentence：_____

Situation 2 : In the forest …

The sentence：_____

Situation 3 : Dishes in this restaurant …

The sentence：_____

Situation 4 : In the zoo …

The sentence：_____

Situation 5 : The library …

The sentence：_____

C 所谓 (so-called)

" 所谓的五岳原本是中国传说中神仙居住的地方。"

"所谓" means "so-called". It is usually placed before a word or phrase that needs an explanation. The explanation follows the word or phrase.

For example

- 所谓"常青藤学校"，是指美国东北部地区的八所名校。
- 所谓"反问句"，就是没有疑问、而又以疑问句形式出现的句子。

Each student is to think up five words or phrases. Explain each of them to your partner using "所谓". Share them with your other classmates and have them comment on whether your explanations are correct.

For Example:

" 龙的传人" ——所谓"龙的传人"，就是指中国人。

从……起 (since)

"从那时起，中国开始形成了一整套封建制度。"

Form two groups. The first group uses "从……起" to describe practices or situations that have persisted over a period of time. The second group uses "从……起" to describe the position or size of something. Each group appoints a representative to present the sentences before the class. The group with more number of correct sentences wins.

① 从_____起，我们这个州就开始_____。（时间）

② 美国太平洋铁路从_____起，直到_____。（空间）

③ _____。

④ _____。

⑤ _____。

⑥ _____。

"从……起" is used to refer to the beginning of something, relative to time or space. In the example sentence, "从……起" has the meaning "since; from then till now". When used to refer to the size or specific location of something, "从……起" has the meaning "from".

For example

■ 从昨天晚上起我一直没吃饭。

■ 前排从左起第三个人就是我们的汉语老师。

 由/通过……+V (by which something is done)

"这些菜早就通过各种途径传到了美国，你想吃什么都很方便的。"

Complete the following sentences using "由/通过… +V".

① 学校的棒球队在比赛中得了冠军，这一消息_____。

② 造纸术是由中国人发明的，后来_____。

③ 中国的瓷器主要是_____。

④ 他考上大学的喜讯_____。

"由/通过… +V" refers to the means by which something is accomplished. The expression may be used for something abstract or concrete.

For example

■ 世界杯足球赛的比赛情况通过电视以及网络传到了全世界各地。

■ 有一些疾病是由动物传给人类的。

COMMUNICATION CORNER

Instructions:

- In groups, choose two or three topics and write them down on cards. Examples of topics may be "famous people in American history", "historical sites and scenic spots in China", "sports celebrities" and "Chinese idioms".

- Your instructor will collect all the cards and deal them out randomly to each group.

- Members of each group then take turns to state what they know about the topic shown on their card, citing at least three points in each case.

- Students evaluate each other's speeches to determine which group delivered the most fluently and naturally, and offered the most complete, accurate and interesting facts.

看谁知道得多

Guidelines:

In the main text, you learned several expressions used in making lists. Try to use these expressions in the following activity.

🗣 In your presentation, you should give as many examples or facts related to the topic as possible. For example, if your card reads "请讲讲汉语中的成语", you could say,

> 汉语的成语都是固定结构，不能分开用。比如有些成语和"龙"有关：画龙点睛、龙飞凤舞、车水马龙、龙争虎斗，另外还有龙马精神、群龙无首、来龙去脉、龙凤呈祥……这实在太有趣了，而且太多，我已经都数不过来了。你还能补充吗？

🗣 If your card reads "对于2008年北京奥运会的吉祥物，你知道些什么？", you may answer,

> 2008年奥运会的吉祥物是五个福娃，它们的名字特别有趣，分别是贝贝、晶晶、欢欢、迎迎、妮妮，合起来意思就是"北京欢迎您"。

WRITING TASK

Instructions:

- Following the example in the main text, use a numbered series to summarize the characteristic features of your school.

- Keep your writing to about 300 words.

我的学校

Guidelines:

First, plan out the features of the school you want to talk about that can be summed up using a numbered series (1,2, …10). For example, your school location, facilities, age-grade distribution, number of teachers, and subjects offered etc. You need to describe at least 5 features. Choose features that best represent your school.

Begin your essay with a brief introduction of your school.

- 我的学校是一个非常有意思的学校，……
- 我在××学校学习了××年，至今我还非常怀念那一段生活。……

Next, describe each feature in detail.

- 我们学校有一个非常美丽的湖，湖里……，还有两个……，三个……
- 像其他学校一样，我们学校有一个校长，但我们的校长很有特点，他……，我们学校的两个××也很有特点，……
- 我们的学校在一个小山坡上，坡上长着两棵……

Finally, summarize your thoughts about your school in your concluding remarks.

- 通过我的介绍，你对我们的学校有一些了解了吧。我的学校是不是……
- 我在这样一个学校里生活了×年，应该说，是一件非常幸运的事。我的学校多么……

The Silk Road

副课文
丝绸之路

Pre-reading

■ 你知道中国古代的丝绸是怎么运到欧洲的吗？
■ 看到上图你想到了什么？

1. 古罗马人是怎样看待丝绸的？

2. 古代商人是怎样和欧洲进行贸易往来的？

3. 商人为什么要用骆驼驮商品？

　　你知道吗？在古代罗马的上层社会中，用丝绸做成的服装被看作是高雅而时髦的。这些丝绸产自遥远的中国，它们是怎样运到欧洲的呢？

　　如果我们今天要从中国的西安去西亚、印度，或者欧洲，无论是乘飞机还是坐火车，都会很快到达目的地。然而，在古代，人们要到这些地方去，至少要花费一两年的时间，而且要克服许许多多的艰难险阻。那些商人们赶着骆驼，冒着风沙，走过荒无人烟的沙漠，将中国的丝绸以及其他一些物品，如茶叶、瓷器等运到西亚、南亚、欧洲，同时把那里的珠宝、玻璃及一些农产品运到中国。在艰难的长途跋涉中，他们走出了一条连接东西方的陆上贸易之路，这就是有名的"丝绸之路"。

4.这条通商道路为什么叫丝绸之路？

5.开通丝绸之路有什么意义？

6."丝绸之路"在什么时候全线开通？其中发挥了最重要作用的人是谁？

7.西域文化对中国文化有什么影响？

8.中国的四大发明是什么？

9.你认为在国际交往中，经济和文化之间有什么联系？

为什么称这条通道为"丝绸之路"呢？因为中国是世界上最早生产丝绸的国家，大量的中国丝织品正是通过这条路运往南亚、西亚以及欧洲、北非的。实际上，丝绸之路不仅是一条贸易之路，更是一条具有历史意义的国际通道，这条通道把古老的中国文化、印度文化、波斯文化和阿拉伯文化以及古希腊、古罗马文化连接了起来。

公元前二世纪，汉朝的张骞出使西域之后，中国就与中亚、南亚、西亚各国之间建立了直接的贸易往来关系，"丝绸之路"也就从那时起全线贯通了。中国的传统文化和富有特色的各种产品从此源源不断地运往西域各国，而西域的文化也不断传到中原。到了唐朝，人们在首都长安也能看到西域的舞蹈，听到西域的音乐，就连当时人们的服装，也受到了西域文化的影响。对中国文化产生深远影响的佛教也是由丝绸之路传到中国的，唐朝初年的玄奘法师历经千辛万苦，从印度取回了大量的佛经，他所走过的，也正是这条丝绸之路。中国的四大发明——造纸术、指南针、火药、印刷术也是通过这条通道传到西方去的。

丝绸之路是一条中外经济、文化交流的通道，千百年来为国际交流发挥了重要的作用。

Xuanzang on his historic pilgrimage to India along the Silk Road

VOCABULARY
副课文 生词表

1	丝绸	sīchóu	n.	silk
2	高雅	gāoyǎ	adj.	elegant; graceful
3	时髦	shímáo	adj	fashionable
4	遥远	yáoyuǎn	adj	distant; remote; far away
5	艰难	jiānnán	adj	difficult; hard
6	险阻	xiǎnzǔ	n. & adj	dangers and obstacles; dangerous and difficult
7	骆驼	luòtuo	n.	camel
8	荒无人烟	huāngwúrényān		desolate, uninhabited
9	玻璃	bōli	n.	glass
10	跋涉	báshè	v. n.	to trudge; to trek
11	贸易	màoyì	n.	trade
12	指南针	zhǐnánzhēn	n.	compass
13	火药	huǒyào	n.	gun powder

文明   civilization

PROPER NOUNS			
14	罗马	Luómǎ	Rome
15	欧洲	Ōuzhōu	Europe
16	波斯	Bōsī	Persia
17	阿拉伯	Ālābó	Arabia
18	古希腊	Gǔxīlà	Ancient Greece
19	张骞	Zhāng Qiān	Zhang Qian (ca. 164-114 B.C.), a Han Dynasty imperial envoy who traveled to Central Asia
20	西域	Xīyù	the Western Regions, an important part of the Silk Road (India, Pakistan, etc)
21	玄奘法师	Xuánzàng fǎshī	Master Xuanzang (602-664), a Tang Dynasty Buddhist monk who traveled to India

UNIT SUMMARY
学习小结

一、语言点

1. 反问句
   你的父亲和哥哥都在，怎么能听到就去做呢？

2. 难怪
   难怪他的学生都那么热爱他、尊敬他呢。

3. 类前缀
   我更愿意把孔子看作是一位富有智慧的、和蔼可亲的长者。

4. 连词"而"
   他们俩一个性格很急躁，……而另一个性格很内向，所以要鼓励他。

5. 既然……就……
   既然我们来到中国，就应该对中国的历史和文化有些了解。

6. 大都
   我们要是跟中国人说话，提起黄河和长江，他们大都会觉得我们对中国有所了解。

7. 所谓
   所谓的五岳原本是中国传说中神仙居住的地方。

8. 从……起
   "丝绸之路"也就从那时起全线贯通了。

9. 由/通过……+V
   这些菜早就通过各种途径传到了美国，现在你想吃什么都很方便的。

二、功能项目

1. 解释性的说明
   "学而时习之，不亦说（悦）乎？"意思是学了一门知识，要不断地复习。

2. 列举
   五岳分别是泰山，华山，衡山，恒山和嵩山。
   北京，西安，洛阳，安阳，开封，杭州，南京都曾经做过中国的首都。

UNIT 6
LITERATURE AND ARTS
文学与艺术

Communicative Goals
- Discuss problems and seek others' advice or opinions amicably and cooperatively
- Describe the process of making something (physical object)

Cultural Information
- *Romance of the Three Kingdoms*, one of the Four Great Classical Novels of Chinese literature
- *Book of Songs*, the earliest existing collection of Chinese poems
- Chinese Papercutting
- *Butterfly Lovers' Violin Concerto*, one of the most famous works of Chinese music outside of China

A Chinese opera performer in elaborate and colorful costume

Warm up

1.　你最喜欢的文学作品是什么？最喜欢的作家是谁？请说一说喜欢的理由。

2.　请你们小组调查一下，在下列这些艺术形式中，哪些是你们最喜欢的，哪些是你们最不喜欢的，哪些是不了解的，并加以具体说明。

Teahouse, a classic play written by Laoshe

"To Borrow Arrows with Thatched Boats"

第十一课
草船借箭

■ 你知道哪些中国的文学作品？请给同学们讲一讲。

■ 你听说过有关中国古代"三国"的故事吗？如果听说过，你最喜欢里面的哪个人物？为什么？

《三国演义》是中国文学史上非常有名的小说，是"四大名著"之一，作者是明朝（公元1368—1644年）的罗贯中。小说主要讲的是汉朝末年到三国时期（公元220—280年）北方的魏国和南方的蜀国、吴国之间争斗的故事。小说里有很多英雄人物和他们的传奇故事，《草船借箭》就是其中的一段。

汉献帝建安十三年（公元208年）冬，丞相曹操率领20万大军进攻东吴。诸葛亮说服孙权与刘备联合作战，孙刘联军就和曹军在长江两岸摆开了阵势。

一天，东吴主帅周瑜请刘备的军师诸葛亮来商议战事。他说："我们就要跟曹军交战了。水上作战，您看用什么兵器最好？"诸葛亮说："弓箭。"周瑜说："您跟我的想法一样。但是现在军中缺箭，想请您负责造十万支箭，怎么样？"诸葛亮说："好！这些箭什么时候用？"周瑜问："十天行吗？"诸葛亮说："既然就要交战了，十天造好，必然误了大事。"周瑜问："您预计几天可以造好？"诸葛亮说："三天。从明天算起，到第三天，请派五百个士兵到江边来搬箭。"

诸葛亮走后，周瑜的参谋鲁肃说："十万支箭十天都未必能造好，三天怎么行呢？我得去看看他怎么造。"

刘备
魏
蜀
吴
孙权

鲁肃见到诸葛亮，诸葛亮说："请你帮我一个忙。"鲁肃说："我能帮您做什么呢？""你借给我二十只船，每条船上三十名士兵。船用青布蒙起来，还要一千多个草把，排在船的两边，我有用处。"

鲁肃把情况告诉了周瑜，他们都觉得很纳闷：诸葛亮造箭不要竹子、羽毛、箭头等材料，却让准备这些不相干的东西，真奇怪！

按照诸葛亮的要求，鲁肃准备好了船及士兵。可是第一天，诸葛亮没有什么动静。第二天，仍然没有动静。到第三天凌晨，诸葛亮悄悄把鲁肃请到船上，说："你陪我一起去取箭。"鲁肃问："到哪里取？"诸葛亮说："不用问，去了就知道了。"诸葛亮吩咐人把二十只船用绳子拴在一起，朝长江北岸的曹军军营开去。

这时候天还没有亮，江面上起了大雾。船靠近曹军水寨后，诸葛亮命令把船头朝西，船尾朝东，一字排开，又叫船上的士兵一边敲鼓一边大喊。鲁肃吃惊地说："如果曹军出来怎么办？"诸葛亮一听，笑了起来："雾这么大，曹操一定不敢派兵出来。"

　　曹操听到鼓声和呐喊声，就下令说："江上雾大，我们看不清敌人的虚实，不要<u>轻易</u>出动。只叫弓箭手向他们射箭，别让他们靠近。"于是一万多名士兵一起朝江中放箭，箭如雨下。诸葛亮又下令把船头掉过来，头朝东尾朝西，仍旧敲鼓呐喊，<u>逼近</u>曹营去受箭。

　　太阳出来了，江面上雾还没有散尽。这时，船两边的草把子上都插满了箭。诸葛亮吩咐士兵们齐声高喊："谢谢曹丞相的箭！"接着就命令二十只船驶回南岸。曹操知道<u>上当</u>了，想派人去追，可是诸葛亮的船顺风顺水，已经驶出很远了。

　　二十只船靠岸的时候，周瑜派来搬箭的五百名士兵也到了。周瑜看到二十只船沿着江岸一字排开，每只船上大约都有五、六千支箭，二十只船总共有十多万支。周瑜一向很<u>自负</u>，但听说诸葛亮轻松"借"回来十万支箭，也<u>赞叹</u>说："诸葛亮神机妙算，我不如他！"

VOCABULARY
生词表

1	四大名著	sì dà míngzhù		four great classical novels

四大名著是明清时代的小说。| 学中国文学的人必读四大名著。

2	传奇	chuánqí	*n.*	legend

【名】传奇的一生 | 玄奘法师是一位传奇式的人物。| 他的一生充满了传奇色彩。

3	丞相	chéngxiàng	*n.*	prime minister

【名】李斯做过秦朝的丞相。| 人们都非常尊敬这位丞相。

4	说服	shuōfú	*v.*	to persuade

【动】说服工作 | 说服老师 | 耐心说服 | 我终于说服了她。| 弟弟已经被说服了。| 我怎么也说不服他。| 大家对他进行了大量的说服工作。

5	联合	liánhé	*v.*	to unite

【动】破坏联合 | 学校之间的联合 | 经济联合 | 他们联合了许多同行。| 这两所大学联合办学，联合招生。

6	作战	zuòzhàn	*v.*	to fight; to battle

【动】参加作战 | 指挥作战 | 联合作战 | 作战经验 | 战士们作战非常勇敢。| 这支部队善于夜间作战。| 双方军队在那里作过战。| 部队按时到达作战地点。

7	联军	liánjūn	*n.*	allied forces

【名】组成一支联军 | 1860 年，英法联军焚烧了圆明园。

8	摆	bǎi	*v.*	to place; to arrange; to set

【动】摆桌椅 | 摆饭菜 | 桌子上摆着两盆花。| 碗筷摆好了，准备吃饭吧！| 柜子里摆了许多工艺品。

9	阵势	zhènshì	*n.*	deployment and formation of troops for battle

【名】阵势严整 | 摆好阵势 | 打乱阵势 | 从对方的阵势看，就可以看出他们很有经验。

10	主帅	zhǔshuài	*n.*	chief commander

【名】一位主帅 | 我军主帅 | 出任主帅 | 作为这场战役的主帅，他的指挥非常得当。

11	军师	jūnshī	*n.*	military counselor; military adviser

【名】一名军师 | 敌军军师 | 你要下象棋，我来给你当"军师"。

12	商议	shāngyì	*v.*	to confer; to discuss

【动】领导们正在商议下半年的工作问题。| 这件事我们要商议一下。| 你们回去再商议商议。

13	交战	jiāozhàn	*v.*	(of two sides) to engage in battle; to be at war; to fight a war

【动】交战的时间 | 交战双方 | 在整个战争中，交战各国的伤亡都很大。| 在和敌人交战的过程中，这位主帅受了伤。

14	兵器	bīngqì	*n.*	weapon; weaponry

【名】冷兵器 | 常规兵器 | 携带兵器 | 兵器知识 | 剑是中国武术中常用的一种兵器。

15	误事	wùshì	*v.*	to bungle things up

【动】别误事 | 我们快走吧，迟了会误事。| 别担心，我不会误了你的事的。| 他办事认真，从来没有误过事。

16	预计	yùjì	*v.*	to estimate/predict

【动】这批货预计明天运到。| 我预计他后天可以到北京。| 这项工程所用的时间比预计的提前了10多天。📖预：事先。📖预报 | 预备 | 预测 | 预定 | 预订 | 预赛 | 预习 | 预见 | 预祝。

17	参谋	cānmóu	*n.*	staff officer

【名】参谋长 | 高级参谋 | 参谋工作 | 他曾经在军队里当参谋。| 参谋的作用非常重要。

18	草把	cǎobǎ	*n.*	bundle of grass

【名】他把草扎成一人多高的草把。📖火把。

19	不相干	bù xiānggān	*v.*	to have nothing to do with sth

【动】这件事和你不相干。| 他找了一份和自己的专业完全不相干的工作。| 她不喜欢和不相干的人交往。

20	动静	dòngjing	*n.*	movement

【名】察看动静 | 这几天敌人一点儿动静也没有。| 只要他有什么动静就马上告诉我。| 领导同意是同意了，可是总没有动静。

21	吩咐	fēnfù	*v.*	to tell; to instruct (repeatedly)

【动】有什么事，请尽管吩咐。| 爸爸刚吩咐完，妈妈又接着吩咐起来。| 你别忘了老师的吩咐。

22	军营	jūnyíng	*n.*	military camp; barracks

【名】闯进军营 | 军营生活 | 由于过度劳累，诸葛亮在军营里病倒了。| 这个好消息很快传遍了整个军营。

23	水寨	shuǐzhài	*n.*	fortified water village

【名】一座水寨 | 那位军师认为应该用火攻打敌人的水寨。

24	呐喊	nàhǎn	*v.*	to shout; to yell

【动】齐声呐喊 | 呐喊起来 | 一声呐喊 | 观众们向运动员摇旗呐喊。| 人群中发出一阵呐喊。| 他们的呐喊震动山谷。

25	虚实	xūshí	*n.*	actual situation

【名】探听虚实 | 辨别虚实 | 虚实不明 | 我试探了一下他们的虚实。| 她不了解这个商场价格的虚实，所以没在那里买东西。| 为了弄清虚实，记者去现场进行了采访。

26	轻易	qīngyì	*adj.*	rashly

【形】他从来不轻易发表自己的看法。| 我一向不轻易相信人。| 他轻易不向别人借钱。| 轻易地下结论往往会犯错误。

27	逼近	bījìn	*v.*	to approach; to press on toward

【动】逼近敌人 | 逼近目标 | 天色已逼近黄昏了。

28	上当	shàngdàng	*v.*	to be taken in

【动】避免上当 | 小心上当 | 上当受骗 | 这次我们要小心，别再上当了。| 我以前上过假广告的当。| 他上过很多次当，现在学聪明了。

29	顺风	shùnfēng	*v.*	to have a favorable wind; to travel or sail with the wind

【动】他顺风闻到了花香。| 今天顺风，船走得很快。| 祝你一路顺风！

| 30 | 自负 | zìfù | *adj.* | think highly of oneself; be conceited |

【形】他是一个很*自负*的人。| 不要那么*自负*！| *自负*的结果就是失败。📖 自：自己。📖 自爱 | 自费 | 自觉 | 自满 | 自学 | 自力更生 | 自高自大。

| 31 | 赞叹 | zàntàn | *v.* | to commend; to highly praise |

【动】*赞叹*不已 | 发出*赞叹* | 不由地*赞叹* | 看到这精美的艺术品，参观的人都不停地*赞叹*。| 游客们用*赞叹*的口气说："这里真美啊！"

| 32 | 神机妙算 | shénjī miàosuàn | | very resourceful and extremely good at ~~planning~~ |

我们都很佩服他的*神机妙算*。| 我们的教练*神机妙算*，算准了他们会采取什么样的战术。

PROPER NOUNS		
33	罗贯中	Luó Guànzhōng	Luo Guanzhong (ca. 1330-1400), author of *Romance of the Three Kingdoms*

人名。元末明初著名的小说家、戏曲家。主要作品是《三国演义》。

| 34 | 三国 | Sānguó | Three Kingdoms Period (220-280) |

指中国历史上魏（公元 220–265）、蜀（公元 221–263）吴（公元 222–280）三国鼎立时期。

| 35 | 汉献帝 | Hàn Xiàndì | Emperor Xian of the Han Dynasty who reigned in the period 190-220 |

皇帝的谥号。原名刘协，公元 190 年到 220 年在位。汉朝最后一位皇帝。

| 36 | 建安 | Jiàn'ān | the reign of Jian'an (196-220) |

年号。是汉献帝的年号，公元 196 年到 220 年。

| 37 | 曹操 | Cáo Cāo | Cao Cao (155-220), the ruler of the Kingdom of Wei |

人名。东汉末年的丞相。著名的政治家、军事家和文学家。

| 38 | 诸葛亮 | Zhūgě Liàng | Zhuge Liang (181-234), the chancellor and a great military strategist of the Kingdom of Shu |

人名。三国时期蜀国的丞相，是著名的政治家、军事家。

| 39 | 孙权 | Sūn Quán | Sun Quan (182-252), the founder of the Kingdom of Wu |

人名。三国时期吴国的君主，吴郡富春县（今浙江富阳）人。

| 40 | 周瑜 | Zhōu Yú | Zhou Yu (175 - 210), a very capable military strategist of the Kingdom of Wu |

人名。三国时吴国大将。

VOCABULARY IN CONTEXT

说服

联合

商议

吩咐

轻易

逼近

自负

赞叹

Fill in the blanks with the words in the list.

A

　　东汉末年，曹操带兵进攻东吴，<u>逼近</u>东吴边境，刘备和孙权_____起来对抗曹军。当时，曹操的部队在长江北岸，孙刘的联军在长江南岸。周瑜和诸葛亮定下了火攻曹军的计划，打算用火船烧毁曹军战船。可是当周瑜_____部下准备好船只以及引火的材料后，他才想起来，这个计划不能实现，因为当时是冬天，刮的是西北风。要想借助风势火烧曹操的战船，必须要刮东南风才行。可是怎么才会有东南风呢？

　　周瑜是个非常_____的人，不愿意和其他人_____解决的办法，自己急得病倒了，没有人知道他的心事。诸葛亮来看望周瑜，猜透了他的心事，给他写下了十六个字的药方：欲破曹公，宜用火攻；万事俱备，只欠东风。周瑜连忙向诸葛亮请教办法。诸葛亮懂得天文，预料几天内会刮东南风，就说自己能用法术借来东南风。后来，果然刮起了东南风，于是吴军火攻成功，曹军大败。

B　Make sentences using the words given for each of the following situations.

Situation 1 ：孩子不想吃早饭……

_____。(说服)

Situation 2 ：班级之间要进行篮球赛……

_____。(联合)

Situation 3 ：妈妈要到外地开会……

_____。(吩咐)

Situation 4 ：学汉语遇到了困难……

_____。(轻易)

Situation 5 ：小王考上了最好的大学……

_____。(赞叹)

LANGUAGE CONNECTION

"未必" indicates a subjective inference. It means "not necessarily; maybe not". Compared with "不一定", "未必" sounds a little more certain.

For example
- 今天下雨，他未必能来。
- 这个计划太理想化了，未必能实现。

A 未必 (not necessarily; maybe not)

"十万支箭十天都未必能造好，……"

Work with your partner to make up the following dialogs based on the given contexts. Refer to the given example. One of you asks the question and the other answers it using "未必".

Situation : Xiao Zhang is thrifty.

Question: 这件衣服那么贵，小张会买吗？

Answer : 小张这人比较节约，她未必会买。

Situation 1 : Wang Hong doesn't like pop music.

Question : _____?

Answer : _____。

Situation 2 : Mr. Wang is over 60 but still looks young.

Question : _____?

Answer : _____。

Situation 3 : Nobody has told Li Li to attend the meeting today.

Question : _____?

Answer : _____。

B 存现句 (Existential Sentence)

"江面上起了大雾。"

An existential sentence can have the structure "(place/direction)+verb+ (person/thing)". The example from the text refers to thick fog (大雾) appearing from the surface of the river (江面).

Other examples

- 对面跑过来一个孩子。(A person appears from somewhere.)
- 刚才旅馆门口开走了一辆出租车。(Something disappears from somewhere.)

An existential sentence can indicate that somebody or something exists somewhere.

For example

- 楼梯底下是他新买的自行车。

An existential sentence can also feature time as the subject of the sentence.

For example

- 上星期转来了两名新生。
- 去年有一千多新生。

Make existential sentences based on the contexts given. Refer to the example.

顾客　　商店里

Sentence: 商店里挤<u>着</u>很多顾客。

① 很多人　　主席台

Sentence: _____

② 花园里　　玫瑰

Sentence: _____

③ 妹妹　　跑

Sentence: _____

④ 左边　　台阶

Sentence: _____

⑤ 朋友　　学校

Sentence: _____

In a sentence that contains a directional adjunct and an object, if the object is a physical object, it can be placed before or after the directional adjunct. In the given example, the sentence can also be expressed as "诸葛亮借回十万支箭来。"

Other examples

- 姐姐寄回来许多照片。
- 姐姐寄回许多照片来。

But if the object is a place, then it must be put between the verb and the directional adjunct.

For example

- 参观的人走进车间去了。
- 参观的人走进去车间了。(×)

C 复合趋向补语 (Directional Adjunct)

"诸葛亮轻松'借'回来十万支箭。"

Rearrange the words to form complete sentences:

① 买 她 回 水果 来 从 一些 商店

_____。

② 哥哥 借 去 几本 我 用 正在 书 的 了

_____。

③ 教室 走 来 外 从 进 一位 老师 男

_____。

④ 搬 房间 小王 自行车 进 去 把 了

_____。

D 复合趋向补语的引申用法

(Extended Usage of Directional Adjuncts)

"船用青布蒙起来。"

Several commonly-used directional adjuncts have other extended usages. In the example sentence, the phrase "蒙起来" has the meaning "to cover up". "起来" here implies the completion of the action.

For example

- 他把桌子上的书收起来了。
- 火车是一节一节连起来的。

Make sentences with directional adjuncts using the given verbs. Refer to the example below.

Verb 笑

Sentence: 看到孩子可爱的样子，妈妈忍不住笑了起来。

① Verb 装

Sentence: _____

② Verb 藏

Sentence: _____

③ Verb 收

Sentence: _____

④ Verb 包

Sentence: _____

⑤ Verb 盖

Sentence: _____

The Adverb "一向" (always, usually)

"周瑜一向很自负。"

The word "一向" in the text is used to describe a certain enduring attribute of someone, a certain characteristic of something or some action or behavior, or a certain state of someone or something.

For example

■ 北京的春天一向比较干旱。

■ 他一向喜欢旅游，一放暑假就出发了。

Complete the following sentences using "一向".

① 蓝天宾馆的价格_____。

② 我的爸爸_____。

③ 我们这个城市的夏天_____。

④ 这个公园_____。

⑤ 食堂的饭菜_____。

 Compare "沿着" and "顺着"

"周瑜看到二十只船沿着江岸一字排开……"

Both "顺着" and "沿着" can be used to mean "along".

For example

■ 我们顺着这条路一直走就到了。

■ 沿着公路走不远就有一个加油站。

However, while "沿着" can collocate with nouns with an abstract meaning, "顺着" collocates only with nouns with a concrete meaning.

■ 沿着正确的道路走下去试验就可以成功。

In the above sentence, only "沿着" can be used.

Make complete sentences with "沿着" or "顺着".

① 这条路   到达

_____。

② 雨水   流下来

_____。

③ 正确的方向   胜利

_____。

④ 小路   有

_____。

COMMUNICATION CORNER

Instructions:

- Your class plans to invite a sinologist to give a lecture in conjunction with the school's Chinese culture and arts festival. You need to liaise with the sinologist on details of the lecture.

- In groups, list the items to be discussed, aside from those already in the table. For big items, note down specific details that need to be addressed.

- In pairs, role-play the conversation between the class representative and the sinologist. The former should explain relevant details about the lecture and seek the latter's opinions. The latter should take the former's perspective into account while expressing his or her views. Revise the plan as necessary to reach a compromise.

- Appoint a representative in your group to announce to the class the final arrangement and the content of the lecture.

- Students evaluate each other's announcements to determine whose announcement is most complete and clear.

您看这样安排怎么样？

Guidelines:

Discussion or negotiation is a common vehicle of communication. During a discussion, you can ask a question directly or express you own opinion first and then ask for the other person's opinion. You have seen several expressions of this nature in the main text. Review how they are used and apply them in this activity.

🗣 First, organize your thoughts, and list all questions and points of the discussion as comprehensively as possible.

商议问题	具体内容	备注
讲座时间	×月×日 15:00 ~ 17:00	
讲座的地点		
主题内容		
需要的设备		
……		

🗣 During the discussion, discuss your list of prepared questions thoroughly with the other party. There is bound to be some differences in opinion, but do not simply give in. Contribute your opinions and ideas actively to encourage a healthy discussion.

🗣 Both parties should speak politely. You could begin like this.

甲：您看我们这次讲座定在什么时候比较方便？×月×日合适吗？

乙：最近这一周我的时间已经排满了，下周怎么样？

甲：下周我们学校有篮球赛，我们是不是改到……您说呢？

甲：这次讲座的主题可不可以是关于"丝绸之路"的内容呢？我们对这方面的话题非常感兴趣。

乙：好啊，我正好……

甲：我们非常希望看看有关的图片……

乙：没问题，到时候我会把电脑带过来，给大家看相关的图片。你们教室的相关设备都没有问题吧？

甲：没有问题。那我们就……，好吗？

乙：一言为定！

In the third part of this activity, the group representative should report not just the results of the discussion, but also give a summary of what transpired during the discussion. In addition, remind the class of any preparatory work for the event.

我和……先生商量决定，我们这次讲座的时间定在……地点是……大家要准时参加。主题是关于……的，本来汉学家希望谈……我告诉他大家希望他讲……他同意了。另外，他要求大家在讲座之前做一些准备……

Before concluding the report, summarize the key points (time, place, etc.) of the event to help students remember.

WRITING TASK

Instructions:

- Write a short story with characters and a plot based on the given poem.

- Keep your writing to about 300 words.

诗歌改写

将仲子

仲子啊，我求求你，
别闯进我家院子里，
别攀折我家柳树枝。
柳树有什么可惜？
怕父母知道这消息。
仲子啊，我怎不把你心上挂？
可父母的责骂，
也真叫人害怕。

仲子啊，听听我劝告，
别从我家围墙跳，
别攀折我家桑树梢。
桑树有什么可惜？
只怕兄长们知道。
仲子啊，我怎不把你心上挂？
可兄长们的训斥，
也真叫人害怕。

Note:

1. 将(qiāng)仲子："将"是"请求"的意思，"仲子"是人名。
2. 本诗出自《诗经·郑风》，用的是《诗经译注》的译文，有删改。
   (This is a modern adaptation of a poem from the "Songs of State Zheng", *The Book of Songs*, which is China's first poetry collection.)

Guidelines:

This poem is written by a girl for her lover. Fearing that her family may disapprove of their relationship, she tells her lover not to visit her. Your essay should develop around this central theme.

You could begin your essay by introducing the main characters.

- 有一个叫××的姑娘，她长得非常漂亮。她和一个小伙子……

- 在古老的中国，结婚的事情一般是由父母决定的。可是，有一个美丽的姑娘……

- 一个小伙子认识了一个美丽的姑娘，可是……

Note that the content of the poem is mainly about the girl making earnest requests to her lover. In your story, try to apply expressions of persuasive negotiation from the main text.

- 小伙子总是寻找机会到姑娘家里来，可他这样做让姑娘很担心，所以姑娘就给小伙子写了一封信，信中写道……

- 姑娘担心父母发现他们的恋情，阻止他们，就给小伙子写了一封信……

Can the girl live happily ever after with her lover? Use your imagination to give your story a good ending.

The "Peach-Blossom Face"

副课文
人面桃花

Pre-reading

■ 你学习过中国有名的"唐诗""宋词"吗？可以背一
首吗？
■ 你可以讲一个文学家（不论中国、美国还是其他国家）
的爱情故事吗？

在中国文学史上，唐朝的诗歌最为著名。据
统计，《全唐诗》收录了唐代2529位诗人的42863首
诗，其中包括像李白、杜甫、白居易、王维这样的
著名大诗人的作品。有些诗歌的背后还有很感人的
故事，崔护的《题都城南庄》就是如此。

题都城南庄

唐　崔护

去年今日此门中，
人面桃花相映红。
人面不知何处去，
桃花依旧笑春风。

这首诗叙述了一个有意思的故事。唐德宗
贞元（公元785-804年）年间，有一个年轻人叫崔
护。这一年他参加科举考试，没有被录取，于是
在京城长安找了个地方住下，继续读书，准备参
加下一次考试。

清明节这一天，崔护独自去城南游览。在
一户农家小院前，他想讨一碗水喝。敲了半天
门，才有一个年轻女子把门打开一条小缝。她从
门缝里看着崔护，问他是什么人。崔护告诉她自
己的姓名，并且告诉她想要一口水喝。姑娘端来
一碗水递给崔护，然后倚着院子里一棵桃树的树
枝，目不转睛地看着崔护。这时正是桃花盛开的
季节，满树鲜艳的桃花映着姑娘粉红色的脸，崔
护看呆了。崔护被姑娘的美貌深深打动，不禁

4.崔护和姑娘见面时的情景是怎样的?

5.你觉得这段描写应该是对诗中那句话的解释?

6.这时男女双方是不是都产生了爱慕之情?你怎么看出来的?

7.相思病是什么病?

8.读了这个故事,你对前面那首诗有了哪些新的理解?

产生了爱慕之情。崔护和姑娘说话,姑娘却不再理他,只是看着他。崔护告别出门,姑娘送到门口,还深情地望着他。

崔护离开后,没有再去找这个姑娘。第二年的清明节,他忽然想起了那个姑娘,就情不自禁地一路寻找过来。他来到那个院子门前,一切依旧,但大门上了锁。于是,他在左边的那扇门板上写下了上面的那首诗。

崔护闷闷不乐地回到了城里。不久后,他再次来访。敲开了院门,一位老人迎了出来。当得知崔护就是那个在门板上写诗的人之后,老人十分愤怒。他指着崔护叫道:"你害死我女儿了!你害死我女儿了!"崔护大吃一惊,仔细一问,才知道自从他上次离开之后,那位年轻女子看到崔护留下的诗歌,得了相思病,马上就要死了。崔护请求老人允许他进入房间向女孩子作最后的告别。崔护见到女孩,抱住她失声痛哭,连声说道:"我在这里!我在这里!"没想到女孩子<u>经</u>过他这么一折腾,竟然慢慢醒了过来。几天以后,她的身体居然完全恢复了健康。老人特别高兴,就把女儿嫁给了崔护。

VOCABULARY
副课文 生词表

1	统计	tǒngjì	v.	to overall count; to add up
2	感人	gǎnrén	adj.	touching; moving
3	依旧	yījiù	adv.	still
4	叙述	xùshù	v.	to narrate; to relate
5	科举	kējǔ	n.	imperial examination
6	录取	lùqǔ	v.	to admit or accept
7	讨	tǎo	v.	to ask for
8	倚	yǐ	v.	to lean on or against
9	目不转睛	mù bù zhuǎn jīng		to gaze steadily (or intently)
10	爱慕	àimù	v.	to carry a torch for; to adore
11	情不自禁	qíng bù zì jīn		cannot refrain from; cannot help doing sth
12	扇	shàn	m.w.	a classifier used with a numeral to modify a noun denoting a door or a window
13	闷闷不乐	mènmèn bù lè		melancholic; depressed; sulky; unhappy
14	相思病	xiāngsībìng	n.	lovesickness
15	允许	yǔnxǔ	v.	to permit
16	失声	shīshēng	v.	to burst out; to burst into
17	折腾	zhēteng	v.	to cause physical or mental suffering; to torment

PROPER NOUNS			
18	唐德宗	Táng Dézōng	Emperor Dezong of the Tang Dynasty (742-805)
19	贞元	Zhēnyuán	the reign of Zhenyuan (785-805)
20	清明节	qīngmíng jié	Tomb-sweeping Day, the traditional day for remembering the dead, on April 5th

Chinese Papercutting

第 十 二 课
中国剪纸

■ 你知道剪纸吗？向同学们介绍一下你了解的情况。

■ 除剪纸外，你还知道哪些民间艺术？跟大家分享一下吧！

剪纸知识

Pre-reading

　　剪纸是中国最为流行的民间艺术之一，至少有一千五百年的历史。现在很多农村地区在过年和婚嫁的时候，人们还会在家中贴上许多剪纸作为装饰。

　　传统剪纸是由手工制作的，常见的方法有两种：一种是用剪刀剪，剪完后再把几张剪纸粘贴起来，最后再用剪刀对图案进行修改加工；另一种是用刀刻，先把纸张折成数叠，并在纸上画好图案，然后用小刀在纸上刻。和用剪刀剪相比，用刀刻的一个优势就是一次可以加工多份剪纸图案。

　　中国剪纸的风格大体上可分为南北两派。北方剪纸淳朴粗放，线条简练，人物特征鲜明，风格朴素，色彩浓艳。南方剪纸注重写实，艺术风格秀丽，工艺复杂精巧。

　　别以为剪纸只是一种消遣、娱乐的玩意儿，在某些农村，剪纸可是每个女孩所必须掌握的一门手艺，甚至还是人们品评新娘的一个标准。

剪纸大师库淑兰

Shulan Ku

　　这幅色彩艳丽的剪纸出自一位叫库淑兰的陕西农村老妇人之手。

　　中国民间的剪纸艺人大多是农村妇女，库淑兰是其中最杰出的代表之一。她的剪纸作品曾获中国民间艺术展大奖、金奖，代表作品被法国、美国、德国和东南亚一些国家收藏，台湾还曾举办过她的剪纸艺术专题研讨会。1986年，她被联合国教科文组织授予"杰出中国民间艺术大师"称号。

　　六十多年前，新婚的库淑兰开始学剪纸。几十年间，她和村里其他女人一样，作品多得不计其数，但是并不为人所知。后来，她的剪纸风格发生了巨大变化，构图、用色都精妙无比，因而也从众多的普通农村剪纸艺人中脱颖而出。

　　库淑兰剪纸时常常是一边说唱一边剪。她唱什么就剪什么，剪什么就唱什么。说唱的词既有自己编的，也有不知道是从什么地方学来的。比如她剪关公，唱词就是关于关公的故事。

　　库淑兰的剪纸构图大胆、色彩鲜丽、人物形象饱满，具有极强的吸引力。她的作品保持了民间美术的特点，形象古朴而又鲜明，画面复杂而又明快，色彩对比强烈而又协调适度。她善于用各种形象拼贴组合起来烘托主要人物形象，整体感、节奏感都很强，使人透过这些浪漫、乐观的画面，看到作者纯真善良的心灵和惊人的艺术心智。

库淑兰这位普通的农村妇女，用她的双手创造了东方民间艺术的奇迹。20世纪80年代，一位中央美术学院的教授带她去法国参加了一次国际艺术大展，没想到顿时轰动了法国，很多人出高价收藏她的作品。

这位老人生长、生活于茫茫的黄土高原，而今已经被茫茫的黄土悄悄掩埋；她的艺术诞生于黄土高原，而她的作品却走出了黄土高原，甚至走向世界，使我们可以在博物馆或收藏家那里体味她作品的永恒魅力。

VOCABULARY
生词表

| 1 | 婚嫁 | hūnjià | n. & v. | wedding; to marry |

【名，动】婚嫁习俗 | 婚嫁年龄 | 准备婚嫁 | 和古时相比，现代人的婚嫁观念有了很大转变。 | 老王有一对双胞胎女儿，都已经婚嫁。

| 2 | 粘贴 | zhāntiē | v. | to stick; to paste |

【动】粘贴标语 | 粘贴邮票 | 便于粘贴 | 仔细地粘贴 | 他用小石子、树叶等东西粘贴成一幅人物像。

| 3 | 修改 | xiūgǎi | v. | to amend; to revise |

【动】修改教材 | 不断地修改 | 这本书我前前后后修改了八遍。 | 这个计划我已经修改过了，你再看看。 | 这篇文章你再修改修改。

| 4 | 叠 | dié | m.w. | stack; pile |

【量】几叠报纸 | 他拿出厚厚的一叠儿钱，放在桌子上。

| 5 | 淳朴 | chúnpǔ | adj. | honest and simple |

【形】民风淳朴 | 非常淳朴 | 生性淳朴 | 他是个淳朴的普通农民。▣朴实 | 质朴 | 简朴。

| 6 | 粗放 | cūfàng | adj. | rough and bold; slipshod |

【形】粗放的线条 | 粗放的风格 | 这部电影在艺术处理上粗放简洁。 | 这一组画色彩明快，气势粗放，给人的印象十分深刻。▣粗狂 | 粗犷 | 粗豪。▣狂放 | 奔放 | 豪放。

| 7 | 线条 | xiàntiáo | n. | line |

【名】粗线条 | 线条清晰 | 明暗的线条 | 这幅画的线条非常柔和。 | 整个壁画人物庄重古朴，线条流畅多变，是壁画艺术中的精品。

| 8 | 简练 | jiǎnliàn | adj. | succinct; concise |

【形】文字简练 | 用词很简练 | 请用几句话简练地概括一下你的发言。 | 漫画常用简练的手法表达丰富的含义。▣简单 | 简短 | 简易 | 简明 | 简略 | 简约。

| 9 | 鲜明 | xiānmíng | adj. | bright; fresh |

【形】主题鲜明 | 立场很鲜明 | 这两个球队的实力形成了鲜明的对比。 | 这篇文章观点十分鲜明。▣鲜艳 | 鲜亮。▣明亮。

| 10 | 朴素 | pǔsù | adj. | simple and plain |

【形】朴素的语言 | 朴素的感情 | 打扮得很朴素。 | 书房布置得朴素大方。 | 他的文章中包含着朴素的人生道理。

| 11 | 浓艳 | nóngyàn | adj. | gaudy |

【形】浓艳的衣服 | 妆化得太浓艳就如同戴了假面具。| 他作画喜欢用浓艳的色调。 | 看过满山红叶，才知道秋色也可以如此浓艳。▣鲜艳 | 艳丽。

| 12 | 注重 | zhùzhòng | v. | to pay attention to; to attach importance to sth |

【动】特别注重 | 不注重 | 注重实用 | 注重传统文化 | 学校一直注重对学生实际能力的培养。▣注意 | 关注 | 重视 | 看重。

| 13 | 写实 | xiěshí | v. | to write or paint realistically |

【动】写实主义 | 写实的手法 | 这幅作品太写实了。 | 在这里，发现了一座一千多年前写实技巧极高的彩色雕像。

| 14 | 消遣 | xiāoqiǎn | v. | to while away time |

【动】供人消遣 | 娱乐消遣 | 他把读书当成是一种有益的消遣。| 终于把工作做完了，他们决定出去消遣消遣。| 养点鱼，种点花，不过是消遣消遣罢了。

| 15 | 玩意儿 | wányìr | n. | plaything |

<口>【名】小玩意儿 | 漂亮玩意儿 | 他经常自己做一些好玩的玩意儿。| 他看见桌子上有一个闪闪发光的玩意儿。| 这玩意儿好玩是好玩，可价钱真贵。

| 16 | 手艺 | shǒuyì | n. | handicraft |

【名】手艺人 | 手艺很高 | 木工手艺 | 靠手艺吃饭 | 这种手艺可不是一时半时能学得会的。艺: 技能；技术。工艺 | 技艺 | 才艺 | 园艺 | 艺高人胆大。

| 17 | 品评 | pǐnpíng | v. | to appreciate and comment |

【动】品评诗文 | 品评产品质量 | 他很善于品评人物。| 她的舞蹈有一种可以反复品评的味道。品茶 | 品味 | 品议 | 品赏 | 品玩。

| 18 | 杰出 | jiéchū | adj. | excellent; outstanding |

【形】杰出贡献 | 杰出人物 | 成就杰出 | 特别杰出 | 他是当代最杰出的作家之一。

| 19 | 不计其数 | bù jì qí shù | | numerous; countless |

一场战争过后，双方死伤不计其数。| 几年来，他们在世界各地演出近千场，观众不计其数。| 他吃过的药不计其数，但病情始终不见好转。

| 20 | 脱颖而出 | tuō yǐng ér chū | | stand out; excel |

她在众多参赛者中脱颖而出，获得比赛第一名。| 青年一代的脱颖而出，离不开老一辈人的扶持和帮助。| 改革使一大批真正有能力有才华的人脱颖而出。

| 21 | 构图 | gòutú | v. | to compose a picture |

【动】构图手法 | 他的绘画作品构图风格十分独特。| 构图离不开线条，就像数学离不开符号。| 他拍的照片构图很有特点。构: 构造；组合。构词 | 构想 | 构思 | 构成。

| 22 | 饱满 | bǎomǎn | adj. | full |

【形】颗粒饱满 | 饱满的热情 | 他精神饱满地走上了领奖台。| 这孩子长着饱满的额头、大大的眼睛，很是招人喜欢。

| 23 | 古朴④ | gǔpǔ | adj. | archaic and plain |

【形】建筑风格古朴典雅 | 古朴秀美的田园风光 | 这个玉瓶外型古朴，花纹简洁。| 他对北京古朴的民风有着很深的体会。

| 24 | 拼贴 | pīntiē | v. | (to make a) collage |

【动】拼贴画 | 仔细拼贴 | 拼贴工艺品 | 这幅画是由各色碎布拼贴而成。

| 25 | 烘托 | hōngtuō | v. | to set out |

【动】烘托气氛 | 起烘托作用 | 这些节目既相互独立，又相互烘托。

| 26 | 乐观 | lèguān | adj. | optimistic |

【形】乐观的精神 | 情况比较乐观 | 不乐观 | 不要盲目乐观。| 他总是非常乐观地对待生活。| 他过分乐观地估计了公司现在的情况。| 大家也不能太乐观了。

| 27 | 纯真 | chúnzhēn | adj. | innocent |

【形】感情纯真 | 非常纯真 | 纯真的笑脸 | 她通过作品要告诉读者的，是对生活的纯真感受。| 她有一颗纯真的爱心。纯洁 | 纯净 | 纯美。

| 28 | 心灵 | xīnlíng | n. | soul |

【名】心灵美 | 幼小的心灵 | 眼睛是心灵的窗户。| 这部小说描写了一个女孩的心灵世界。

29	心智	xīnzhì	*n.*	mind

【名】心智健康｜陶冶心智｜语言是了解人类心智的窗口。｜真正的散文是作者情感和心智的表露。

30	顿时	dùnshí	*adv.*	immediately

【副】听他这么一说，我顿时明白了。｜喜讯传来，人们顿时欢呼起来。｜一阵狂风吹过，乌云顿时散开了。

31	茫茫	mángmáng	*adj.*	boundless

【形】白茫茫｜茫茫无际｜人海茫茫｜茫茫的草原上到处开满了野花。

32	掩埋	yǎnmái	*v.*	to bury

【动】掩埋尸体｜掩埋在地下｜风沙渐渐掩埋了农田，掩埋了房屋。⊗掩：遮盖。⊗掩盖｜掩藏｜掩蔽｜掩护｜掩饰。

33	体味	tǐwèi	*v.*	to appreciate and understand

【动】细细体味｜体味人生苦乐｜有些深刻的感情，没有经历过的人是很难体味到的。⊗体会｜体认。

34	永恒	yǒnghéng	*adj.*	eternal

【形】永恒的友谊｜永恒的纪念｜具有永恒意义｜爱是人类艺术作品中永恒的主题。

PROPER NOUNS

35	联合国教科文组织	Liánhéguó – Jiàokēwén Zǔzhī	United Nations Educational, Scientific and Cultural Organization – UNESCO

联合国专门机构名，即联合国教育、科学及文化组织的简称。总部设在法国巴黎。其宗旨是通过教育、科学和文化促进各国间合作，对和平和安全作出贡献。

36	关公	Guāngōng	Lord Guan Yu (160-219), a remarkable general during the Three Kingdoms Period

即关羽（公元 160 年—公元 219 年），字云长。三国时期最著名的人物之一，蜀国著名将领。被后人尊为"武圣"，各地都有纪念他的庙宇，叫关帝庙。

37	黄土高原	Huángtǔ Gāoyuán	Loess Plateau in northern China

中国四大高原之一，位于内蒙古高原以南，北起长城，南达秦岭，面积约 50 万平方千米。是世界上最大的黄土分布区，高原约 60% 的地面为黄土所覆盖。

VOCABULARY IN CONTEXT

The following sentences are part of a dialog but they are placed out of sequence. Read the sentences once to get the main idea of the conversation, and then fill in the blanks with the words from the list. Note that not all the words will be used.

粘贴

修改

注重

玩意儿

杰出

顿时

体味（动词）

Ⓐ

① 你最近都在画什么呢？

② 真棒！没想到这样一改，_____感觉不一样，简直是一幅_____的作品！

③ 那我改一改，电脑绘画的优势就是可以随时_____。

④ 画面色彩很特别，但是有太多的绿色，似乎和其他颜色的搭配不协调。

⑤ 都是画一些小_____。来看看这幅吧，你觉得色彩怎么样？

⑥ 现在感觉呢？

⑦ 是吗？我要把这幅画_____到我的博客(Blog)上，让更多人欣赏！

Ⓑ Put the sentences of the dialog into the correct order.

LANGUAGE CONNECTION

Instructions:

In pairs, tell your partner about a topic of your choice (e.g. your school, your community, your classmate) using the deductive method of narration. One of you will then present it before the class. The class comments on whether you have used the method correctly.

 叙述的总分式 (The Deductive Method of Narration)

In deductive narration, you start by stating the main idea, and then go on to provide specific details and examples in support of the idea.

The first part of the text uses deductive narration to introduce Chinese papercutting:

剪纸是中国最为流行的民间艺术之一，至少有一千五百年的历史。现在很多农村地区在过年和婚嫁的时候，人们还会在家中贴上许多剪纸作为装饰。

The writer first introduces papercutting as one of China's most popular folk arts that has existed for thousands of years, and states that Chinese people use these works as decorations on important occasions. He then goes on to describe the different methods and styles of paper cutting, and the significance of this art form to some rural areas. The second part of the text uses the same narrative method to introduce Shulan Ku, a master of color papercutting.

为……所……

"但是并不为人所知。"

"为…… 所……" means "被……所……". It is a passive construction and is usually used in written Chinese. The word after "所" is a verb and the word following "为" is the agent of the action.

For example
- 环境问题为全世界所关注。
- 一定要了解真实情况，不要为他的谎言所欺骗。

Rewrite the following sentences using "为……所……". Refer to the example given:

大家都很喜爱大熊猫。→大熊猫为大家所喜爱。

① 大家都熟知这一段历史。→
② 人们痛恨这种行为。→
③ 美丽的外表经常会欺骗我们。→

 V$_1$ + 什么 + 就 + V$_2$ + 什么

"她唱什么就剪什么，剪什么就唱什么。"

This construction signifies the common object involved in or related to different actions. The object can be an indefinite pronoun.

In the example, the object is "什么" which is an indefinite pronoun and the sentence means what she sings is the same as what she cuts. Here are more examples:
- 他学什么就会什么，真是个聪明的孩子。
- 她看见什么就买什么，一点计划也没有。

The object can also be a noun phrase. The sentence above can be rewritten as:
- 她看见衣服就买衣服，看见裙子就买裙子，一点也没有计划。

In pairs, write a sentence with the words given below. Refer to the example provided. Read out your sentence to the class and have the class discuss if it is correct:

喜欢→每天吃饭的时候，弟弟总是喜欢什么就吃什么，妈妈说，这样对他的身体没有好处。

① 有 →
② 看见 →
③ 知道 →
④ 喜欢 →

D 类后缀 (Quasi-Suffix)

"库淑兰的剪纸构图大胆、色彩鲜丽、人物形象饱满，具有极强的吸引力。"

"她善于用各种形象拼贴组合起来烘托主要人物形象，整体感、节奏感都很强。"

A quasi-suffix is a word that can be placed after the stem of another word or words to form new words.

For example

化——绿化
　　现代化
　　信息化
　　年轻化
吧——酒吧
　　网吧
　　水吧
　　氧吧

In pairs, form words with the following quasi-suffixes and see which pair forms more words more quickly and accurately.

① 性

② 型

③ 业

④ 界

⑤ 员

E 排比 (Parallelism)

"她的作品保持了民间美术的特点，形象古朴而又鲜明，画面复杂而又明快，色彩对比强烈而又协调适度。"

When two or more clauses with related meanings, a similar structure or a similar number of characters are placed side by side, they form a construction known as parallelism. The three clauses in the given example "形象……，画面……，色彩……" are parallel clauses.

For example

■ 爱心是什么？它是湿润的雨，它是凉爽的风，它是温暖的阳光。

■ 她就是这样一个人，工作马马虎虎，做人斤斤计较，穿着随随便便。

■ 中国的传统节日都有很多习俗：春节要包饺子，中秋节要赏月，端午节要赛龙舟，元宵节要看花灯。

Complete the following sentences using parallel clauses.

Example:

早上上街卖菜，中午回家做饭，晚上打扫卫生，她每天都是那么忙碌。

① 这是一个幸福的大家庭，_____。

② _____，傍晚的景色漂亮极了。

③ 作为一个成功的现代人，_____。

COMMUNICATION CORNER

Instructions:

Option One:

- Describe the steps in making a craft of your choice.

- Pick a handmade item such as a Chinese knot, a kite, a clay sculpture, a music video or an art piece.

- Gather all information and visual aids (e.g. actual items, tools, materials, models, drawings, videos) that can help you explain the making process.

- Give a presentation to the class with the help of the materials you have collected.

Option Two:

- Describe the process of making something based on what you see in the photographs.

一步一步慢慢来

Guidelines:

In the text, you learned many useful expressions for giving a clear description of a process. You need to describe clearly and completely the process. Use parenthetical remarks or give an explanation when necessary.

Describing the activities or procedure involved is an important part of demonstrative speech. In your speech, you need to describe clearly and completely what to do in each step. Also, pay attention to how you begin and close your speech. Here are some examples to help you get started.

◀ 今天我给大家介绍……的制作过程。第一步……，第二步……，然后……，最后……就可以了。

◀ ……是一种非常有意思的工艺品，下面我来简单介绍一下它是怎样制作出来的。首先……，然后你需要把……，再把……，这时，它就变成了……

◀ 注意这一步可能你看起来比较奇怪，实际上就是……，刚开始是……，接下来是……。好了！现在大家已经能够理解……的制作了，你们可以回家试一试，非常有意思。

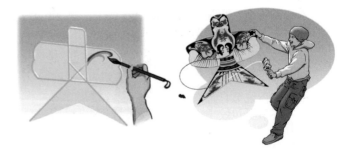

WRITING TASK

Instructions:

- Describe the steps in making a souvenir.
- Keep your writing to about 300 words.

我是这样制作纪念品的

Guidelines:

You will soon be graduating from your high school. Please make a souvenir to show your appreciation for your teacher or a friend.

 You can begin your essay by explaining the occasion, what souvenir you have made and who you gave it to.

- 为了纪念我的中学生活，我做了一个××送给老师……
- 我要去……留学了，就要和我的好朋友分别了，临分别前，我做了一个××送给他。
- 我的朋友要回家了，我送给他一个××，这是我自己制作的，很有意思……

 Next, describe the sequence of steps in making the souvenir, using time transition words such as "首先" "然后" "接着" "最后". Your instructions should be complete and easy for someone to follow to recreate the item.

 When describing the making process, you could use "其中" to highlight a particular step. For example:

- 开始做很容易，可是越做越难，其中……

 Once you have finished making your souvenir, present it to your teacher or friend. We are sure they will love it!

The Butterfly Lovers

副课文

小提琴协奏曲《梁祝》

Pre-reading

■ 你喜欢音乐吗？最喜欢什么风格的乐曲？

■ 你看过中国京剧、听过中国音乐吗？谈谈你的印象和感受。

1.小提琴协奏曲《梁祝》是谁创作的？

2.这个爱情故事的男女主人公是谁？

3.祝英台用什么方法向梁山伯表达爱情？

4.祝英台为什么不能嫁给梁山伯？

5.祝英台在梁山伯墓前祭拜时发生了什么事情？

50年前，两个来自中国南方、在上海音乐学院就读的学生——23岁的陈刚和25岁的何占豪合作创作了一首小提琴协奏曲，名叫《梁祝》。这首曲子很快成为用西洋乐器演绎中国故事的最有名的乐曲。

小提琴协奏曲《梁祝》用优美的音乐叙述了一个美丽动人的爱情故事，深深打动了亿万人的心。

传说在东晋时期，浙江有个聪明美丽的女子，叫祝英台。为了到杭州读书，她把自己打扮成男子的模样。在去杭州途中，她遇上了另一个读书人梁山伯，两人成了特别好的朋友。

二人在杭州同学三年，英台逐渐爱上了山伯，但山伯却始终不知她是女子。后来英台家中有事要离开杭州，山伯送她到十八里以外，他们依依不舍。临别之前，英台不断向山伯暗示自己爱他，但忠厚淳朴的山伯却一点也不懂。英台没办法，只能假称家中有个妹妹，和自己一模一样，她愿替山伯做媒。可是梁山伯家里很穷，没能及时到祝家求婚。等到山伯去祝家求婚时，英台已经被许配给别人了。二人见面后，十分悲痛。临别时，他们立下誓言：活着不能结合，死也要埋葬在一起！

后来梁山伯因为思念英台，不久就生病去世了。英台在被迫出嫁的时候，特地绕道去梁山伯

墓前祭拜。这时雷电大作，风雨交加，山伯的坟墓突然裂开，英台立刻跳入坟墓，坟墓又合拢起来。风雨停歇之后，阳光灿烂，彩虹高悬，梁山伯与祝英台化为一对美丽的蝴蝶，在空中比翼双飞。

《梁祝》全曲大约二十八分钟，开始的五分钟主要以小提琴和大提琴分别代表祝英台和梁山伯来叙述爱情主题，然后是快乐的学习生活，接着是"十八相送"。从第十一分钟开始到第二十二分钟为第二段，表现的是祝英台回家抗婚不成，二人在楼台相会，最后是"哭灵"。从第二十三到二十八分钟是最后一段，"化蝶"的主旋律再现。乐曲中采用了一些中国民族乐器，融合了京剧和越剧中的音乐成分，而小提琴也经常运用中国民族音乐的演奏手法，甚至直接模仿民族乐器来演奏，把中西音乐元素融合得天衣无缝。

梁祝的故事在中国家喻户晓，根据这个故事创作的小提琴协奏曲《梁祝》自然也容易得到人们的认可。《梁祝》首演时担任小提琴独奏的俞丽拿（女），以及日本小提琴演奏家西崎崇子（女）和旅美华人小提琴家吕思清演奏的都是最经典的版本。梁祝的故事伴随着优美的小提琴协奏曲传向世界。

6. 在听《梁祝》乐曲时，对于不同的乐章，你有怎样的感受？

7. 你能感受到《梁祝》与西方乐曲在表达手法上的不同吗？

8. 比较一下不同版本的《梁祝》乐曲，选出你最喜欢的版本，并说明理由。

1	合作	hézuò	v.	to cooperate; to collaborate
2	协奏曲	xiézòuqǔ	n.	concerto
3	演绎	yǎnyì	v.	to act; to play out
4	打动	dǎdòng	v.	to touch, to move
5	依依不舍	yīyībùshě		reluctantly
6	暗示	ànshì	v.	to hint
7	忠厚	zhōnghòu	adj.	loyal, honest and good-natured
8	做媒	zuòméi	v.	to act as a matchmaker
9	求婚	qiúhūn	v.	to propose (marriage)
10	许配	xǔpèi	v.	to betroth
11	祭拜	jìbài	v.	to hold a memorial ceremony for sb; to pray to
12	比翼双飞	bǐyìshuāngfēi		fly side by side
13	融合	rónghé	v.	to integrate
14	元素	yuánsù	n.	element
15	天衣无缝	tiānyīwúfèng		seamless
16	家喻户晓	jiāyùhùxiǎo		known to every household; known to all
17	认可	rènkě	v.	to approve of
18	经典	jīngdiǎn	adj.	classic

PROPER NOUNS			
19	东晋	Dōngjìn	Eastern Jin Dynasty (317-420)

UNIT SUMMARY
学习小结

一、语言点

1. 副词"未必"≈不间得
   十万支箭十天都未必能造好。

2. 存现句
   江面上起了大雾。

3. 趋向补语和宾语的位置
   诸葛亮轻松"借"回来十万支箭。

4. 复合趋向补语的引申用法
   船用青布蒙起来。

5. 副词"一向"
   周瑜一向很自负。

6. 比较"沿着"与"顺着"
   周瑜看到二十只船沿着江岸一字排开。

7. 叙述的总分式

8. 为……所……
   但是并不为人所知。

9. V₁ + 什么+就 + V₂ + 什么
   她唱什么就剪什么，剪什么就唱什么。

10. 类后缀
    具有极强的吸引力。
    整体感、节奏感都很强。

11. 排比
    她的作品保持了民间美术的特点，形象古朴而又鲜明，画面复杂而又明
    快，色彩对比强烈而又协调适度。

二、功能项目

1. 商议-
   您看用什么兵器最好？
   十天行吗？
   想请您负责造十万支箭，怎么样？

2. 实用性操作说明
   用剪刀剪，剪完后再把几张剪纸粘贴起来，最后再用剪刀对图案进行修改
   加工。
   先把纸张折成数叠，并在纸上画好图案，然后用小刀在纸上刻。

VOCABULARY INDEX 生词索引

　　本表按音序编排。表格最后一列指生词所在课，如"9.1"指第九课主课文，"11.2"指第十一课副课文。

兵器	兵器	bīngqì	*n.*	weapon; weaponry	11.1
病魔	病魔	bìngmó	*n.*	serious illness	4.1
玻璃	玻璃	bōli	*n.*	glass	10.2
波斯	波斯	Bōsī		Persia	10.2
博爱	博愛	bó'ài	*v.*	to have universal love	9.2
博学	博學	bóxué	*adj.*	learned	9.1
捕鱼	捕魚	bǔyú	*v.*	to catch fish	4.1
不妨	不妨	bùfáng	*adv.*	might as well, there is no harm	5.2
不计其数	不計其數	bù jì qí shù		numerous; countless	12.1
不相干	不相干	bù xiānggān	*v.*	to have nothing to do with sth	11.1
不虚此行	不虛此行	bù xū cǐ xíng		It's been a worthwhile trip	9.2
不知不觉	不知不覺	bùzhī bùjué		without realizing	1.1
部	部	bù	*m.w.*	a classifier used with a numeral to modify nouns denoting books, film, etc	9.1

C					
猜	猜	cāi	*v.*	to guess	3.1
猜测	猜測	cāicè	*v.*	to guess, conjecture	6.1
彩球	彩球	cǎiqiú	*n.*	colored ball	4.1
彩云	彩雲	cǎiyún	*n.*	colorful clouds	7.1
参谋	參謀	cānmóu	*n.*	staff officer	11.1
操心	操心	cāoxīn	*v.*	to concern oneself with; to worry about	7.1
曹操	曹操	Cáo Cāo		Cao Cao (155-220), the ruler of the Kingdom of Wei	11.1
草把	草把	cǎobǎ	*n.*	bundle of grass	11.1
册	冊	cè	*m.w.*	volume	8.1
曾	曾	céng	*adv.*	ever	1.1
差异	差異	chāyì	*n.*	difference	8.2
婵娟	嬋娟	chánjuān	*n.*	the moon	4.1
产物	產物	chǎnwù	*n.*	outcome	6.2
长假	長假	chángjià	*n.*	long vacation	3.1
长袍	長袍	chángpáo	*n.*	long gown	5.2
嫦娥	嫦娥	Cháng'é		Chang'e, the moon Goddess	4.1
嫦娥奔月	嫦娥奔月	Cháng'é bēn yuè		a legend about Chang'e who flew to the moon	4.1
超市	超市	chāoshì	*n.*	supermarket	1.1
朝代	朝代	cháodài	*n.*	dynasty	10.1
称心如意	稱心如意	chènxīn rúyì		perfectly matching expectation	3.2
城堡	城堡	chéngbǎo	*n.*	castle, fortification	6.2
盛	盛	chéng	*v.*	to fill	2.2
乘	乘	chéng	*v.*	to take (a bus, car, train, etc.)	5.1

沟通	溝通	gōutōng	*v.*	to communicate	2.2
构图	構圖	gòutú	*v.*	to compose a picture	12.1
购物	購物	gòuwù	*v.*	to shop, to buy things	1.1
孤独	孤獨	gūdú	*adj.*	being alone	8.2
古朴	古樸	gǔpǔ	*adj.*	archaic and plain	12.1
古希腊	古希臘	Gǔxīlà		Ancient Greece	10.2
鼓励	鼓勵	gǔlì	*v.*	to encourage	9.1
鼓乐	鼓樂	gǔyuè	*n.*	drumbeats	4.1
固定	固定	gùdìng	*adj.*	fixed; regular	9.1
固然	固然	gùrán	*conj.*	certainly, of course	1.1
故宫	故宫	Gùgōng		the Forbidden City, in Beijing	5.1
故乡	故鄉	gùxiāng	*n.*	hometown	4.1
关爱	關愛	guān'ài	*n.*	care and concern	2.1
关公	關公	Guāngōng		Lord Guan Yu (160-219), a remarkable general during the Three Kingdoms Period	12.1
关切	關切	guānqiè	*adj.*	deeply concerned	5.2
管¹	管	guǎn	*v.*	to discipline	2.1
管²	管	guǎn	*v.*	to bother about sth	10.1
馆长	館長	guǎnzhǎng	*n.*	curator	2.1
光线	光線	guāngxiàn	*n.*	light	8.1
广东	廣東	Guǎngdōng		Guangdong Province	3.1
规范	規範	guīfàn	*n.*	standard, the norm	2.1
果仁	果仁	guǒrén	*n.*	kernel	4.1
过渡	過渡	guòdù	*v.*	to evolve, develop	6.2

H

哈萨克族	哈薩克族	Hāsākèzú		The Kazak people, one of China's ethnic minority groups	7.2
哈达	哈達	hǎdá	*n.*	Long piece of silk used as greeting gift	7.1
海拔	海拔	hǎibá	*n.*	above sea level	6.1
海南	海南	Hǎinán		Hainan Province	3.1
海外	海外	hǎiwài	*n.*	overseas	5.2
害羞	害羞	hàixiū	*adj.*	shy, timid	5.1
含蓄	含蓄	hánxù	*adj.*	implicit	2.1
汉朝	漢朝	Hàncháo		the Han Dynasty (206 B.C.-220A.D.)	6.2
汉献帝	漢獻帝	Hàn Xiàndì		Emperor Xian of the Han Dynasty who reigned in the period 190-220	11.1
杭州	杭州	Hángzhōu		Hangzhou, a city, in Zhejiang Province	5.1
好像	好像	hǎoxiàng	*adv.*	to seem like	1.1
和蔼	和藹	hé'ǎi	*adj.*	amiable	2.1

合家团圆	闔家團圓	héjiā tuányuán		family reunion	3.1
合作	合作	hézuò	*v.*	to cooperate, to collaborate	12.2
禾苗	禾苗	hémiáo	*n.*	rice or wheat seedlings	4.1
嗨	嗨	hēi	*interj.*	hi, hey	5.1
恒山	恒山	Héng Shān		Mount Heng in Shanxi Province	10.1
衡山	衡山	Héng Shān		Mount Heng in Hunan Province	10.1
烘托	烘托	hōngtuō	*v.*	to set out	12.1
红包	紅包	hóngbāo	*n.*	a traditional Chinese red packet with money inside	3.1
红枣	紅棗	hóngzǎo	*n.*	red date	4.2
胡同	胡同	hútòng	*n.*	alley, lane	5.1
花瓣	花瓣	huābàn	*n.*	petal	7.1
花灯	花燈	huādēng	*n.*	festive lantern	3.1
花好月圆	花好月圓	huāhǎo yuèyuán		a wish for family happiness	4.1
化解	化解	huàjiě	*v.*	to resolve	8.2
华清池	華清池	Huàqīngchí		Huaqing Hot Spring, in Shaanxi Province	5.1
华山	華山	Huà Shān		Mount Hua in Shaanxi Province	10.1
怀念	懷念	huáiniàn	*v.*	to miss; to cherish the memory of sth	8.1
欢腾	歡騰	huānténg	*v.*	to be elated	4.1
荒无人烟	荒無人煙	huāngwúrényān		desolate, uninhabited	10.2
皇帝	皇帝	huángdì	*n.*	emperor	10.1
皇家马德里	皇家馬德里	Huángjiā Mǎdélǐ		Real Madrid	1.1
黄河	黃河	Huánghé		the Yellow River	5.1
黄山	黃山	Huáng Shān		The Yellow Mountain in Anhui Province	10.1
黄土高原	黃土高原	Huángtǔ Gāoyuán		Loess Plateau in northern China	12.1
回	回	huí	*m.w.*	a measure work (for number of occasions)	3.1
回味	回味	húiwèi	*v.*	to reminisce	7.1
会馆	會館	huìguǎn	*n.*	club, association	8.2
婚嫁	婚嫁	hūnjià	*n. & v.*	wedding; to marry	12.1
婚姻	婚姻	hūnyīn	*n.*	marriage	2.2
浑身	渾身	húnshēn	*n.*	all over (the body)	7.2
火锅店	火鍋店	huǒguōdiàn	*n.*	hot-pot restaurant	1.1
火炬	火炬	huǒjù	*n.*	torch	6.1
火塘	火塘	huǒtáng	*n.*	fireplace	7.1
火腿	火腿	huǒtuǐ	*n.*	ham	4.1
火药	火藥	huǒyào	*n.*	gun powder	10.2
货币	貨幣	huòbì	*n.*	money; currency	10.1

J

机场	機場	jīchǎng	*n.*	airport	5.1
吉庆	吉慶	jíqìng	*adj.*	auspicious occasion	4.1

录取	録取	lùqǔ	v.	to admit or accept	11.2
《论语》	《論語》	Lúnyǔ		The Analects of Confucius	9.1
罗贯中	羅貫中	Luó Guànzhōng		Luo Guanzhong (ca. 1330-1400), author of Romance of the Three Kingdoms	11.1
罗马	羅馬	Luómǎ		Rome	10.2
骆驼	駱駝	luòtuo	n.	camel	10.2
M					
麻辣粉	麻辣粉	málàfěn		a spicy vegetable and noodle dish	5.1
马褂	馬褂	mǎguà	n.	mandarin jacket	5.2
骂	罵	mà	v.	to scold	2.2
麦克尔·乔丹	麥克爾·喬丹	màikè'ěr·Qiáodān		Michael Jordan	6.1
漫	漫	màn	v.	to overflow	4.2
曼彻斯特联队	曼徹斯特聯隊	Mànchèsītè Liánduì		Manchester United	1.1
茫茫	茫茫	mángmáng	adj.	boundless	12.1
蟒蛇	蟒蛇	mǎngshé	n.	python	4.1
毛	毛	máo	m.w.	10 cents	3.1
贸易	貿易	màoyì	n.	trade	0.2
煤炉	煤爐	méilú	n.	coal stove	8.1
媒体	媒體	méitǐ	n.	media	6.1
门槛	門檻	ménkǎn	n.	threshold	7.1
闷闷不乐	悶悶不樂	mènmèn bù lè		melancholic; depressed; sulky; unhappy	11.2
孟姜女	孟姜女	Mèngjiāngnǚ		Mengjiangnu, a legendary woman from ancient China	6.2
绵延	綿延	miányán	v.	to stretch/reach far	6.1
面积	面積	miànjī	n.	area; surface area	10.1
民间故事	民間故事	mínjiān gùshi	n.	folk tale	6.2
民权	民權	mínquán		the principle of democracy	9.2
民生	民生	mínshēng		the principle of people's livelihood	9.2
鸣沙山	鳴沙山	Míngshāshān		Mingsha Mountain, in Gansu Province	5.1
名胜	名勝	míngshèng	n.	place of interest	5.1
莫高窟	莫高窟	Mògāokū		the Mogao Caves, in Gansu Province	5.1
莫名其妙	莫名其妙	mò míng qí miào		baffling	7.1
母亲河	母親河	mǔqīnhé	n.	mother river	10.1
目不转睛	目不轉睛	mù bù zhuǎn jīng		to gaze steadily (or intently)	11.2
牧场	牧場	mùchǎng	n.	pasture	7.2
墓穴	墓穴	mùxué	n.	burial pit	9.2
N					
呐喊	呐喊	nàhǎn	v.	to shout; to yell	11.1
纳闷儿	納悶兒	nàmènr	v.	to feel puzzled	2.1
奶茶	奶茶	nǎichá	n.	milk tea	7.2

南北朝	南北朝	Nán Běi Cháo		Northern and Southern Dynasties (420-589)	10.1
难度	難度	nándù	*n.*	level of difficulty	6.1
脑海	腦海	nǎohǎi	*n.*	brain, mind	5.2
内向	內向	nèixiàng	*adj.*	introvert	9.1
能手	能手	néngshǒu	*n.*	expert	7.2
年糕	年糕	niángāo	*n.*	Chinese New Year cake	3.1
牛郎	牛郎	Niúláng		Zhinü's husband, a cowherd	3.2
农耕	農耕	nónggēng	*v.*	to grow crops	6.2
农历	農曆	nónglì	*n.*	the Chinese lunar calendar	3.2
农牧	農牧	nóngmù		farming	6.2
浓艳	濃豔	nóngyàn	*adj.*	gaudy	12.1
暖气	暖氣	nuǎnqì	*n.*	central heating	8.1
糯米	糯米	nuòmǐ	*n.*	glutinous rice	4.2
O					
欧洲	歐洲	Ōuzhōu		Europe	10.2
P					
牌坊	牌坊	páifāng	*n.*	archway	9.2
泡	泡	pào	*v.*	to soak	4.2
陪伴	陪伴	péibàn	*v.*	to accompany	8.2
皮带	皮帶	pídài	*n.*	leather belt	0.1
疲倦	疲倦	píjuàn	*adj. & n.*	tired; fatigue	8.1
脾气	脾氣	píqi	*n.*	temper	2.2
撇	撇	piē	*v.*	to cast aside, neglect	2.1
拼贴	拼貼	pīntiē	*v.*	(to make a) collage	12.1
品评	品評	pǐnpíng	*v.*	to appreciate and comment	12.1
品种	品種	pǐnzhǒng	*n.*	breed, kind	4.1
平辈	平輩	píngbèi	*n.*	person of the same generation	2.1
菩萨	菩薩	púsa	*n.*	Bodhisattva	4.1
朴素	樸素	pǔsù	*adj.*	simple and plain	12.1
Q					
期望	期望	qīwàng	*n.*	hope, expectation	2.1
七夕	七夕	qīxī	*n.*	the seventh evening of the seventh month of the Chinese Lunar Year	3.2
其次	其次	qícì	*conj.*	secondly	1.1
祈祷	祈禱	qídǎo	*v.*	to pray	3.2
奇迹	奇蹟	qíjì	*n.*	miracle	5.2
岂	豈	qǐ	*adv.*	used in formal Chinese to achieve the effect of a rhetorical question	8.2
起舞	起舞	qǐwǔ	*v.*	to dance	4.1
迁	遷	qiān	*v.*	to move	2.1

钱币	錢幣	qiánbì	*n.*	coin	1.2
前夕	前夕	qiánxī	*n.*	eve	4.2
强迫	強迫	qiǎngpò	*v.*	to force; to compel	9.1
亲戚	親戚	qīnqi	*n.*	relative	3.1
亲切	親切	qīnqiè	*adj.*	kind; amiable	9.1
亲情	親情	qīnqíng	*n.*	feelings of kinship	8.2
侵袭	侵襲	qīnxí	*v.*	to invade, attack	6.2
秦国	秦國	Qínguó		the State of Qin during the Warring States period (475B.C.-221B.C.)	4.2
秦始皇	秦始皇	Qínshǐhuáng		Qinshihuang, the first emperor of a united China	5.1
清	清	Qīng		Qing Dynasty (1616-1911)	10.1
清明节	清明節	qīngmíng jié		Tomb-sweeping Day, the traditional day for remembering the dead, on April 5th	11.2
轻轨	輕軌	qīngguǐ	*n.*	light rail	5.1
轻易	輕易	qīngyì	*adj.*	rashly	1.1
青藏铁路	青藏鐵路	Qīng Zàng tiělù		the Qinghai-Tibet railway	5.2
情不自禁	情不自禁	qíng bù zì jīn		cannot refrain from; cannot help doing sth	11.2
情人节	情人節	qíngrénjié	*n.*	Valentine's Day	3.2
请教	請教	qǐngjiào	*v.*	to ask for advice	9.1
球队	球隊	qiúduì	*n.*	team (in a ball game)	1.1
球星	球星	qiúxīng	*n.*	star athlete (in a ball game)	1.1
求婚	求婚	qiúhūn	*v.*	to propose (marriage)	12.2
屈原	屈原	Qū Yuán		a minister from the state of Chu during the Warring State period (475B.C.-221B.C.)	4.2
取暖	取暖	qǔnuǎn	*v.*	to warm oneself	8.1
鹊桥	鵲橋	quèqiáo		the Maggie Bridge	3.2

R					
人次	人次	réncì	*m.w.*	people (number of times)	6.2
人力三轮车	人力三輪車	rénlì sānlúnchē	*n.*	trishaw	5.1
人之初，性本善	人之初，性本善	rén zhī chū, xìng běn shàn		At the beginning people are good by nature.	10.1
认可	認可	rènkě	*v.*	to approve of	12.2
日月潭	日月潭	Rìyuètán		Sun Moon Lake, in Taiwan	4.1
融合	融合	rónghé	*v.*	to integrate	12.2
绒毛	絨毛	róngmáo	*n.*	fluff, down	7.1
儒家	儒家	Rújiā		Confucian school (of thought)	9.1
入侵	入侵	rùqīn	*v.*	to invade	6.2

S					
赛里木湖	賽里木湖	Sàilǐmùhú		Lake Sayram, the largest alpine lake in Xinjiang	7.2
三国	三國	Sānguó		Three Kingdoms Period (220-280)	11.1

三峡大坝	三峽大壩	Sānxiá dàbà		the Three Gorges Dam	5.2
《三字经》	《三字經》	sānzìjīng		Three-Character Textbook for children in ancient China	10.1
纱巾	紗巾	shājīn	*n.*	scarf	7.1
山海关	山海關	Shānhǎiguān		Shanhai Pass on the Great Wall	6.2
扇	扇	shàn	*m.w.*	a classifier used with a numeral to modify a noun denoting a door or a window	11.2
伤感	傷感	shānggǎn	*v.*	to feel sad, emotional	8.2
商品房	商品房	shāngpǐnfáng	*n.*	commodity housing	8.1
商议	商議	shāngyì	*v.*	to confer; to discuss	11.1
赏月	賞月	shǎngyuè	*v.*	to enjoy looking at the moon	4.1
上当	上當	shàngdàng	*v.*	to be taken in	11.1
上街	上街	shàng jiē	*v.*	to go shopping	1.1
射箭	射箭	shèjiàn	*n.*	archery	10.1
伸	伸	shēn	*v.*	to stretch, extend	2.1
神机妙算	神機妙算	shénjī miàosuàn		very resourceful and extremely good at planning	11.1
神态	神態	shéntài	*n.*	expression; manner	9.1
神仙	神仙	shénxiān	*n.*	supernatural being; celestial being; immortals	10.1
婶婶	嬸嬸	shěnshen	*n.*	aunt, the wife of someone's father's younger brother	5.1
声调	聲調	shēngdiào	*n.*	tone	1.2
生肖	生肖	shēngxiào	*n.*	the animals of the Chinese zodiac	3.1
圣人	聖人	shèngrén	*n.*	sage	9.1
师傅领进门，修行在个人	師傅領進門，修行在個人	shīfu lǐng jìng mén, xiūxíng zài gèrén		The master reaches the trade, but an apprentice is self-made.	1.1
失声	失聲	shīshēng	*v.*	to burst out; to burst into	11.2
施瓦辛格	施瓦辛格	Shīwǎxīngé		Arnold Schwarzenegger	6.1
实践	實踐	shíjiàn	*n.*	practice	9.1
时髦	時髦	shímáo	*adj.*	fashionable	10.2
十三陵	十三陵	Shísānlíng		the Ming Dynasty Tombs, in Beijing	5.1
实用性	實用性	shíyòngxìng	*n.*	practicality	1.1
识字	識字	shízì	*v.*	to learn to read; to become literate	10.1
市民	市民	shìmín	*n.*	urban residents	1.2
逝世	逝世	shìshì	*v.*	to die; to pass away	9.2
收拾	收拾	shōushi	*v.*	to pack; to sort out	8.1
守护	守護	shǒuhù	*v.*	to guard, defend	4.1
手段	手段	shǒuduàn	*n.*	means	9.1
手忙脚乱	手忙腳亂	shǒumáng jiǎoluàn		(caught) in a flurry	8.1
手腕	手腕	shǒuwàn	*n.*	wrist	7.1
手艺	手藝	shǒuyì	*n.*	handicraft	12.1

手杖	手杖	shǒuzhàng	*n.*	walking stick	2.1
首先	首先	shǒuxiān	*conj.*	first of all	1.1
书柜	書櫃	shūguì	*n.*	bookcase; book shelf	8.1
数	數	shǔ	*v.*	to count	10.1
属	屬	shǔ	*v.*	to be born in the year of	3.1
率领	率領	shuàilǐng	*v.*	to lead	6.1
拴	拴	shuān	*v.*	to fasten	7.1
水寨	水寨	shuǐzhài	*n.*	fortified water village	11.1
顺从	順從	shùncóng	*v.*	to obey; to submit	7.2
顺风	順風	shùnfēng	*v.*	to have a favorable wind; to travel or sail with the wind	11.1
说服	説服	shuōfú	*v.*	to persuade	11.1
丝绸	絲綢	sīchóu	*n.*	silk	10.2
思想家	思想家	sīxiǎngjiā	*n.*	thinker	9.1
四大名著	四大名著	sì dà míngzhù		four great classical novels	11.1
四合院	四合院	sìhéyuàn	*n.*	a Chinese courtyard, quadrangle	5.2
宋	宋	Sòng		Song Dynasty (960-1279)	10.1
苏轼	蘇軾	Sū Shì		a famous writer from the Song Dynasty	8.1
苏州	蘇州	Sūzhōu		Suzhou, a city, in Jiangsu Province	5.1
隋	隋	Suí		Sui Dynasty (581-618)	10.1
孙权	孫權	Sūn Quán		Sun Quan (182-252), the founder of the Kingdom of Wu	11.1
孙中山	孫中山	Sūn Zhōngshān		Dr. Sun Yat-sen (1866-1925), leader of modern China's democratic revolution	9.2
T					
泰山	泰山	Tài Shān		Mount Tai in Shandong Province	10.1
檀香山	檀香山	Tánxiāngshān		Honolulu	9.2
探	探	tàn	*v.*	to crane, stretch forward	6.1
唐德宗	唐德宗	Táng Dézōng		Emperor Dezong of the Tang Dynasty (742-805)	11.2
堂兄弟	堂兄弟	tángxiōngdì	*n.*	paternal cousins	5.1
讨	討	tǎo	*v.*	to ask for	11.2
特殊奥林匹克运动	特殊奧林匹克運動	Tèshū Àolínpǐkè Yùndòng		the Special Olympics	6.1
特制	特製	tèzhì	*v.*	specially made (for a specific purpose or by a special process)	4.1
提起	提起	tíqǐ	*v.*	to mention; to speak of	10.1
提醒	提醒	tíxǐng	*v.*	to remind	7.1
体会	體會	tǐhuì	*v.*	to understand, experience	1.1
体味	體味	tǐwèi	*v.*	to appreciate and understand	12.1
天安门	天安門	Tiān'ānmén		Tiananmen, in Beijing	5.1
天昏地暗	天昏地暗	tiānhūn dì'àn		bad weather coupled with strong winds	6.2

天伦之乐	天倫之樂	tiānlún zhī lè		the happiness of family life	8.2
天南海北	天南海北	tiānnán hǎiběi		talk about a wide range of subjects	1.2
天坛	天壇	Tiāntán		the Temple of Heaven, in Beijing	5.1
天下为公	天下爲公	tiānxiàwéigōng		the world or country for all; the whole world or country as one community	9.2
天性	天性	tiānxìng	n.	natural disposition	2.1
天衣无缝	天衣無縫	tiān yī wú fèng		seamless	12.2
天真	天真	tiānzhēn	adj.	innocent	2.1
挑战	挑戰	tiǎozhàn	v.	to challenge	10.1
挑战性	挑戰性	tiǎozhànxìng	n.	challenge	1.1
铜锣湾	銅鑼灣	Tóngluówān		Causeway Bay, a district in Hong Kong	4.1
统计	統計	tǒngjì	v.	to overall count; to add up	11.2
统一	統一	tǒngyī	v.	to unify	10.1
筒子楼	筒子樓	tǒngzilóu	n.	tube-shaped dormitory building [with one corridor, public toilets and a kitchen]	8.1
头巾	頭巾	tóujīn	n.	headscarf	7.1
头饰	頭飾	tóushì	n.	headwear	7.1
图案	圖案	tú'àn	n.	design	3.1
团圆饭	團圓飯	tuányuánfàn	n.	family reunion dinner	3.1
推翻	推翻	tūifān	v.	to overthrow; to overturn	9.2
托	托	tuō	v.	to hold up, support by hand	4.1
脱口而出	脫口而出	tuō kǒu ér chū		blurt out	1.2
脱颖而出	脫穎而出	tuō yǐng ér chū		stand out; excel	12.1
W					
外地	外地	wàidì	n.	other places	3.1
玩意儿	玩意兒	wányìr	n.	plaything	12.1
晚会	晚會	wǎnhuì	n.	an event/party that takes place in the evening	3.1
王母娘娘	王母娘娘	Wángmǔ Niángniang		the Queen Mother of Heaven	3.2
望子成龙	望子成龍	wàngzǐ chénglóng		to have high expectation for your children	2.1
威严	威嚴	wēiyán	n.	authority; dignity	9.1
围墙	圍牆	wéiqiáng	n.	surrounding wall	1.1
唯一	唯一	wéiyī	adj.	only, sole	2.1
苇叶	葦葉	wěiyè	n.	reed leaf	4.2
位置	位置	wèizhi	n.	position; place	9.1
温情	溫情	wēnqíng	n.	tender	2.1
文学馆	文學館	wénxuéguǎn	n.	hall of writer	2.1
文学家	文學家	wénxuéjiā	n.	great writer	6.1
无地自容	無地自容	wúdìzìróng		feel extremely ashamed	1.2
吴刚	吳剛	Wú Gāng		Wu Gang, the wood cutter on the moon	4.1

五谷丰登	五穀豐登	wǔgǔ fēngdēng		a good harvest	4.1
五霸	五霸	wǔbà	*n.*	five powers; five hegemonic states; five overlords	10.1
五帝	五帝	wǔdì	*n.*	five emperors	10.1
五岳	五岳	wǔ yuè	*n.*	five famous high mountains in China	10.1
武警	武警	wǔjǐng	*n.*	armed police	6.1
误会	誤會	wùhuì	*v.*	to misunderstand	7.2
误事	誤事	wùshì	*v.*	to bungle things up	11.1
X					
西双版纳	西雙版納	Xīshuāngbǎnnà		Xishuangbanna, the Dai autonomous area in Yunnan	7.1
西域	西域	Xīyù		the Western Regions, an important part of the Silk Road	10.2
西周	西周	Xīzhōu		Western Zhou Dynasty (1046-771 B.C.)	10.1
嬉皮笑脸	嬉皮笑臉	xīpíxiàoliǎn		grin cheekily	7.2
喜鹊	喜鹊	xǐquè	*n.*	magpie	3.2
细节	細節	xìjié	*n.*	details	9.1
细致	細緻	xìzhì	*adj.*	attentive to detail	2.1
夏	夏	Xià		Xia Dynasty (ca. 2070-1600 B.C.)	10.1
夏威夷	夏威夷	Xiàwēiyí		Hawaii	9.2
先后	先後	xiānhòu	*adv.*	successively; one after another	9.1
鲜明	鮮明	xiānmíng	*adj.*	bright; fresh	12.1
仙女	仙女	xiānnǚ	*n.*	the Chinese fairy	3.2
显然	顯然	xiǎnrán	*adj.*	obviously	6.1
险要	險要	xiǎnyào	*n.*	treacherous terrain with strategic value	6.2
险阻	險阻	xiǎnzǔ	*n. & adj.*	dangers and obstacles; dangerous and difficult	10.2
馅儿	餡兒	xiànr	*n.*	filling	4.1
羡慕	羨慕	xiànmù	*v.*	to envy, to admire	8.1
线条	線條	xiàntiáo	*n.*	line	12.1
相传	相傳	xiāngchuán	*v.*	to pass from generation to generation	3.2
相反	相反	xiāngfǎn	*adj.*	opposite; on the contrary	9.1
香格里拉	香格里拉	Xiānggélǐlā		Shangri-la, the Tibetan autonomous area in Yunnan	7.1
相思病	相思病	xiāngsībìng	*n.*	lovesickness	11.2
想念	想念	xiǎngniàn	*v.*	to miss	4.1
向来	向來	xiànglái	*adv.*	always	2.1
象征¹	象徵1	xiàngzhēng	*v.*	to symbolize	4.1
象征²	象徵2	xiàngzhēng	*n.*	symbol, token	6.1
消遣	消遣	xiāoqiǎn	*v.*	to while away time	12.1

小贩	小販	xiǎofàn	*n.*	street vendor, hawker	1.1
小区	小區	xiǎoqū	*n.*	housing estate	8.1
小雁塔	小雁塔	Xiǎoyàntǎ		the Small Wild Goose Pagoda, in Xi'an	5.1
协议	協議	xiéyì	*n.*	agreement	2.2
协奏曲	協奏曲	xiézòuqǔ	*n.*	concerto	12.2
写实	寫實	xiěshí	*v.*	to write or paint realistically	12.1
辛亥革命	辛亥革命	Xīnhài Gémìng		the Republican Revolution of 1911	9.2
心灵	心靈	xīnlíng	*n.*	soul	12.1
心灵手巧	心靈手巧	xīnlíng shǒuqiǎo		clever and capable (with one's hands)	3.2
心智	心智	xīnzhì	*n.*	mind	12.1
新疆	新疆	Xīnjiāng		the Xinjiang Uygur autonomous region	5.1
欣赏	欣賞	xīnshǎng	*v.*	to appreciate	1.1
星巴克	星巴克	Xīngbākè		Starbucks	5.2
兴高采烈	興高采烈	xìnggāocǎiliè		in high spirits; excited	1.2
性相近，习相远	性相近，習相遠	xìng xiāng jìn, xí xiāng yuǎn		Their natures are similar, but their habits are different.	10.1
兴致勃勃	興致勃勃	xìngzhì bóbó		with great interest	6.1
胸有成竹	胸有成竹	xiōngyǒu chéngzhú		have a well-thought-out plan in one's mind; confidently	1.2
羞	羞	xiū	*v.*	to blush	7.2
修改	修改	xiūgǎi	*v.*	to amend; to revise	12.1
修养	修養	xiūyǎng	*n.*	self-cultivation	9.1
修整	修整	xiūzhěng	*v.*	to repair	6.2
绣花	繡花	xiùhuā	*v. & n.*	to embroider; embroidery	7.1
秀丽	秀麗	xiùlì	*adj.*	beautiful	7.1
虚实	虛實	xūshí	*n.*	actual situation	11.1
许配	許配	xǔpèi	*v.*	to betroth	12.2
叙述	敘述	xùshù	*v.*	to narrate; to relate	11.2
玄奘法师	玄奘法師	Xuánzàng fǎshī		Master Xuanzang (602-664), a Tang Dynasty Buddhist monk who traveled to India	10.2
学说	學說	xuéshuō	*n.*	theory; doctrine	9.1
学无常师	學無常師	xué wú cháng shī		One can treat anyone with more knowledge than oneself as a teacher	9.1
熏	燻	xūn	*v.*	to be filled with fumes	8.1
Y					
鸭绿江	鴨綠江	Yālùjiāng		the Yalujiang River	6.2
压岁钱	壓歲錢	yāsuìqián	*n.*	money given to children as a gift during Chinese New Year	3.1
燕	燕	Yān		the State of Yan during the Zhou Dynasty	6.2
严肃	嚴肅	yánsù	*adj.*	serious; solemn; earnest	9.1

沿线	沿線	yánxiàn	*n.*	along the route	6.2
延续	延續	yánxù	*v.*	to extend, to last for	6.2
演讲	演講	yǎnjiǎng	*v.*	to make a public speech	10.1
掩埋	掩埋	yǎnmái	*v.*	to bury	12.1
演绎	演繹	yǎnyì	*v.*	to act; to play out	12.2
洋车	洋車	yángchē	*n.*	richshaw	5.2
洋人	洋人	yángrén	*n.*	foreigner	9.2
杨澜	楊瀾	Yáng Lán		a famous TV program hostess in China	2.1
羊肉泡馍	羊肉泡饃	yángròupàomó		a Xi'an specialty made with lamb and dough	5.1
邀请	邀請	yāoqǐng	*v.*	to invite	7.1
摇篮	搖籃	yáolán	*n.*	cradle	10.1
遥远	遙遠	yáoyuǎn	*adj.*	distant; remote; far away	10.2
一辈子	一輩子	yībèizi		all one's life	9.1
一口气	一口氣	yīkǒuqì	*adv.*	at one go, without a break	3.1
一统天下	一統天下	yītǒng tiānxià		to unify the whole country, to monopolize the world	10.1
一无所知	一無所知	yī wú suǒ zhī		to know nothing	10.1
一言不发	一言不發	yī yán bù fā		without saying a word	7.2
一致	一致	yīzhì	*adj.*	in agreement with	2.2
衣食住行	衣食住行	yī shí zhù xíng		basic necessities	2.1
依旧	依舊	yījiù	*adv.*	still	11.2
依依不舍	依依不捨	yī yī bù shě		reluctantly	12.2
遗憾	遺憾	yíhàn	*n.*	regret	4.1
颐和园	頤和園	Yíhéyuán		the Summer Palace, in Beijing	5.1
意识	意識	yìshi	*v.*	to be aware, conscious of; to realize	1.2
意味着	意味着	yìwèizhe	*v.*	to mean	1.1
倚	倚	yǐ	*v.*	to lean on or against	11.2
阴谋	陰謀	yīnmóu	*n.*	conspiracy	4.2
银河	銀河	Yínhé	*n.*	the Milky Way	3.2
印第安人	印第安人	Yìndì'ānrén		American Indians	5.2
印象	印象	yìnxiàng	*n.*	impression	7.1
英姿勃勃	英姿勃勃	yīngzībóbó		handsome and spirited	7.2
永恒	永恒	yǒnghéng	*adj.*	eternal	12.1
勇气	勇氣	yǒngqì	*n.*	courage	1.1
游牧	遊牧	yóumù	*v.*	to move about in search of pasture	6.2
有份儿	有份兒	yǒufènr	*v.*	to have a share	8.1
有害无益	有害無益	yǒu hài wú yì		harmful, not beneficial	1.1
有趣	有趣	yǒuqù	*adj.*	interesting	3.1
有所	有所	yǒusuǒ	*v.*	to some extent; somewhat	10.1

有所作为	有所作爲	yǒusuǒ zuòwéi		promising, able to accomplish sth	7.1
浴缸	浴缸	yùgāng	*n.*	bathtub	8.1
预计	預計	yùjì	*v.*	to estimate	11.1
玉兔	玉兔	Yùtù		Yutu, the jade hare on the moon	4.1
圆明园	圓明園	Yuánmíngyuán		ruins of the Old Summer Palace, in Beijing	5.1
元	元	Yuán		Yuan Dynasty (1206-1368)	10.1
元首	元首	yuánshǒu	*n.*	the head of state	6.2
元素	元素	yuánsù	*n.*	element	12.2
元宵	元宵	yuánxiāo	*n.*	glutinous rice dumplings	3.1
元宵节	元宵節	yuánxiāojié		the Lantern Festival (on the 15th night of the first lunar month)	3.1
原则	原則	yuánzé	*n.*	principle	9.1
院落	院落	yuànluò	*n.*	courtyard	8.1
院子	院子	yuànzi	*n.*	courtyard	4.1
约束	約束	yuēshù	*v.*	to restrict, restrain	21
越南	越南	Yuènán		Vietnam	8.2
月牙泉	月牙泉	Yuèyáquán		Crescent Lake, in Gansu Province	5.1
允许	允許	yǔnxǔ	*v.*	to permit	11.2
Z					
赞叹	讚嘆	zàntàn	*v.*	to commend; to highly praise	11.1
葬	葬	zàng	*v.*	to bury	9.2
粘贴	粘貼	zhāntiē	*v.*	to stick; to paste	12.1
战国	戰國	Zhànguó		Warring States Period (475-221 B.C.)	10.1
站台	站臺	zhàntái	*n.*	platform	2.1
张骞	張騫	Zhāng Qiān		Zhang Qian (ca. 164-114 B.C.), a Han Dynasty imperial envoy who traveled to Central Asia	10.2
张望	張望	zhāngwàng	*v.*	to look out	6.1
长辈	長輩	zhǎngbèi	*n.*	the older generation	3.1
长者	長者	zhǎngzhě	*n.*	venerable elder	9.1
帐篷	帳篷	zhàngpeng	*n.*	tent	7.2
赵	趙	Zhào		the State of Zhao during the Zhou Dynasty	6.2
折腾	折騰	zhēteng	*v.*	to cause physical or mental suffering; to torment	11.2
珍藏	珍藏	zhēncáng	*v.*	to treasure; to keep or store sth in good condition	7.1
贞元	貞元	Zhēnyuán		the reign of Zhenyuan (785-805)	11.2
阵势	陣勢	zhènshì	*n.*	deployment and formation of troops for battle	11.1
征求	徵求	zhēngqiú	*v.*	to solicit; seek; ask for	9.1
整理	整理	zhěnglǐ	*v.*	to tidy up	8.1
证明	證明	zhèngmíng	*v.*	to prove	1.1

自尊心	自尊心	zìzūnxīn	*n.*	self-esteem	8.2
总统	總統	zǒngtǒng	*n.*	president	9.2
粽子	粽子	zòngzi	*n.*	steamed rice dumpling	4.2
租	租	zū	*v.*	to rent	5.1
琢磨	琢磨	zuómo	*v.*	to ponder, think over	2.1
做媒	做媒	zuòméi	*v.*	to act as a matchmaker	12.2
作战	作戰	zuòzhàn	*v.*	to fight; to battle, to combat	11.1

Abbreviations of Parts of Speech

【名】	名词	名詞	noun	*n.*
【动】	动词	動詞	verb	*v.*
【形】	形容词	形容詞	adjective	*adj.*
【数】	数词	數詞	numeral	*num.*
【量】	量词	量詞	measure word	*m.w.*
【代】	代词	代詞	pronoun	*pron.*
【副】	副词	副詞	adverb	*adv.*
【介】	介词	介詞	preposition	*prep.*
【连】	连词	連詞	conjunction	*conj.*
【助】	助词	助詞	particle	*part.*
【叹】	叹词	嘆詞	interjection	*interj.*
【助动】	助动词	助動詞	auxiliary verb	*aux. v.*

All photos are from **Getty Images** unless indicated below:

Quanjing Photos (全景图片库): p.106 (*1st row: 1st and 2nd images*), p.107, p.108 (*top*), p.132, p.139 (*right*), p.140, p.152, p.167, p.172 (*2nd row*), p.190 (*right*)
CNS Photo (中国新闻图片网): p.106 (*1st row: 3rd and 4th images, and 2nd row*), p.108 (*center*), p.109, p.117, p.119, p.120, p.123 (*bottom*)
China Foto Press (五洲传播图片库): p.141 (*top*), p.157 (*far right*), p.165 (*bottom*), p.191 (*top*), p.192
Xinhua Multimedia Database (新华社多媒体数据库): p.51 (*bottom*), p.69 (*bottom right*), p.168, p.172 (*background*)
Other Sources: p.63-64 (*from Tiger*), p.153 (*background, from Christopher Han, Punahou School, Hawaii*)